GU01111784

About the Authors

Grant Bourne is a New Zealander whose fascination with other lands and cultures has taken him through much of Asia, Africa, the Near East and Europe. He has written and illustrated numerous travel guides, the main focus being on Germany and New Zealand. His love of the outdoors has taken him not only along the magnificent tramping tracks of his native country, but also up the slopes of Mt Kenya in Africa, through the steamy jungles of Yucatan, the hills of northern Thailand and the trekking trails of Nepal. Now living in the beautiful Rhine Valley, Germany, he keeps himself (and his dog) fit by walking the many excellent trails along the Rhine, together with frequent walking holidays in the Bavarian and Swiss Alps. Visit Grant at www.grantbourne.com.

Sabine Körner-Bourne is a native of Germany and, like her husband Grant, is a keen hiker. Together they have explored numerous trails in exotic parts of the world. Nevertheless, Sabine has never lost her affection for the many beautiful tracks to be found in her home country. She accompanied Grant on many of the walks in this guide, helped with background information and also contributed some of the photographic material.

WALKING IN
THE BAVARIAN ALPS

WALKING IN THE BAVARIAN ALPS

by
**Grant Bourne and
Sabine Körner-Bourne**

CICERONE

2 POLICE SQUARE, MILNTHORPE, CUMBRIA LA7 7PY
www.cicerone.co.uk

Second edition 2007
ISBN-13: 978-1-85284-497-4

© G. Bourne and S. Körner-Bourne 2007

First edition 1997
ISBN-10: 1-85284-229-6

A catalogue record for this book is available from the British Library.

DEDICATION
Für meine Frau

Advice to Readers
Readers are advised that while every effort is taken by the author to ensure the accuracy of this guidebook, changes can occur which may affect the contents. It is advisable to check locally on transport, accommodation, shops, and so on, but even rights of way can be altered. The publisher would welcome notes of any such changes.

Mountain walking can be a dangerous activity, carrying a risk of personal injury or death. It should be undertaken only by those with a full understanding of the risks and with the training and/or experience to evaluate them. Whilst every care and effort has been taken in the preparation of this book, the user should be aware that conditions can be highly variable and can change quickly, thus materially affecting the seriousness of a mountain walk.

Therefore, except for any liability which cannot be excluded by law, neither Cicerone nor the author accepts liability for damage of any nature (including damage to property, personal injury or death) arising directly or indirectly from the information in this book.

Front cover: Tegernseer Hut is perched like an eagle's nest just below the Buchstein summit (Route 41)

CONTENTS

Preface 11

Introduction 13
Getting There 14
Transport 16
Accommodation 18
Mountain Huts 20
Climate 23
Flora and Wildlife 23
Clothing and Equipment 27
Safety in the Mountains 28
Language 29
Expenses 29
How to Use this Book 29
Maps 31

Part I The Allgäu Alps 33
1 The Nagelfluhkette: A Ridge Walk between the Mittagberg and Stuiben 39
2 Over the Großer Ochsenkopf to Riedberger Horn 43
3 A Ridge Walk between Sonnenkopf and Falken Alpe 46
4 The Rubihorn 49
5 Edmund-Probst-Haus to the Oytal 51
6 Prinz-Luitpold-Haus to Landsberger Hut/Tannheim 56
7 Gerstruben 61
8 From the Gerstrubental to the Oytal 64
9 Kanzelwandbahn to Fellhorn and Söllereck 66
10 Fiderepaß Hut 70
11 Gottesacker Plateau 73
12 Around the Großer Widderstein 76
13 Tannheim to Vilsalpsee 81
14 Füssener Jöchl to Bad Kissinger Hut 86

Part II The Ammergau Alps 89
15 Kalvarienberg 93
16 A Walk above Hohenschwangau 95
17 Bad Kohlgrub to Oberammergau 99
18 Over the Laberjoch to Ettal 103
19 The Kofel 105

20 Along the Sonnenberggrat to August-Schuster-Haus and Linderhof 109
21 The Notkarspitze 112

Part III The Wetterstein, Ester and Walchensee Mountains...................115
22 Wank, Esterberg Alm and Gams Hut...121
23 Partenkirchen to the Krottenkopf..124
24 Wamberg, Berggasthof Eckbauer and the Partnachklamm...........................127
25 Schachen Haus and the Königs Haus..131
26 Schachenhaus/Meiler Hut to Leutasch 134
27 The Zugspitze...137
28 Kreuzeck, Knappenhäuser and the Höllentalklamm.....................................142
29 Soiern Haus, Schöttelkarspitze and Seinskopf 148
30 Dammkar Hut, Hochland Hut and Wörnersattel..152
31 Kranzberg, Grünkopf and Ederkanzel..157
32 The Brunnsteinspitze 161
33 Herzogstand and Heimgarten..164
34 The Jochberg...168

Part IV The Tegernsee and Schliersee Mountains 171
35 Brauneck, Achselköpfe and Benediktenwand 176
36 The Seekarkreuz 179
37 Above Tegernsee...183
38 Wallberg and Risserkogel..186
39 Wildbad Kreuth to the Schildenstein...189
40 The Blauberge...192
41 The Roßstein...195
42 The Wendelstein..199
43 The Breitenstein..203
44 Taubensteinbahn – Soinsee – Taubenstein Haus...205
45 Jägerkamp, (Aiplspitz), Taubenstein and Taubenstein Haus.........................209
46 Tatzelwurm – Brünnstein – Tatzelwurm..212

Part V The Chiemgau Alps 215
47 From the Kampenwand to the Geigelstein 219
48 Marquartstein to the Hochgern 224
49 To Hindenburg Hut, Straubinger Haus and the Fellhorn.............................227
50 Winklmoos Alm and Dürrnbachhorn...231
51 Winklmoos Alm to the Steinplatte...234
52 The Hochfelln..238
53 The Rauschberg 241
54 From Inzell-Adlgaß to the Zwiesel 245
55 The Aibleck 246

Part VI The Berchtesgaden Alps	251
56 The Lattengebirge (Predigtstuhl)	254
57 To the Alm Meadows above Ramsau	258
58 The Reiteralpe Massif: Hintersee to Neue Traunsteiner Hut	262
59 The Hochkalter Massif: Ramsau to Blaueis Hut	265
60 Wimbachklamm, Wimbachtal and Wimbachgrieß Hut	267
61 Kühroint Alm (Watzmann Haus and Hocheck)	271
62 The Untersberg Massif	275
63 The Schellenberg Ice Cave	279
64 The Almbachklamm	281
65 Kehlstein: The Eagle's Nest	284
66 The Jenner	287
67 The Hagengebirge above Königssee	291
68 A Three-day Hike through Berchtesgaden National Park	295

Part VII Multi-Day Tours: The Via Alpina	301
69 Via Alpina: The Bavarian section of the Purple Trail	303
70 Via Alpina: The Bavarian section of the Red Trail	305

Valley Walks

i	The Breitachklamm	38
ii	To the Freibergsee	38
iii	The Eibsee	120
iv	Grubsee and Barmsee	146
v	Leutaschklamm	146
vi	Mühlbach – Laßeln – Holz – Mühlbach	175
vii	Around the Spitzingsee	198
viii	To Kronberger Alm	198
ix	The Smuggler's Trail	218
x	Around the Falkenstein	237
xi	Around the Frillensee	237
xii	Around the Thumsee	253
xiii	The Zauberwald	257
xiv	The Malerweg	257
xv	The Salzhandelsweg	257

Appendix A: Further Reading	306
Appendix B: Alpine Hut Accommodation	307
Appendix C: Useful Addresses	314
Appendix D: Glossary	316

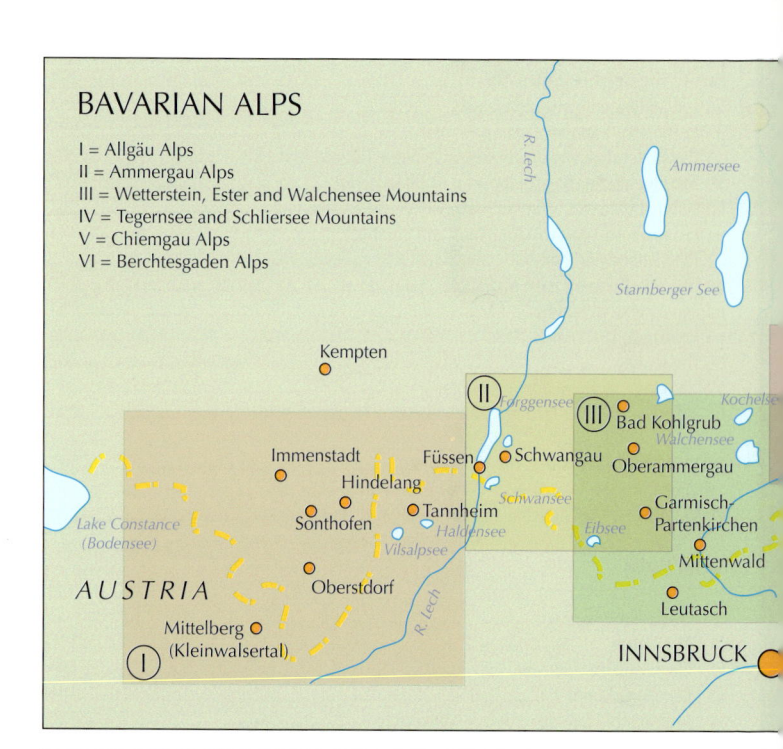

BAVARIAN ALPS

I = Allgäu Alps
II = Ammergau Alps
III = Wetterstein, Ester and Walchensee Mountains
IV = Tegernsee and Schliersee Mountains
V = Chiemgau Alps
VI = Berchtesgaden Alps

Ammersee
R. Lech
Starnberger See

Kempten

Forggensee
Kochelsee
Bad Kohlgrub
Walchensee
Immenstadt Füssen Schwangau Oberammergau
Hindelang *Schwansee*
Sonthofen Tannheim Garmisch-
Lake Constance *Haldensee* *Eibsee* Partenkirchen
(Bodensee) *Vilsalpsee* Mittenwald
AUSTRIA Oberstdorf *R. Lech*
Mittelberg Leutasch
(Kleinwalsertal)
(I) INNSBRUCK

Map Key

⬤ ◦	town (large, small)
■	very small settlement, cluster of houses
⌂	hut, only refreshment
▲ (filled)	hut/hotel with accommodation
⌂	abandoned hut/alp
⌂	hut, no accommodation, no refreshment
✝	church/chapel
✦	point of interest or orientation
▲	mountain
𝘈	campsite
Ⓑ	bus stop
🅿	car park
☀	lookout point

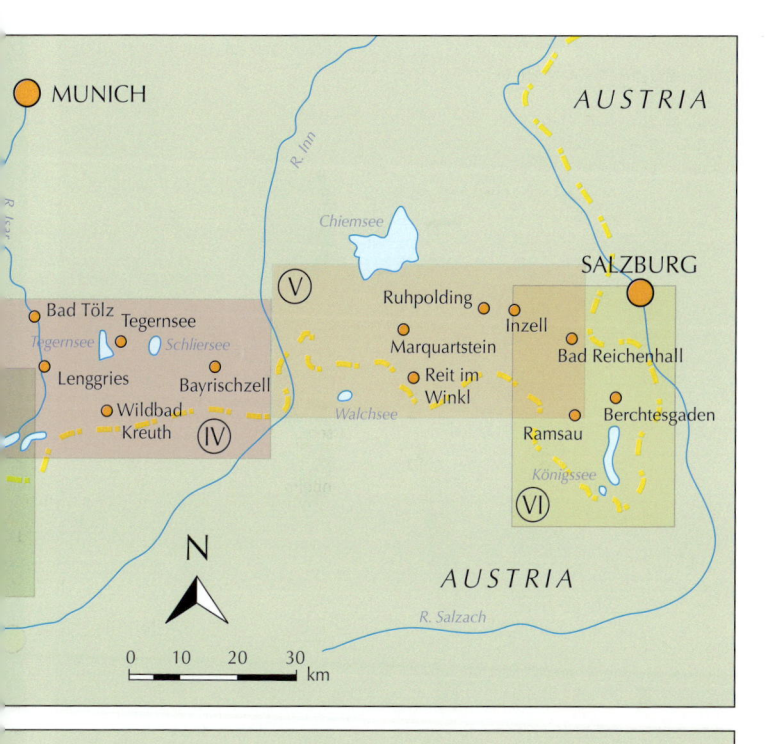

Map

MUNICH

AUSTRIA

R. Isar · R. Inn · Chiemsee · **SALZBURG**

Bad Tölz · Tegernsee · *Tegernsee* · *Schliersee* · Ruhpolding · Inzell

Lenggries · Bayrischzell · Marquartstein · Bad Reichenhall

Wildbad Kreuth · Reit im Winkl · Berchtesgaden

Walchsee · Ramsau · *Königssee*

Ⅳ · Ⅴ · Ⅵ

N

AUSTRIA

R. Salzach

0 10 20 30 km

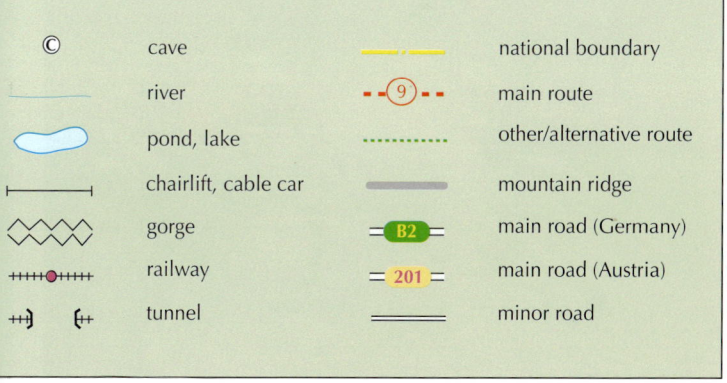

Legend

©	cave	┄┄	national boundary
	river	┄⑨┄	main route
⬭	pond, lake	┄┄┄┄	other/alternative route
├──┤	chairlift, cable car	▬▬▬	mountain ridge
⋈⋈⋈	gorge	═B2═	main road (Germany)
┼┼┼●┼┼┼	railway	═201═	main road (Austria)
⊢) (⊣	tunnel	══	minor road

Atop the Rubihorn (Route 4)

PREFACE

As far as most non-German mountain walkers are concerned the Bavarian Alps lie very much in the shadow of the Austrian and Swiss Alps. This is a shame, for what this border region lacks in terms of the comparative height and extent of its mountains is more than compensated for by the diversity of its landscape and cultural attractions.

This second, expanded edition of the guidebook hopes to bring that diversity to the attention of more outdoor enthusiasts. Moving from west to east the guidebook starts with a look at the Allgäu, a region renowned for its wildflowers, tranquil alpine pastures and the impossibly steep grass slopes that characterise many of its well-known peaks. Moving further east mountain trails lead past famous castles such as Neuschwanstein, which seems to have materialised from the pages of a storybook. In the vicinity of Garmisch-Partenkirchen you can sunbathe on the grassy summit of the Wank while enjoying a fantastic bird's-eye view over the world-famous alpine resort. At the foot of the Zugspitze, Germany's highest mountain, a trail skirts the shores of the beautiful Eibsee, a pristine lake surpassed in beauty only by the Königssee, visited in the final section of the guidebook. Here, in the Berchtesgaden Alps, trails in the shadow of the mighty Watzmann massif lead you through a landscape of Wagnerian grandeur.

There is, of course, much more to discover along these mountain trails. Upland moors, an ice cave, remote other-worldly karst landscapes like the Steinernes Meer and wild mountain gorges such as the Höllentalklamm, Leutaschklamm and Partnachklamm are just a few of the highlights. New additions include an ascent of the Zugspitze (possible even for those without climbing experience), a climb up to Hitler's 'Eagle's Nest' and a two-day hike from Garmisch-Partenkirchen to Leutasch in Austria.

All the sketch maps have been redrawn, and many new photographs have been added to illustrate the routes. The expanded introduction includes more practical information for planning your walking holiday so that you should not need to carry another general guidebook.

Though every attempt has been made to ensure the accuracy of the information given on the routes, floods and other natural events can erase landmarks, make it necessary to modify routes, or occasionally render a section of track unwalkable. However, a look at an up-to-date map, or a chat with hut wardens and other hikers on the spot, will ensure that such inconveniences are kept to a minimum.

Grant Bourne and Sabine Körner-Bourne, 2007

The ridge walk looking towards August-Schuster-Haus (Route 20)

INTRODUCTION

Those seeking alpine superlatives in the Bavarian Alps will search in vain. There are no peaks that can compete with the Matterhorn or Mont Blanc in terms of height, no glaciers of considerable extent, and even the ski slopes have a rather provincial aspect when compared to such famous resorts as Zermatt or St Moritz. Nevertheless, even without superlatives the Bavarian Alps still have their fair share of dramatic scenery. Their position between the lowlands to the north and the higher alpine regions further south offers a dramatic contrast in landscapes, and the proximity of Austria adds further to the region's charms.

For the walker the advantages of this location are many. For example, it is never far from the valley bottom to the top of a rugged mountain peak, from a picturesque village nestling in the lush green foothills to a lonely alpine tarn. A day in the mountains could be followed by an outing to historic Salzburg (especially if you are based in either Bad Reichenhall or Berchtesgaden) or Munich from where, on a clear autumn day, the mountains seem only a stone's throw away. One need not even go that far to enjoy a lazy day, for strung along the edge of the Alps is a succession of beautiful lakes (many of which are suitable for bathing), fairy-tale castles (around Füssen), ancient monasteries and opulent baroque churches. Folklore traditions are particularly strong in this part of Bavaria, evident in the numerous *Heimatabende* (evenings of folk dancing and songs) and the not-uncommon aspect of gnarled old men sporting flowing white beards and wearing *lederhosen*.

Of the many hundreds of excellent walking trails to be explored in the Bavarian Alps only a small selection are

Trail to Gams Hut (Route 22)

VIA FERRATA

The great majority of routes described can be undertaken by anybody who is reasonably fit. Ambitious protected routes (Klettersteige/Via Ferrata) which (may) require the use of ropes or special equipment are not described. However, it is worth mentioning a few of the more famous for those who are capable of attempting them (the inexperienced are strongly advised to leave them alone).

- **The Heilbronner Weg (Allgäu)** Rappensee Hut – Kemptner Hut. 2 days (6–7hrs). Depart Oberstdorf. Climbing experience not necessary, but this high-altitude route should not be underestimated.

- **The Mindelheimer Klettersteig (Allgäu)** Fiderepaß Hut – Mindelheimer Hut. 2 days (9–10hrs). Depart Mittelberg. Mountaineering or rock-climbing experience essential.

- **The Hindelanger Klettersteig (Allgäu)** Nebelhorn – Großer Daumen. 7–8hrs. Depart Oberstdorf. Most difficult Klettersteig in the Allgäu.

- **The Mittenwalder Höhenweg (Karwendelgebirge)** Westliche Karwendelspitze – Tiroler Hut – Brunnstein Hut. 6–7hrs. Depart Mittenwald. Similar in difficulty to Heilbronner Weg.

described in detail in this book. They vary in length from a half-day to four or five days and many are circular (convenient if you have to get back to your car). Where possible suggestions have been made for longer tours, but with the help of the recommended maps it should be possible to work out your own variations and additional routes.

GETTING THERE

By Rail

Many of the base towns in this book can be reached by train, and for those travelling from Great Britain this can be a very relaxing way of reaching their destination. Using the Eurostar from London's Waterloo station to Brussels, and onward via German ICE high-speed trains, it would take about 10hrs to reach Munich. **Note** The overall cost might be higher than flying with a low-cost airline.

For more information on tickets visit the Rail Europe website www.raileurope.com. For details on train routes through Germany visit www.bahn.de.

By Road

If travelling by car the excellent German motorways (*Autobahn*) are the quickest way south. From Frankfurt the A3, A7 and A8 take you via Munich from where the western, central and eastern regions of the Bavarian Alps are only a relatively short drive away. From Karlsruhe (near the French border and southeast of Luxemburg) the A8 and A7 provide a speedy connection to the Allgäu Alps. As an example of the distances involved Dunkirk to Munich is 969km, Munich to Garmisch-Partenkirchen 90km.

By Air
The closest international airports are Munich (www.munich-airport.de) in Germany, together with those at Salzburg (www.salzburg-airport.com) or Innsbruck (www.innsbruck-airport.com) in Austria. From Munich all destinations in the Bavarian Alps are quickly reached by either train, bus or car. For international travellers the main point of entry into Germany is Frankfurt International Airport (www.frankfurt-airport.com). A railway station at the airport allows comfortable train connections to Bavaria.

Budget flights to Germany
Note that budget airlines come and go, routes change and that even large national carriers offer budget fares that may compare to those of the 'cheap' airlines (from Britain and Ireland). Check with your local travel agent or search the Internet for current bargains. For bargain fares from Great Britain, Ireland, North America and elsewhere in the world visit (among others) www.travel.yahoo.com, www.expedia.com, www.travelocity.com and www.statravel.com (for student travel).

Ryanair's main port of call in Germany is Frankfurt-Hahn Airport. Flights to Frankfurt-Hahn depart from London Stansted, Glasgow's Prestwick Airport, Dublin, Shannon and Kerry. There are also flights to Salzburg in Austria from London Stansted, East Midlands, Liverpool and Dublin. For more information visit www.ryanair.com.

Garmisch-Partenkirchen nestles in the mountains (Part III, as seen from Route 22)

WALKING IN THE BAVARIAN ALPS

Cable cars save a long uphill climb on many routes

EasyJet offers flights from London Stansted to Munich (www.easyjet.com). SkyEurope (www1.skyeurope.com) offers flights from Manchester to Salzburg.

TRANSPORT

All the base towns and mountain groups in this guidebook can be easily reached via bus or train, or a combination of both. The transport system is efficient and reliable and will get you to the smallest village and the start of many routes. The bus system in Oberstdorf is especially well organised, and makes dispensing with the car a real pleasure! The 'Alex' trains from here to Munich also provide a comfortable connection for a day in the big city.

Details on transport to the start of a route, or from the end of a track, are given at the start of each route description. However, some routes may begin in town (for example, in Füssen, Mittenwald and Oberammergau). Oberammergau is especially interesting if you are without a car as the starting points of most of the routes described can be reached by foot.

Whether you travel around by car or bus depends on how you want to spend your holiday. Those who want to do a lot of travelling will find a car the most comfortable option. If you are content to stay in one place, or intend to spend a lot of time in mountain huts, then you can probably do without a car.

Information on timetables (*Fahrpläne*) for trains and buses can be obtained from the German Federal Railway's website at www.bahn.de (also in English), and for the local bus network in Oberbayern from www.rvo-bus.de (German).

Discounts are available on the regional transport services. As they are subject to change it pays to enquire at the local tourist offices about current offers (or visit one of the above websites). They can also help you with timetables and so forth. Some of the most interesting possibilities are listed below.

Discount tickets within Oberbayern (Upper Bavaria)

Gästekarte The free *Kurkarte* or *Gästekarte* (visitor's card) that you receive from either your host or the local tourist office usually allows free or discounted travel on the town buses. In Oberstdorf (Allgäu) and the towns of the Kleinwalsertal it is known as the Allgäu-Walser Card. As an extra you can book an *Urlaubskarte* (holiday card or pass) directly onto your Allgäu-Walser Card.

Allgäu-Walser Card with Urlaubskarte Allows unlimited travel on all bus and train lines in the southern Oberallgäu and the Kleinwalsertal. Travel on IC (InterCity) trains is not included. It can be purchased for a period of 7 or 14 days. Children under 15 years old, accompanied by an adult, travel free of charge. The Urlaubskarte can be purchased from local tourist offices.

Urlaubsticket Berchtesgadener Land Similar to the Urlaubskarte for the Allgäu, it allows unlimited travel on (nearly) all RVO buses in the Berchtesgaden region. The ticket is valid for 6 days. It can be purchased on showing a valid *Kurkarte* from the local tourist offices.

Werdenfelsticket Allows unlimited travel on all local trains and buses in the Werdenfels region (Garmisch-Partenkirchen, Mittenwald, Oberammergau, Kochel). It is valid from Mon–Fri from 09.00–03.00 on the following day. On weekends it is valid all day without any limits. Adults can take their own children or grandchildren up to the age of 14 free of charge. The ticket can be purchased from the bus driver, at railway station ticket counters and automatic ticket machines.

Discount tickets for Bavaria and travel throughout Germany

Bayern-Ticket Useful for long-distance travel on local trains (second class) and buses throughout Bavaria. It allows travel on any day Mon–Fri from 09.00–03.00. On weekends and public holidays it is valid all day. Up to 5 people can travel, or parents with children (any number) under 15 years. Discounts are available at various attractions in the region on presentation of the ticket, which can be bought from any DB Reisezentren (travel centres) at railway stations or from automatic ticket machines.

Bayern-Ticket Single For individual travellers, children under 6 travel free of charge. Otherwise as above.

Schönes-Wochenende-Ticket Similar to the Bayern-Ticket, except it is only valid on a Sat or Sun from 00.00–03.00 on the following day. It allows travel throughout Germany.

RVO Bus Pass Allows unlimited travel on the entire RVO bus network in Oberbayern. It is valid for 5 days of your choice within the period of 1 month.

ACCOMMODATION

Campsites, rustic farmhouses, simple bed and breakfasts or luxury hotels combined with stunning alpine views; the Bavarian Alps offers the whole gamut of possibilities to satisfy the varied budgets of tired mountain walkers seeking shelter for the night. For those who cannot bear to leave the tops well-equipped mountain huts ensure a measure of comfort, some even with the comfort of hot showers and double rooms.

All the base towns in this guidebook, along with many other towns along the alpine fringe, are *Kurorte* (spa or health resorts). All visitors staying in such towns are required to pay a visitor's tax. This daily surcharge (up to €2 per person, per day) is paid to your host on top of your accommodation costs, and is used to provide and maintain the various amenities offered by the resorts. All guests receive a *Kurkarte* or *Gästekarte* (visitor's card) which entitles them to various reductions on local attractions and free use of town buses.

Local tourist offices (contact details are given at the start of base town descriptions) are the best bet for information on accommodation in a specific area. It is often possible to book accommodation via their websites or by phone. For Bavaria as a whole try www.tiscover.de. Refer also to the comments under the categories listed below.

Campsites

There are numerous campsites scattered throughout the region. Standards are high and one can usually expect facilities for camper vans (mobile homes) or caravans, an attached restaurant and small shop for daily necessities. The local tourist office in your base town will be able to provide addresses of those in the vicinity. Try also www.eurocampings.co.uk. **Note** Wild camping is forbidden in Germany.

View over the Reintal to the Zugspitzplatt from the lookout pavilion near Schachen Haus (Route 25)

The Reintal near Reintalanger Hut (Route 27)

Youth Hostels

German youth hostels (*Jugendherberge*) are open to anyone holding a current membership card. The German network is affiliated with Youth Hostelling International. For more information and a listing of sites in Bavaria and Germany visit www.jugendherberge.de or contact DJH Service GmbH, Bismarckstrasse 8, D-32756 Detmold, Germany. Information is also available from the international site www.hihostels.com.

Bed and Breakfast, Guesthouses

Known in Germany as *Gasthöfe*, *Gästehäuser*, *Pensionen* or *Privatzimmer* the range and quality of the accommodation is as varied as the terminology. The common denominator, however, is that breakfast is usually included in the price of a room.

Generally speaking a *Gasthof* or *Gasthaus* is a small, privately run hotel or inn and is usually more expensive than a *Pension* or *Privatzimmer*. The *Privatzimmer* are always just that: a room in a private home. They are the cheapest alternative and the local tourist offices provide lists on their websites, along with other forms of accommodation. For addresses in Munich and other towns in Germany try www.bed-and-breakfast.de.

Many German B&Bs offer reductions for stays of three days or more; some also offer reductions for children. These usually apply to children up to 12 years of age, but it is best to enquire beforehand. At some establishments there will be a surcharge for a stay of only one night.

Holiday Flats

Self-catering holiday flats (*Ferienwohnung*) are excellent value for those who want to stay in a place for three days or longer; many landlords require a minimum of one week. This is an especially good option for families or if you are travelling in a group. Facilities vary according to price but may include a fully equipped kitchen, a lounge and separate bedrooms. Once again the websites of local tourist offices are the best place to search for this kind of accommodation. Other websites for holiday flats in Bavaria and elsewhere in Germany include www.novasol.co.uk, www.interhome.co.uk and www.interhome.us.

Hotels and Mountain Inns

There is a wide range of hotel accommodation within the area. They are usually rated from one to five stars in line with international standards. Especially attractive for hikers are mountain inns, some of which are only accessible by cable car or on foot. These are mentioned (see Appendix B) if they occur on or near a route. Hotels can often be booked directly via the tourist office website of the relevant base town. Other useful websites for hotel reservations and addresses include www.hotel.de, www.hotellerie.de, www.hotelguide.de and www.leithammel.de.

MOUNTAIN HUTS

Mountain huts belonging to the German (DAV) or Austrian (OeAV) Alpine Clubs are open to everybody, but those who are members of either organisation are entitled to discounts of up to 50 percent at both DAV and OeAV huts. Accommodation is also available in huts run by other organisations such as the Naturfreunde (Naturefriends) or in some privately run alm huts.

Note Near the start or towards the end of the walking season (June to late October) it is advisable to ring the huts in advance to see if they are open (see Appendix B).

Most Alpine Club (AV) huts provide simple meals and snacks which makes it unnecessary to carry large amounts of food. However, if you are a member it is a good idea to carry teabags or instant coffee and so on as you are entitled to *Teewasser* (tea-water). This is usually about a litre of hot water and the price is much more modest than that for a *Haferl* (mug) of tea with which non-members have to content themselves. Those with a thermos can always refill it at the hut. Another 'privilege' for members is the *Bergsteigeressen* (mountaineer's food). This dish is somewhat cheaper than the others on the menu, but is not always the best buy. Beer and other alcoholic drinks are also available.

At Alpine Club huts you can sleep in either a *Matrazenlager* or smaller bunkroom. The *Matrazenlager* is the cheapest and generally consists of a large room with mattresses usually placed very close together. A pillow and blanket is provided. To get a smaller bunkroom you need to ask for *Betten* (beds). Pillow, blankets and perhaps a warm eiderdown are provided. As these rooms usually accommodate a maximum of four people they are the better option for a good night's sleep. Some huts even offer double rooms, the ultimate in luxury! Please note: if you do not specify *Betten* you will invariably end up in the *Matrazenlager*.

MOUNTAIN HUTS

Most huts have washing facilities, even if that amounts to no more than a basin with cold running water. A few of the more luxurious huts provide hot showers, but you will have to pay extra.

Alpine Club huts are divided into three categories:

- **Cat I** Usually at least an hour's walk away from any mechanised transport (chairlifts and so on). Members have priority over non-members for sleeping accommodation; age has priority over youth. Non-members are not assigned a bed or mattress before 19.00. Beds or mattresses may only be used with a sleeping bag. Non-members cannot reserve accommodation in advance.
- **Cat II** Can be reached by mechanical means and generally offer better facilities. Once again members have priority over non-members for beds or mattresses, but non-members may also reserve their accommodation in advance. The huts are usually open all year and not just in summer (as is the case with many Category I huts).
- **Cat III** Accessible by car or cable railway, catering mainly for day visitors. Facilities for an overnight stay are limited. *Bergsteigeressen* and *Teewasser* are not available.

Appendix B lists those huts mentioned in the route descriptions. A comprehensive list of AV huts and those belonging to other alpine clubs in the Bavarian and Austrian Alps is published by Bergverlag Rother: *Die Alpenvereinshütten, Band I: Ostalpen*. On the Internet a complete data base of AV huts (in German) is available at www.dav-huettensuche.de.

There is a full listing of NaturFreunde Huts (Naturefriends) at the German language site www.naturfreunde.de. For more information visit the British website www.naturefriends.org.uk.

The mountain huts often have stunning locations with spectacular views (Rotwand Haus, Route 44)

TRAVELLING WITH A DOG

Walking with man's (or woman's) best friend in the mountains is – for both – great fun, but not without problems. Coming from the UK you will need to make sure your dog is inoculated against rabies, which is prevalent in many parts of Europe including the Bavarian Alps. Information on other necessary inoculations (and formalities) can be obtained from your veterinarian.

Germans are as fond of dogs as the British, and your four-legged friend will be welcome in most restaurants and many hotels and other accommodation.

However, it always pays to ask beforehand. Depending on the discretion of the hut warden or the rules of the alpine section to which the hut belongs, dogs are not usually welcome in mountain huts belonging to the Alpine Clubs. Your best chance will be in those with *Betten* (small bunkrooms) or rooms for two. If you come when demand is relatively low (spring or autumn) your chances will increase. Those huts only offering *Matrazenlager* (large dormitories) do not permit dogs.

With a bit of planning nothing stands in the way of taking your dog on a walking holiday

You will usually be able to find a place to stay in the valleys. Small dogs have the advantage over large breeds, though if the dog is obedient (and quiet) size should not be a problem. Most establishments charge a small extra daily fee.

In *Naturschutzgebiete* (nature reserves) or the *Nationalpark Berchtesgaden* dogs should be held on a leash. Where there is a lot of hunting (for instance the Kleinwalsertal, Austria) keep your dog on a leash regardless of whether it is the hunting season. The same applies to areas where sheep or cows are grazed. If your dog is absolutely obedient you can let it roam free, but be aware that many farmers will react aggressively if they think your dog endangers their livestock.

Where meadows are near habitation (for instance Ramsau or Oberstdorf) dogs should not be allowed to defecate on the fields, a source of hay and therefore animal feed.

FLORA AND WILDLIFE

Average temperatures (°C) and precipitation figures (mm) for Garmisch-Partenkirchen in the region of the Wetterstein, Ester and Walchensee Mountains

	Jan	Feb	Mar	Apr	May	Jun	Jul	Aug	Sep	Oct	Nov	Dec
Temp.	-3	-1	3	7	11	14	15	15	12	7	2	-2
Precip.	76	55	78	99	123	176	185	162	123	76	63	80

Austrian Alpine Club (Section Britannia) The Austrian Alpine Club is affiliated with the German Alpine Club, and its members are entitled to all the privileges mentioned above. Postal address: 12a North Street, Wareham, Dorset BH20 4AG; tel: (01929) 556 870, fax: (01929) 554 729, e-mail: manager@aacuk.org.uk, www.aacuk.org.uk.

CLIMATE

The climate in the Bavarian Alps is characterised by relatively cool summers with high rainfall and mild winters which usually (recent years have been somewhat disappointing for skiers) bring plenty of snow. This is largely due to the influence of the prevailing westerly winds which deposit moist oceanic air masses in the form of clouds on the northern fringes of the Alps. Precipitation in the valleys can be as high as 1500mm per annum and in the alpine regions as high as 2500mm. In other words waterproof gear is essential.

A guarantee for fine weather, however, is the *Föhn* (known as *Chinook* in the American Rockies). This dry, warm wind brings crystal clear air and blue skies to the mountains when the lowlands to the north are hidden below a thick blanket of cloud. It makes its presence felt especially in autumn, one of the best times to go walking.

Note When walking in the Alps remember that with every 100m of altitude the temperature drops by 1°C.

Walking season

The walking season starts in the valleys in April, and with a bit of luck peaks over 1500m are free of snow by the end of May. The mountain walking season proper begins in June and finishes in late October. January is the coldest month and – being in the middle of winter – one might think it a time when only skiers are to be found on the mountain slopes. However, a growing number of people are discovering the joys of snow-shoeing through isolated alpine valleys, far away from the crowded ski slopes. A description of suitable routes goes beyond the scope of this book but it is an interesting possibility for those who want to try something a little different.

FLORA AND WILDLIFE

In all mountain regions different plant communities grow at different altitudes. A walk from the valley floor to the top of an alpine peak will take you through

WALKING IN THE BAVARIAN ALPS

In late spring and early summer the mountain paths are lined with a profusion of wildflowers

several vegetation zones: cultivated fields and woodland lower down, shrublands and alpine meadows as you ascend. Due to the extreme climatic conditions the higher alpine regions are only relatively sparsely vegetated. In the Bavarian Alps the *Latsche* or dwarf pine (*Pinus mugo*) is the most characteristic plant above the treeline (1700–1900m). Related to the pine (*Pinus sylvestris*) it grows at altitudes up to 2700m and has the appearance of a bush rather than a tree.

Below 1700m the forests are characterised by conifers such as spruce and fir, but large stands of beech are still found in those areas which have not been over-exploited by the forestry industry. Relatively untouched mountain forests are dominated by a mixture of pine and beech (800–1400m), and in recent years efforts have been made to establish healthier mixed forests (less susceptible to disease and insect pests) by planting more deciduous species along with the quick-growing conifers. In autumn the sycamore and European larch are especially noticeable as their leaves turn to a striking golden-yellow.

Human influence on the local plant communities is most evident on the lower mountain slopes and in the valleys. Fields of wildflowers – that many may think represent a natural, undisturbed environment – in fact result from the grazing of alpine pastures over many centuries. Without this grazing, or the mowing of grass for hay, the mountain pastures would soon be overgrown by weeds and eventually forest would take over. Various species of orchid, gentian and globeflower are just a few of the many that can be seen in the course of a walk through alm pastures. Probably the best known and most characteristic of the flowering plants at higher altitudes (up to 2800m) is the alpenrose with its pink-red flowers. Among the rarest plants found in the region are the famous edelweiss and the beautiful lady's slipper orchid.

The last brown bears were exterminated in the Bavarian Alps in the 19th century and the wolf and lynx fared no better – small populations have managed to survive, however, in a few isolated regions elsewhere in the Alps. In the absence of predators the herbivores have managed to do quite well, though even here a few species have been reintroduced after over-hunting and loss of habitat decimated local populations. Among the larger animals you are most likely to encounter are red deer (in the

Larches provide a vivid splash of colour in autumn

Hellebore (above left). Stemless gentian (above right), a common sight along many routes in spring and summer. Chamois (below) are quite commonly seen on the higher level walks.

lower forested regions), chamois and ibex. Large birds such as the capercaillie and black grouse are very rare, while the golden eagle and bearded vulture are still struggling to re-establish themselves after being brought to the verge of extinction.

If the above sounds like a rather depressing litany of ecological disaster it might be a relief to know that the alpine chough is quite common and continues to amuse mountain walkers with its acrobatic flight techniques and the undivided interest it shows in the contents of one's lunch box. Ptarmigan are found in high alpine regions where their plumage blends in perfectly with the light grey rocks. In winter they turn snow-white (like the snow hare) so it takes a bit of luck, and a keen eye, to see them at any time of the year. Marmots usually leave you in no doubt as to their existence by emitting a shrill warning cry as soon as you approach. In some places they have grown so used to the presence of people that they are content to just stare back at you from the vicinity of their holes. The burrows which these small, furry rodents dig are quite impressive: up to 10m long and 3m deep.

Among the smaller representatives of the animal kingdom worth special mention are two species of salamander. The spotted or fire salamander (*Salamandra salamandra*) is found at lower altitudes on forested slopes, whereas the black alpine salamander (*Salamandra atra*) may be found at altitudes of up to 3000m (see also Route 48). Both species are best observed in the early morning when dew still lies on the ground, or just after it has rained. Less common (in spite of the name) is the common viper or adder (*Vipera berus*), a poisonous snake which inhabits upland moors. However, as it is very shy you are unlikely to see one.

This brief survey of alpine flora and wildlife is of course by no means complete, and space precludes listing all the colourful butterflies and other insects that you may encounter during a sojourn in the mountains. See Appendix A for some useful book titles.

CLOTHING AND EQUIPMENT

When walking in the mountains always carry wet weather gear and warm clothes as an insurance against sudden changes in the weather. Good walking boots are essential, although jogging shoes are sufficient for some valley walks.

Though there are usually huts en route where you can buy refreshments it is nevertheless important to carry some kind of light snack (chocolate, dried fruit, nuts, and so on) and plenty to drink.

A passport should always be carried where routes run close to or cross national borders. You will probably never be asked to show it, but if you are you'd better have it!

For most routes in this book a small, light inner-frame rucksack is all that is required. For longer tours a narrow inner-frame rucksack with a volume of up to 40 litres should be sufficient. Wide packs with external frames can be very cumbersome, and even dangerous on narrow alpine paths.

Those staying in huts need slippers of some kind as boots are not permitted in the sleeping areas. If staying in a *Matrazenlager* it is wise to bring earplugs. There is *always* somebody who snores! A sleeping bag (a light YHA-style cloth sleeping bag will do) is required in AV huts belonging to Category I.

As most alpine trails in the Bavarian Alps are usually very well waymarked many people do not bother with a compass. It is, however, a wise precaution to carry one and to know how to use it in conjunction with a topographical map. Also useful is a GPS device, though as they require batteries it is sensible to carry an ordinary compass as a back-up.

Other useful pieces of equipment are sunglasses, suncream, a hat (the sun's UV rays should not be underestimated in the mountains), a whistle for emergencies and perhaps gaiters if you are expecting to encounter snow on the trail. A pair of spiked walking poles (known in German as *Wanderstöcke* and available at any local sports shop) aid balance and help ease the strain on the knees when going downhill. On longer excursions a torch can be very handy.

SAFETY IN THE MOUNTAINS

There are mountain rescue (Bergwacht) teams based near all the main resorts in the Bavarian Alps.
- Emergency telephone number: 112
- Weather report: 089 295070 (German)

Note Mobile phone coverage can be patchy in alpine regions, so do not rely on your mobile phone alone.

Safety checklist
- Inform somebody of your intentions before departure.
- Do not walk alone, especially in remote alpine regions.
- Check the current weather forecast (your host, hut wardens or the local tourist office can help here).
- Make sure you are properly equipped (see Clothing and Equipment above).
- Ensure that your abilities match the level of difficulty of the proposed route.
- Be prepared to turn back in the event of adverse conditions.

International distress signal
To be used in an emergency only.
- Six blasts on a whistle (and flashes with a torch after dark) spaced evenly for one minute, followed by a minute's pause. Repeat until located by a rescuer.
- Response: Three signals per minute followed by a minute's pause.

Rack railway to Wendelstein summit (Route 42)

LANGUAGE

German is spoken in Bavaria and Austria, although it is often flavoured by the various local dialects which can make it difficult to understand even for those who are otherwise fluent. However, English is widely spoken and visitors will usually have no trouble finding someone who speaks at least a little English at ticket offices, hotels, restaurants and so forth. The staff at tourist information offices are generally quite fluent and can help with advice on English-speaking doctors, timetables, accommodation and other matters. Nevertheless, a good phrase book will help clarify any communication problems that might arise (see also Appendix D).

EXPENSES

A strong argument in favour of the Bavarian Alps as opposed to other regions in the European Alps is the cost factor. When compared to Austria the overall costs are around 5 percent lower, and in the case of Switzerland nearly 20 percent lower! This differential soon becomes obvious in terms of restaurants, shopping and accommodation.

For those on a walking holiday camping is the cheapest and most flexible form of accommodation. There are plenty of campsites spread along the fringes of the Bavarian Alps, and it is often possible to leave your car at the campsite, and to just pay for your empty tent (*leeres Zelt*) if you are walking from hut to hut. *Pensions* or bed and breakfasts are also quite reasonably priced and ideal if you intend to base yourself in an area for several days (most offer discounts for a stay of a week or more) and are not planning to stay in the mountain huts. Every tourist office has a *Gästeverzeichnis* (accommodation list), and it pays to get hold of a copy.

HOW TO USE THIS BOOK

In this book the Bavarian Alps are divided into six mountain groups, described from west to east. The divisions are more or less in accordance with those stipulated by the Alpine Club (AV).

The routes have been grouped around base towns in order to make planning a walking holiday as easy as possible. A brief portrait of each town has been included to help walkers choose the most suitable place to stay. Apart from the mountain routes which are described in detail the authors have also included some shorter valley walks. These walks are generally no longer than 3hrs in length and suitable for all ages.

At the start of each route is a box with information to help you plan your route, including the distance, height gain, height loss, grade of difficulty, recommended map, accommodation in huts and so forth. Contact details of the huts are given in Appendix B under the mountain group where the route is located.

Details of transport to the starting point of each route (by bus, cable car and so on) are given, with information on how to return to the start at the end of the day. Where a route starts in the base town and can be reached on foot or by local bus from, say, a nearby village where you may be staying, 'local bus' is noted. Parking details are also given.

Grading of Routes

The following grades are only intended as a rough guide to the difficulty of the individual routes. How hard or difficult a route is for any given person at any given time depends on such variables as the weather, track conditions and personal fitness. None of the routes described requires climbing skills or experience in snow or ice conditions – though snow may sometimes be encountered on the higher routes, especially in early spring or late autumn.

- **Grade 1** Clearly waymarked, involve no dangerous passages and suitable for anybody who is reasonably fit.
- **Grade 2** Clearly waymarked, but either longer or cross more difficult terrain. A higher standard of fitness and at least sure-footedness is required.
- **Grade 3** Suitable only for those who are fit and have sufficient mountain experience; often require a head for heights and in some (very few) cases pathfinding ability.

The walking times given are only approximate and do not take into account refreshment stops and so forth. Bad weather or track conditions can also prolong a walk and these factors should always be taken into consideration. As a rough guideline you could add 1–2hrs for 'enjoying the scenery'.

The trail above Knorr Hut, near the Zugspitzplatt (Route 27)

From the very start the trail offers fine views towards the main chain of the Allgäu Alps (Route 3)

MAPS

The sketch maps are only intended to serve as an initial means of orientation. They **should not be used** in place of a proper walking map.

The relevant maps are listed at the start of each route description to enable walkers to quickly locate the map they need. **Note** The maps listed are all to the scale 1:50,000. Where possible a choice of maps has been given. In researching this guidebook the Kompass maps were used as a basis for describing routes, though it should be possible to follow them using maps from other publishers. All the maps mentioned are readily available at bookshops in Germany or from:

- **Edward Stanford Ltd** 12–14 Long Acre, London WC2E 9LP www.stanfords.co.uk
- **The Map Shop** 15 High Street, Upton-upon-Severn, Worcs WR8 OHJ www.themapshop.co.uk
- **Mapsworldwide** (British online map shop) www.mapsworldwide.com
- **Omni Resources** 1004 South Mebane Street, PO Box 2096, Burlington, NC 27216-2096, USA e-mail: inquiries@omnimap.com, www.omnimap.com

Apart from the two main series listed below there are also maps produced by smaller, locally based publishers, often in conjunction with local tourist offices. These maps are usually of a high standard and are often available at a scale of 1:25,000.

1 Kompass-Wanderkarten 1:50,000 (for certain areas also 1:30,000 or 1:35,000) A useful feature of the Kompass series is the fact that the map legend is in both German and English. All the trails are very clearly marked, and the maps frequently updated. The most recent ones are GPS compatible.

Kompass has also brought out some digital maps that are relevant to the area covered. Currently available are *Allgäuer Alpen Kleinwalsertal*, *Füssen-Ausserfern*, *Zugspitze-Mieminger Kette* and the

Karwendelgebirge. The digital maps can be used in conjunction with a GPS device, and with suitable software the maps can be transferred to a Palm or Pocket PC.

2 Umgebungskarten (UK) mit Wanderwegen (Area Maps with Walking Trails) Usually 1:50,000. The Bavarian State Survey Office (Landesamt für Vermessung und Geoinformation) puts out excellent maps. The topographical detail exceeds that of the Kompass maps, but they are not as readily available in local bookshops. Though topographical maps are also available at 1:25,000 these usually show the trails less clearly. For an overview of the areas covered visit www.geodaten.bayern.de.

FAST FACTS

Currency Germany belongs to the Euro (€) zone, as does most of Central Europe including Austria. €1 = 100 cents.

Formalities Members of EU countries with either a valid passport or national identity card do not require a visa to enter Germany. Citizens of the USA, Canada, Republic of Ireland, New Zealand and Australia do not require a visa for stays of up to three months. South African nationals do require a visa.

Language German or dialects of German are spoken in Bavaria and Austria. English is widely spoken.

Health No special health precautions are necessary for travel in Germany. UK residents are covered by reciprocal health schemes while in the country. In order to receive coverage a European Health Insurance Card (EHIC) is required, available via your local post office. Not all expenses are covered by these schemes and so it is wise to take out extra insurance in case of accidents – mountain rescue is expensive! www.dh.gov.uk/travellers.

International Dialling Code The international dialling code for calls to Germany from abroad is 0049 and to Austria 0043. When dialling the UK from Germany the code is 0044, then drop the first zero of the following area code. Most public phones in Germany are card-operated. Telephone cards (*Telefonkarten*) can be bought at post offices, newspaper kiosks and some bookshops.

Location The Bavarian Alps are located in Germany along the border with Austria. More specifically they are situated in Oberbayern (Upper Bavaria), the southernmost region of the state of Bavaria. The Allgäu, at the western extreme of the region, is treated as a separate entity.

Brentenjoch from Bad Kissinger Hut (Route 14)

PART I
THE ALLGAU ALPS

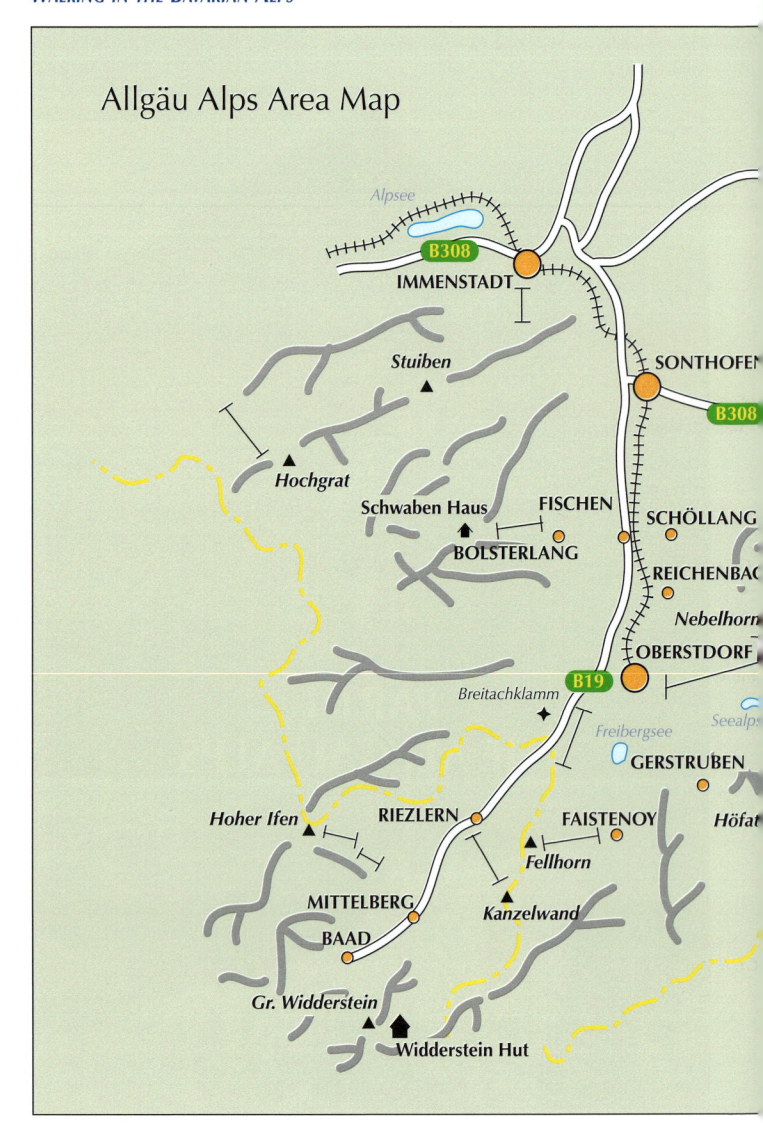

Allgäu Alps Area Map

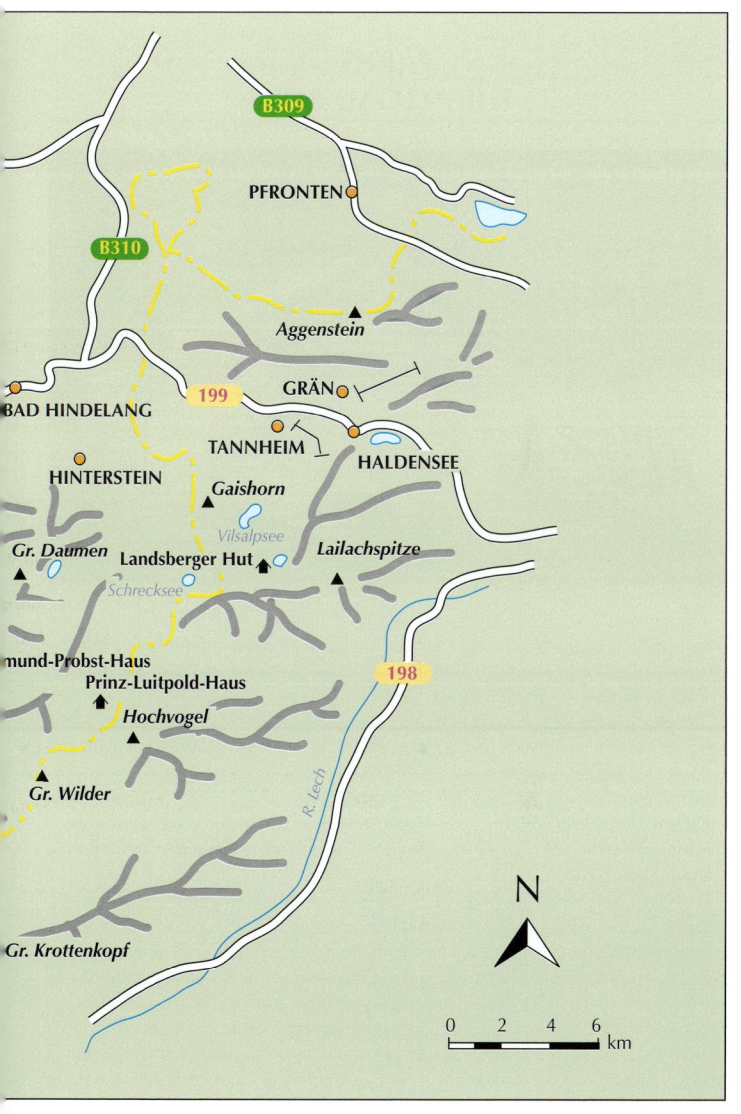

Part I – The Allgau Alps

PART I
THE ALLGAU ALPS

The region is almost as well known for its cows as for its mountains (Route 6)

The main chain of the Allgäu Alps forms the German–Austrian border between the rivers Iller and Lech and is located within the Allgäu, a popular tourist region encompassing that part of the northern Limestone Alps and the alpine foothills between Lake Constance (Bodensee) and the River Lech. Included within the Alpine Club's definition of the group is the area known as the Allgäuer Voralpen to which such peaks as the Fellhorn (2037m) and Hoher Ifen (2230m) as well as the Gottesacker Plateau (2017m) belong. Among the highest peaks in the Allgäu Alps in German territory are the Mädelegabel (2645m), Hochvogel (2593m) and Nebelhorn (2224m). The highest peak is Großer Krottenkopf (2657m) on the Austrian side of the border. Also covered here is the Kleinwalsertal, which lies in Austria, but is only accessible by road from the German state of Bavaria.

Though not the driest region in the Alps (precipitation averages between 1000mm per year in the valleys, and 2000mm per year in the alpine regions), the Allgäu is blessed with a relatively mild climate which, combined with its great diversity of soil types, has contributed to a richly varied flora. There is no other region in the Alps where so many different species of wildflower grow so close together. In spring soldanellas and crocus push their way up through the retreating snow, while dark blue gentians dot the drier slopes. Early summer is the time for red alpenrose, yellow gentian, monk's hood and alpine aquilegia to decorate the mountainsides. Those who are lucky might

PART I – THE ALLGÄU ALPS

even find the rare lady's slipper orchid or the famed edelweiss. In autumn carline thistles and purple autumn crocus (meadow saffron) offer some compensation for the shorter days and cooler temperatures.

THE KLEINWALSERTAL

This valley was settled by farmers from the Valais, a canton in Switzerland, in the 13th century. Though it has belonged to Austria since 1453 it is only easily accessible from Germany. This caused problems for farmers when it came to selling their produce within Austria as they had to cross high alpine passes to get to markets in the south. In winter they were completely isolated from the motherland. This difficult and economically disastrous state of affairs came to an end in 1891 when Austria and Germany signed a treaty which exempted the 'Walser' from the need to pay duty on goods brought to and from Germany.

The valley is entered at Walserschanz (no customs post), only a few kilometres southwest of Oberstdorf. For mountain walkers the Kleinwalsertal provides plenty of carefully waymarked trails and magnificent scenery. A bus (Walserbus) runs daily (May–October, every 30mins) from Oberstdorf railway station to Baad at the end of the valley.

OBERSTDORF

*Tourist office: Tourist-Information und Kurverwaltung (main office), Marktplatz 7, D-87561 Oberstdorf. Tel: (08322) 700-0, fax: (08322) 700 236; **www.oberstdorf.de**, e-mail: info@oberstdorf.de. Tourist-Information, Bahnhofplatz (opposite railway station). Tel: (08322) 700 217 (accommodation service).*

Oberstdorf can be reached by train from Munich and is popular as a tourist resort in both summer and winter. Though not unattractive, this modern-looking town lacks the

Oberstdorf enjoys a magnificent situation at the foot of the Allgäu Alps; near the centre of the picture is the Hoher Ifen in the Kleinwalsertal (Route 4)

rural charm of some of the smaller settlements in this region (in 1865 a devastating fire destroyed most of the older buildings). It is well served with a good range of accommodation (campsite, youth hostel and hotels in all price categories) and offers all the usual tourist facilities.

VALLEY WALKS
Map: Kompass-Wanderkarte No 3.

i **BREITACHKLAMM (1½hrs)** The Breitachklamm (open 08.00–17.00) is 1½km long and considered by many to be one of the most picturesque gorges of its size in Central Europe. Over a period of some 10,000 years the Breitach stream has cut its way through the limestone to a depth of 90m, and at some points the sheer rock walls are not much more than 2m apart. The *Klamm* is by no means an 'undiscovered' attraction and is best avoided on weekends, and even during the week it is unlikely that you will have it all to yourself. **Note** There is an entrance charge.

The *Klamm* is situated to the southwest of Oberstdorf. From the ticket office near Gasthaus Breitachklamm follow a well-kept path into the gorge. As short as this walk is, it provides an impressive example of how water has sculpted, and continues to sculpt, many of the more spectacular features in the Limestone Alps. At the other end keep left and continue towards Gasthaus Walserschanz. From here walk a few minutes along the road in the direction of Oberstdorf, then turn left along a track (the Zwingsteig) that brings you to a small bridge which crosses the gorge at height of 80m. On the other side the track zigzags uphill for a short stretch and then it is an easy stroll through woods and fields back to the start. (*Refreshments available at Alpe Dornach, before you reach the car park.*)

ii **TO THE FREIBERGSEE (2¼hrs)** From the centre of Oberstdorf follow the Weststrasse to the Schlechtenbrücke over the Stillach. Directly after the bridge cross the road to Birgsau and follow a small asphalt road uphill to the left in the direction of Café Waldesrüh. From the café continue climbing at a moderate gradient through woods in the signposted direction of Freibergsee. After passing a turn-off to the Söllereck cable railway the next destination, Restaurant Bergkristall, is 30mins away. From here an attractive trail runs downhill through woods on a broad gravel path (Probstweg). Pass the Naturfreundehaus (*refreshments*), and after roughly 20mins pleasant walking you will be suddenly confronted with a view of the wooded shores of the Freibergsee. Follow the path left to reach Strandcafé Freibergsee (*refreshments, boat hire, swimming*), which is beautifully located directly on the lake shore.

For the return route to Oberstdorf climb briefly up from the lake, then descend through woods towards the Untere Renksteg. On reaching the Stillach cross the covered wooden bridge, then follow a level gravel path on the river's right bank back to the Schlechtenbrücke and Oberstdorf – 1hr from the covered bridge.

ROUTE 1
The Nagelfluhkette: A Ridge Walk between the Mittagberg and Stuiben

Start	Immenstadt, north of Oberstdorf
Parking	Car park next to Mittagbahn chairlift
Transport	Regular trains from Oberstdorf
Distance	13.5km/8 miles
Height gain	298m (997ft)
Height loss	1018m (3340ft)
Time	5hrs
Grade	2
Refreshments	Bergstation Mittagbahn, Alpe Gund
Map	Kompass-Wanderkarte No 3: Allgäuer Alpen – Kleinwalsertal

The Nagelfluh Chain extends for some 25km from Mittagberg, near Immenstadt, to the Hohe Häderich in Austria. It takes its name from the characteristic 'nagelfluh' rock, a type of conglomerate composed of smaller stones cemented together millions of years ago during the Pleistocene. In many ways this walk introduces much that is typical of walks in the region: unobstructed views of the main Allgäu chain and the lowlands to the north; in spring and summer a profusion of wildflowers; tracks flanked by steep grassy slopes on the one side and sheer cliffs on the other; the tinkling of cowbells from lonely alpine pastures; and alm huts offering milk and cheese produced on the spot.

The two-stage Mittagbahn chairlift brings walkers comfortably to the top of the **Mittagberg**, thus saving a roughly 2hr ascent. From the Bergstation (upper terminus) an easy trail leads in a southwesterly direction to the **Bärenkopf** (10–15mins), an unremarkable peak marked by a wooden cross just below the actual summit (1463m). The onward route is clearly visible from here: at first continue comfortably a short distance along grassy slopes then, on reaching a

Though this route offers no extreme difficulties, some exposed sections require care. It is best undertaken in dry and stable weather conditions.

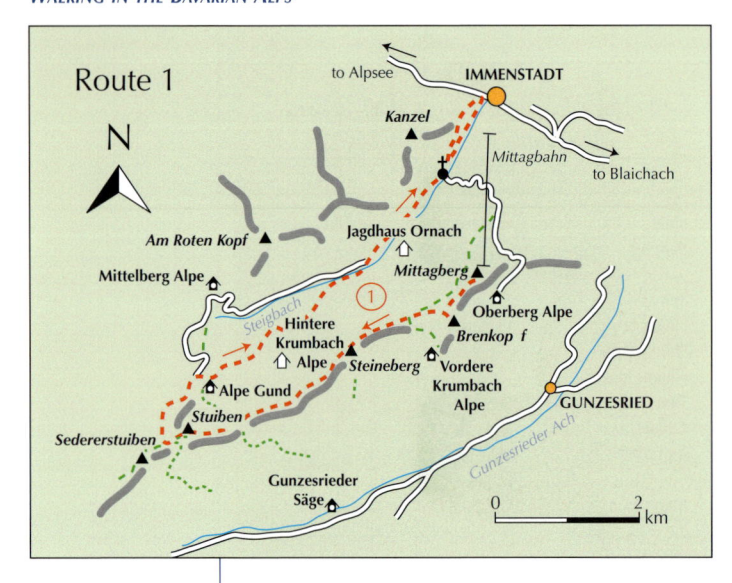

WALKING IN THE BAVARIAN ALPS

lightly wooded, narrow section of the ridge the trail begins its steep – and, in summer, very sweaty – ascent to the Steineberg.

Shortly before the last section of the climb to the **Steineberg** summit cross the *Normalweg* (easy route) swings sharp left, before climbing steeply to the cliffs below the summit. A more difficult and exposed route (*Nur für Geübte*) is also signposted. Both routes will bring you to the ladder, which climbs directly to the summit cross. ◂

> To avoid the ladder follow a narrow trail, which continues from the ladder and below the cliffs, before curving back to the summit along a harmless grass slope.

From here it is fairly easy going along the ridge towards the Stuiben, which is already visible in the distance. Wire ropes aid walkers on a few more exposed sections of track and most usefully along one easy traverse down a bare rock face. In early summer, the grass slopes along the trail are dotted with dark blue gentians, wild orchids and other wildflowers.

Not long after passing the intersection with the trail leading directly down to Alpe Gund, the track begins its steep climb up the **Stuiben**. Just before the summit wire ropes aid your ascent along a steeply falling section of rock.

ROUTE 1 – THE NAGELFLUHKETTE

Ladder to Steineberg summit

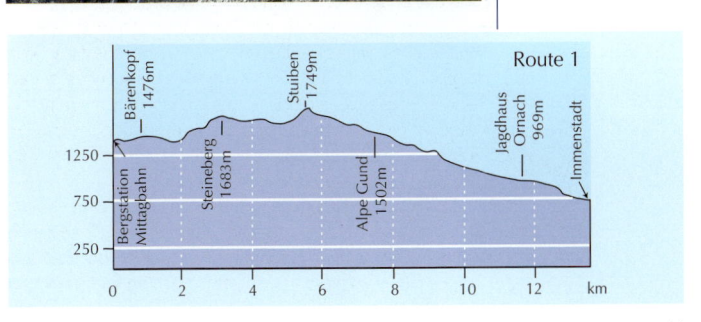

Then it is an easy stroll to the summit cross and a splendid panoramic view.

Descend from the summit along a clear trail, which takes you in around 20mins to **Alpe Gund** (*accommodation and simple refreshments in summer*). Continue from the east side of the alm hut in a (signposted) northeasterly direction – this route does not follow the gravel road down to Immenstadt on the other side of the hut. Pass a trail up to the Steineberg and follow the signposted track to Immenstadt. It winds attractively through fields and lightly wooded slopes to **Hintere Krumbach Alpe**. After reaching the broad meadows below the alm hut the trail crosses a simple log bridge over a stream, climbs briefly left, then descends through the woods. It takes you in roughly 40mins to the gravel road from Alpe Gund.

Now follow the road past **Jagdhaus Ornach** (hunting lodge) to a small wooden chapel and picnic tables. A bit further on you have the choice of continuing along the road, or you can follow the more interesting Tobelweg, which runs just below the road through a lovely little gorge. Once the outskirts of **Immenstadt** are reached (15–20mins from the turn-off along the Tobelweg), it is no more than 10mins back to the valley station of the Mittagbahn or to the railway station.

Ridge walk between Steineberg and Stuiben

ROUTE 2
Over the Großer Ochsenkopf to Riedberger Horn

Start	Bolsterlang
Parking	Car park at the Bolsterlanger Hörnerbahn
Transport	Regular bus service from Oberstdorf
Distance	12.2km/7.5 miles
Height gain	286m (938ft)
Height loss	845m (2772ft)
Time	4½hrs
Grade	1
Refreshments	Schwaben Haus, Bolgen Alpe, Zunkleiten Alpe
Accommodation	Schwaben Haus
Map	Kompass-Wanderkarte No 3: Allgäuer Alpen – Kleinwalsertal

Though not alpine in character the ridge walk between Ochsenkopf and Riedberger Horn offers plenty of fine views to the higher mountains further south, and provides a good impression of the alm pastureland that is so typical of the Allgäu's grass-covered lower peaks. It is an easy walk with no major climbs and can be walked from spring to late autumn.

The **Bolsterlanger Hörnerbahn** (gondola-lift) takes you in less than 10mins to an altitude of 1500m. At the top there is a magnificent view over the Iller Valley, and both the Großer Ochsenkopf and Riedberger Horn, the goals of this walk, are clearly visible to the west.

From the upper station of the gondola-lift an almost level path leads to Schwaben Haus. Most walkers who want to climb the Riedberger Horn continue straight ahead from the hut. This is a very easy but rather monotonous route. It is much more interesting to turn right just before the hut and to climb steeply uphill towards the Großer Ochsenkopf. After

WALKING IN THE BAVARIAN ALPS

Route 2

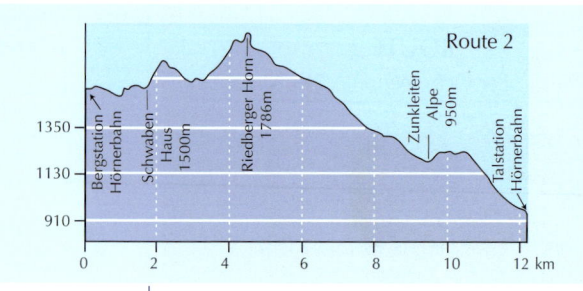

Bergstation Hörnerbahn — Schwaben Haus 1500m — Riedberger Horn 1786m — Zunkleiten Alpe 950m — Talstation Hörnerbahn

To the north the Nagelfluhkette ridge (see Route 1) is clearly visible.

gaining about 100m in altitude the path from the Weiherkopf is joined and followed left along the ridge (westwards) to the summit of the **Ochsenkopf** (1662m). Marked by a wooden cross, and covered by bilberry (blueberry) bushes, there are nevertheless enough grassy patches where you can recline and admire the views. ◄

From the Großer Ochsenkopf descend through the bilberry bushes and go past a small upland moor. The track always keeps to the ridge passing en route the fork to Printschen Hut (private). In summer alpenrose provide a splash of red colour to the predominating browns and greens of the landscape. Shortly before you reach the Riedberger Horn there is a steep rocky section that you have to scramble up, but it is not too difficult. After 1hr walking (from Ochsenkopf) a final climb leads up a grass slope to the summit of the **Riedberger Horn**.

On fine weekends the summit is usually crowded with walkers, most of whom have taken the shorter route up from Grasgehren Hut (car park) in the Schönberger Achtal. The views are good in all directions: apart from the main chain of the Allgäu Alps to the southwest, you can also make out the distinctive rock wall of the Gottersackerwände (south, see Route 11) and to the west the snow-tipped peaks of the Swiss Alps.

The descent presents no problems. At first you walk in the direction of Grasgehren Hut. At the saddle turn left, and then walk for a while in the direction of Schwaben Haus. Eventually a signpost points you to the right towards Sonderdorf. After passing Obere Bolgen Alpe (*Alp(e)* = alm

Route 2 – Over the Großer Ochsenkopf to Riedberger Horn

Trail to Schwaben Haus

in the Allgäu) a partially asphalted road is joined. From here it is not far to **Bolgen Alpe** (*refreshments*).

From the alm hut keep to the road until **Zunkleiten Alpe**. Leave the road here on a path to the left. Ignore a left-hand turn-off further along the route to the gondola's Mittelstation and continue to the **Sonderdorfer Kreuz** (cross). The trail now follows the Bergblick-Hohenweg (panorama trail) back to the valley station of the Hörnerbahn.

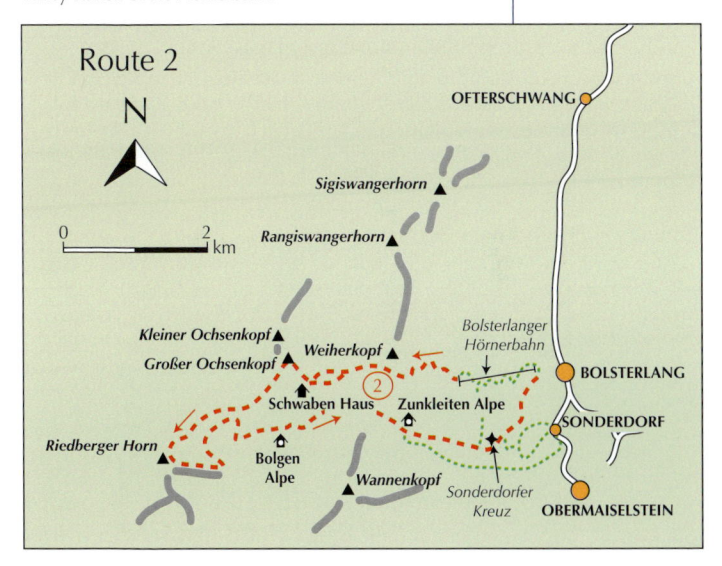

ROUTE 3
A Ridge Walk between Sonnenkopf and Falken Alpe

Start	Schöllang (north of Oberstdorf)
Parking	Car park on the bypass to Altstädten
Transport	Regular bus service from Oberstdorf
Distance	10.7km/6.5 miles
Height gain	952m (3123ft)
Height loss	952m (3123ft)
Time	5–6hrs
Grade	2
Refreshments	Gais Alpe
Map	Kompass-Wanderkarte No 3: Allgäuer Alpen – Kleinwalsertal

As this walk involves a big ascent a good standard of fitness is required, but otherwise there are no difficulties worth mentioning. Schöllang is a very pretty little village, where just about every house seems to have its balcony adorned with bright red or pink geraniums. Those with a car might find staying in a *Pension* or *Gasthaus* here an interesting alternative to Oberstdorf. The tourist office is located at Schelchweg 1, tel: (08326) 7197.

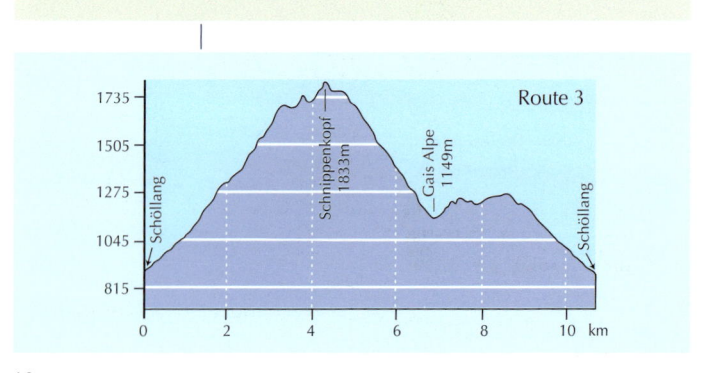

ROUTE 3 – A RIDGE WALK BETWEEN SONNENKOPF AND FALKEN ALPE

Instead of driving into Schöllang (where parking is very limited) follow the bypass in the direction of Altstädten, and you will come to a parking bay at the side of the road. The route to Entschen Alpe and the Sonnenkopf is clearly signposted, so it is just a matter of following the Eybach stream uphill until you come to a bridge. The easiest way to Entschen Alpe is to follow the road left over the bridge, but the more attractive route is to follow the **Tobelweg** (gorge walk) straight ahead along the stream. If the Tobelweg is chosen it brings you to a wooden footbridge, from where the path zigzags its way up through the woods and eventually links up with the alm access road which is followed to the right. After heavy rain it is advisable to choose the easier alternative, as the steep and narrow Tobelweg can get very slippery, and the track may be washed away in places.

Before reaching Entschen Alpe hut, however, our path swings left (signposted), away from the road, and winds its

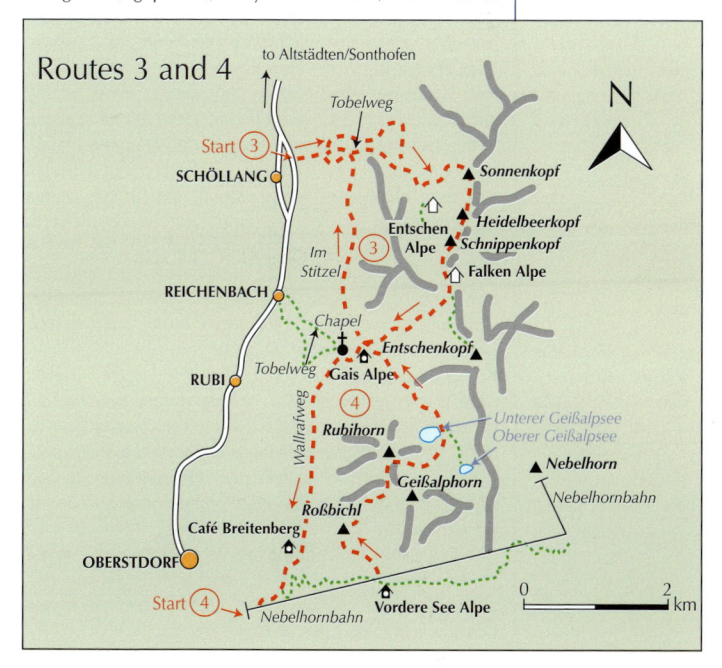

Situated at the intersection of several tracks, Gais Alpe is a popular stop

way up through fields and then into the woods. After passing a small clearing with views to the north (good spot for a rest), it is no longer far to the summit cross of the **Sonnenkopf** (1712m). Magnificent views down into the Retterschwang Valley and across to the Daumen massif.

Continuing along the ridge you descend into a trough, and then climb very steeply up to the summit of the **Heidelbeerkopf** (1767m). The same sweaty procedure has to be repeated en route to the **Schnippenkopf** (1833m), but the dramatic alpine scenery to the left of the track is compensation enough. This peak offers the best views on the entire walk, and the outlook is only hindered by the imposing bulk of the Entschenkopf to the south. ◀

As the summit plateau is broad and grassy it would make a good picnic spot. Those who have moved relatively quickly will have required 3hrs up to this point.

Compared to the preceding climb the descent to **Falken Alpe** is reasonably gradual. A little further down a trail branches left off the main track to the Entschenkopf, but as this is a climb that can only be recommended to the experienced it is best to continue downhill through woods to **Gais Alpe**. The restaurant here is quite popular, as it also lies on the route to the Nebelhorn and Rubihorn.

To get back to Schöllang head north through the woods via **Im Stitzel**. If the weather has deteriorated, or if your legs just will not take you any further, then you can also have a taxi arranged to pick you up from Gais Alpe.

ROUTE 4
The Rubihorn (1957m)

Start	Oberstdorf
Parking	Car park next to cable railway (Nebelhornbahn)
Transport	Local buses
Distance	11.4km/7 miles
Height gain	683m (2241ft)
Height loss	1132m (3714ft)
Time	5hrs
Grade	3
Refreshments	See Alpe, Gais Alpe, Café Breitenberg
Map	Kompass-Wanderkarte No 3: Allgäuer Alpen – Kleinwalsertal

As the paths along this route are often very steep and narrow, and require in some places at least sure-footedness, they are best left to the more experienced. However, those who would like to visit the lovely Geißalpsee, and avoid the exposed stretch around the Rubihorn, could do so by starting out in Reichenbach (north of Oberstdorf) and then following the Tobelweg to Gais Alpe. From there continue on the track up to the Geißalpsee. Return the same way.

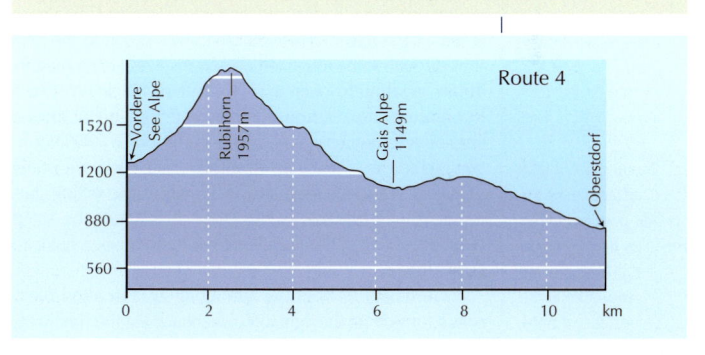

WALKING IN THE BAVARIAN ALPS

Resting at the Niedereck Saddle, shortly before the summit

The Nebelhorn cable railway is taken as far as **Vordere See Alpe** (1274m), the first stop, thus saving 1hr uphill walking. From the restaurant head in a northerly direction through pastureland towards the **Roßbichl** (1465m). The path now curves its way sharply uphill, offering little shade on the way, to the narrow Niedereck Saddle between the Geißalphorn on the right and the Rubihorn on the left. From here a narrow trail, with wire ropes securing exposed sections, passes the route down to Geißalpsee on its way to the **Rubihorn** summit.

For the descent return to the turn-off passed on the way to the summit and follow the zigzagging path down the mountain's steep eastern slopes to the **Unterer Geißalpsee** (Lower Geißalpsee). Note that the route down to the lake runs through some rough terrain and involves losing roughly 400m in altitude over a very short distance. With the Rubihorn as a backdrop, the lake and Älpele Hut form a very picturesque ensemble, and a better place for a mountain picnic can scarcely be imagined. Once you have finally managed to drag yourself away from this idyllic setting continue in a northwesterly direction, first along the steep wooded slopes of the Entschenkopf, then through fields to **Gais Alpe**. ◄

If you did not take advantage of the picnic possibilities by the lake, then a bite to eat and drinks are available at the restaurant here.

Go downhill from the alm along an asphalted road, pass a turn-off on the right to Reichenbach via the Tobelweg, then near a roadside chapel veer left along the Wallrafweg (Gaisalpweg) back to Oberstdorf. For the most part this easy path runs through woods. Just before town you pass **Café Breitenberg**, then the trail joins the road linking Oberstdorf to Vordere See Alpe.

ROUTE 5
Edmund-Probst-Haus to the Oytal (Oy Valley)

Start	Oberstdorf
Parking	Car park (parking fee) next to Nebelhornbahn
Transport	Local buses
Distance	20.5km/13 miles
Height gain	250m (820ft)
Height loss	1355m (4445ft)
Time	6–6½ hrs
Grade	2–3
Refreshments	Käser Alpe, Untere Guten Alpe, Oytal Haus, Café Jägerstand
Accommodation	Edmund-Probst-Haus
Map	Kompass-Wanderkarte No 3: Allgäuer Alpen – Kleinwalsertal

This is one of the most scenically rewarding routes in the entire Allgäu Alps. Though there are a few very narrow and somewhat exposed sections of track, where sure-footedness is a prerequisite, it requires above all stamina. Apart from a few steep climbs, and the long descent into the Oytal, it is mostly relatively easy walking along a fairly level, clearly defined alpine trail. In spite of this, the route should not be attempted in unstable weather conditions.

Considering the length of this route it is best to go up with one of the first gondolas (09.00 before, and 08.30 after, 1 July). If there are enough people queuing the cable railway might even start ½hr or so earlier. The trip up takes around 20mins and brings you to the Höfatsblick restaurant, situated below the Nebelhorn summit at an altitude of 1929m. ▶

At the valley station ask for a ticket to the *Bergstation*, not the *Gipfelstation* which is at the very top.

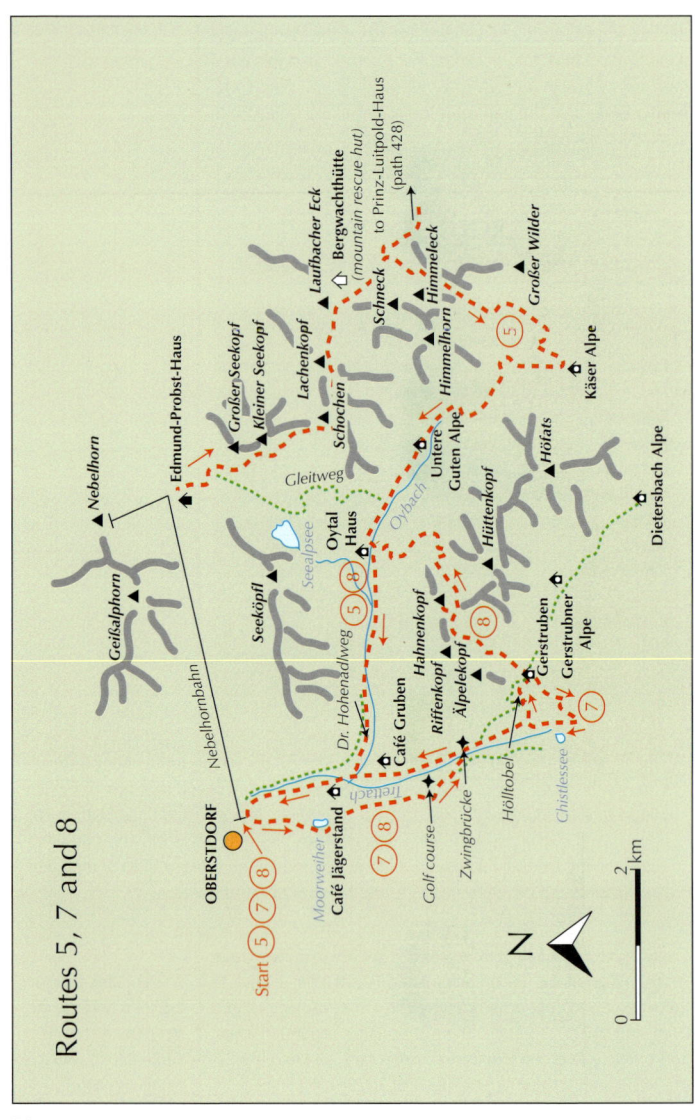

WALKING IN THE BAVARIAN ALPS

Routes 5, 7 and 8

Route 5 – Edmund-Probst-Haus to the Oytal (Oy Valley)

The Seealpsee

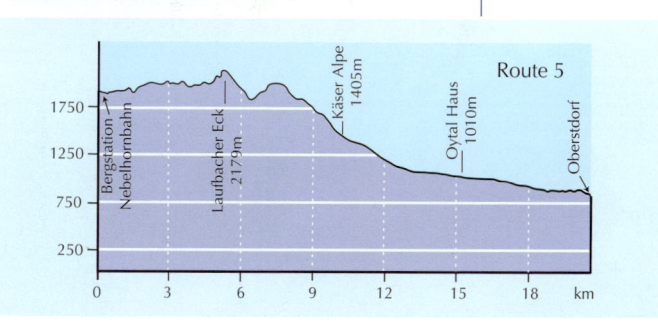

WALKING IN THE BAVARIAN ALPS

Because the excursion to the summit of the Nebelhorn (2224m) itself involves a rather lengthy detour, it is best to leave the ascent for another day and to continue south past **Edmund-Probst-Haus** towards the saddle between the Hüttenkopf and the Zeiger (the route is signposted 'Laufbacher Eck/Himmeleck/Oytal'), a mere 15mins away. Directly below the saddle, nestled at the foot of the Seeköpfel like a glistening blue gem, is the pretty Seealpsee.

A steep track goes down past the Seealpsee and would bring you in roughly 2hrs directly to Oytal Haus. However, the section of the trail known as the Gleitweg is exposed in places and should be avoided in wet conditions. On no account attempt to walk directly down from the tarn! Slippery grass slopes lead to an abrupt drop over the cliffs of the Seewände.

The route continues along path 428, past the two Seeköpfe to the point where the track curves around the **Schochen** (2100m). It is often possible to observe chamois grazing on the steep grass slopes near here. They are quite used to walkers and anyone equipped with a telephoto lens (at the very least 200mm) might get a few nice portraits. To

The Hochvogel from Laufbacher Eck

ROUTE 5 – EDMUND-PROBST-HAUS TO THE OYTAL (OY VALLEY)

the south the Höfats and Großer Wilder rise high above the Oytal, dwarfing the tiny Käser Alpe hut, which is located on the basin between. Behind them are lofty peaks belonging to the main Allgäu chain: the three Trettachspitze, the Mädelegabel and the Kratzer.

Turning sharply east the trail (marked on the map as Laufbacheckweg) now heads towards the Laufbacher-Eck. Before reaching it, however, it is first necessary to cross a steep rock face below the **Lachenkopf**. This very short section of track does not present any real problems (a wire rope is provided), but the rock is very smooth and some care is necessary if it is wet. After successfully navigating this obstacle it is not long before you begin the steep ascent up to the saddle just below the **Laufbacher Eck** (2179m). The summit is quickly reached from here. Tremendous panorama: to the north the view is dominated by the chain of mountains stretching from the Nebelhorn to the Breitenberg (the route of the famous Hindelanger Klettersteig or Via Ferrata), to the northeast is the Rauhhorn and neighbouring peaks, while southeast it is the mighty rock pyramid of the Hochvogel that claims attention.

From the saddle descend quite steeply down a slippery, pebble-strewn path towards (but not right down to) a mountain rescue hut (**Bergwachthütte** on map). This stretch usually coincides with the midday heat, but before climbing up to the Himmeleck there is a good spot where you can pause for lunch below the Schneck, a distinctive rock pinnacle which, when observed from a position further south, takes on the appearance of an immense snail crawling downhill. At the Himmeleck Saddle (2001m) you can stop for another breather. ▸

A track to the right goes up a grass slope to the **Himmeleck** summit (2151m).

> This spot is known among botanists because of the edelweiss that grows here. These rare flowers are protected and picking them is strictly forbidden.

> Instead of continuing on from below the Schneck to Himmeleck, this route can be extended into a multi-day tour by continuing along path 428 to Prinz-Luitpold Haus. Shortly after passing Schönberg Hut the trail crosses the Stierbach stream and goes past the track (to the left) down to Giebel Haus in the Bärgündeletal. From here Prinz-Luitpold-Haus is soon reached on a good trail – 1hr from Schneck. Spend the night at the hut, then continue next day to Landsberger Hut in Austria (see Route 6).

The rest of the route back to Oberstdorf is all downhill. Already on the way to Wildenfeld Hut the trail loses about 300m in altitude. The stretch of track that passes below the scree-covered slopes of the Großer and Kleiner Wilder is quite badly eroded in places and can be extremely slippery if wet. Chamois are often seen in the vicinity. At the small hut turn right. The trail now zigzags steeply down to **Käser Alpe**. Surrounded by craggy peaks, the hut has a magnificent situation (*refreshments available for walkers from July–late October*).

For the final leg of the walk continue downhill along a gravel road into the Oytal. An attraction en route is the impressive Stuibenfall waterfall, only 10mins or so further on from the hut. After descending to **Untere Guten Alpe** (1048m) the road is quite flat and easy to walk. Continue along it past **Oytal Haus**, but then turn left along the Dr. Hohenadlweg (signposted). This picturesque trail runs directly along the Oybach stream as far as a bridge. From here the River Trettach is followed north towards **Café Jägerstand**. Cross another bridge below the café, and then follow the west bank of the river back to **Oberstdorf**. This track brings you back to the Nebelhornbahn and car park in around 20mins.

ROUTE 6
Prinz-Luitpold-Haus (1846m) to Landsberger Hut/Tannheim

Start	Prinz-Luitpold-Haus (Bad Hindelang-Hinterstein)
Parking	In Oberstdorf (see Route 5) or Hinterstein
Transport	Bus to Hinterstein from Bad Hindelang, then bus from Hinterstein to Giebel Haus; buses run to Bad Hindelang from Oberstdorf via Sonthofen; bus from Tannheim to Sonthofen

ROUTE 6 – PRINZ-LUITPOLD-HAUS TO LANDSBERGER HUT/TANNHEIM

Distance	12km/7.5 miles
Height gain	318m (1043ft)
Height loss	354m (1161ft)
Time	1½ days (2½ days from Edmund-Probst-Haus)
Grade	2–3
Refreshments	(Giebel Haus), Prinz-Luitpold-Haus, Landsberger Hut
Accommodation	Prinz-Luitpold-Haus, Landsberger Hut
Maps	Kompass-Wanderkarte No 3: Allgäuer Alpen – Kleinwalsertal and No 4: Füssen – Ausserfern

Prinz-Luitpold-Haus enjoys a superb position on the edge of a cirque, above a small mountain lake. Surrounded by stunning mountain scenery the hut is a popular base for rock climbing (grades I–VIII) on the Fuchskarspitze (2314m), as well as for the ascent of nearby peaks such as the Hochvogel (2593m) and Wiedemerkopf (2163m). It is also the starting point for a beautiful alpine walk, which follows the Jubiläumsweg (also a section of the Via Alpina) and the Saalfelder Höhenweg to Landsberger Hut in Austria.

Prinz-Luitpold-Haus is perched attractively above a tarn

Of the various routes to Prinz-Luitpold-Haus two of the most attractive (and easiest) for average mountain walkers are mentioned here. Assuming you take advantage of the bus to Giebel Haus the shortest route is from Hindelang-Hinterstein – the walk from Hinterstein along the lovely Ostrach valley would require 2½hrs and an overnight stay at the hut. The longer alternative from Edmund-Probst-Haus has the advantage that the trail already starts at a high altitude, with no major climbs or descents all the way to Prinz-Luitpold. Combined with this high-level section of Route 5 from Edmund-Probst-Haus as far as the Schneck, this route becomes a magnificent multi-day alpine tour – long stretches also form part of the Via Alpina long-distance trail.

From Edmund-Probst-Haus via Laufbacher Eck (4½hrs)
See Route 5 for a description of this scenic alpine route to **Prinz-Luitpold-Haus** from Oberstdorf. Spend the night at the hut.

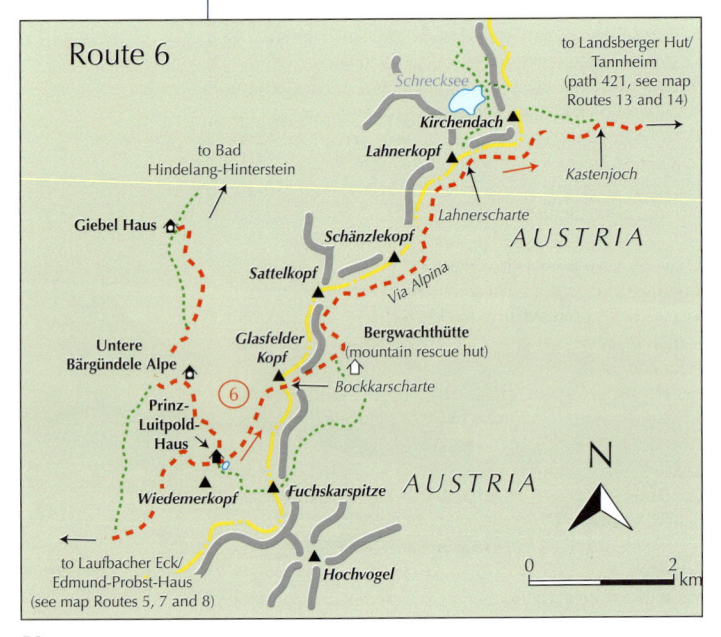

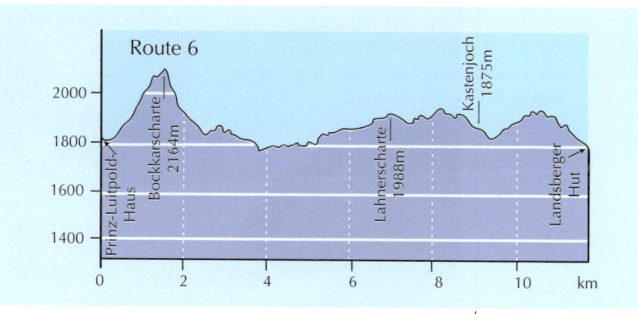

ROUTE 6 – PRINZ-LUITPOLD-HAUS TO LANDSBERGER HUT/TANNHEIM

Ascent from Giebel Haus (2hrs)
From the large car park 'Auf der Höh' in Bad Hindelang-Hinterstein catch the bus to **Giebel Haus** (1066m; 20min trip). Cross a bridge just south of the restaurant, and continue uphill along an asphalt road (closed to private cars). After about 50mins on this shady stretch through the Bärgündeletal a signposted track bears left off the road. It descends to the Bärgündelesbach, which is crossed on a footbridge. Now the trail climbs picturesquely through woods and past an impressive waterfall to Untere Bärgündele Alp (refreshments in summer). From the alp the trail climbs steeply along grassy slopes sprinkled with flowers, and past more waterfalls, to **Prinz-Luitpold-Haus** (70mins from Bärgündele Alp).

Onwards from Prinz-Luitpold Haus
Continue along the Jubiläumsweg (path 421) in a northeasterly direction towards the **Bockkarscharte** (2164m). The saddle is reached after a steep 1hr climb. Splendid views from here of the Höfats and Schneck to the southwest and the Hochvogel to the south, while in the east it is possible to make out the Lailachspitze in the Tannheim Valley. Ahead the onward route is plainly visible: a steep zigzag descent over loose rock below the **Glasfelder Kopf** (2271m), then more comfortably past the **Sattelkopf** to the **Schänzlespitz**.

En route to the **Lahnerkopf** and the **Lahnerscharte** there are fine views down into the Austrian Schwarzwassertal – the trail has been running through Austrian territory since

Climbing the Bockkarscharte (from the direction of Landsberger Hut) in early summer!

leaving the Bockkarscharte. At the saddle itself the view extends down to the idyllically situated Schrecksee, on the German side of the border. Instead of taking the trail left, down to the lake, continue right along the Saalfelder Höhenweg (path 421) towards Landsberger Hut. At the **Kastenjoch** (1875m), where a trail on the left runs northwest back to Schrecksee, the track connects with the route from Landsberger Hut described in Route 13. This section of Route 13 is now done in reverse, skirting the western flanks of the Steinkarspitze and passing below the Rote Spitze before reaching the hut (5hrs from Prinz-Luitpold-Haus, 7hrs from Giebel Haus).

The next day descend along path 425 via Traualpsee to the northern end of Vilsalpsee (1½hrs). Here it is possible to catch a bus to Tannheim, or you can walk down in 1hr. As an alternative follow the route described in Route 13 to the Neunerköpfle and the gondola-lift in reverse (2hrs).

ROUTE 7
Gerstruben

Start	Oberstdorf
Parking	Car park (parking fee) next to Nebelhornbahn
Transport	Local buses
Distance	12.2km/7.5 miles
Height gain	328m (1076ft)
Height loss	328m (1076ft)
Time	3½hrs
Grade	1
Refreshments	Gasthof Gerstruben, Café Gruben, Café Jägerstand
Map	Kompass-Wanderkarte No 3: Allgäuer Alpen – Kleinwalsertal

The tiny settlement of Gerstruben was founded centuries ago by Valaisian migrants from Switzerland. Its picturesque farmhouses are reminiscent of those that can still be found in the Valais to this day. The small church with the Höfats in the background is a popular photo motif. Light refreshments and meals are available at Gasthof Gerstruben.

Start at the bridge over the Trettach, a short distance south of the Nebelhorn cable railway. Do not cross the river, but remain on its true right, and follow a track through woods which climbs up and away from the river – signposted Moorweiher. A bit further on, at a fork, take the trail signposted Moorschwimmbad – Moorweiher. Pass through meadows then, at the Moorschwimmbad (Moor Baths),

WALKING IN THE BAVARIAN ALPS

Route 7 elevation profile: Oberstdorf – Moorweiher – Zwingbrücke – Gerstruben 1154m – Zwingbrücke – Oberstdorf; elevations 755, 865, 975, 1520; distance 0–12 km.

In the Hölltobel (gorge)

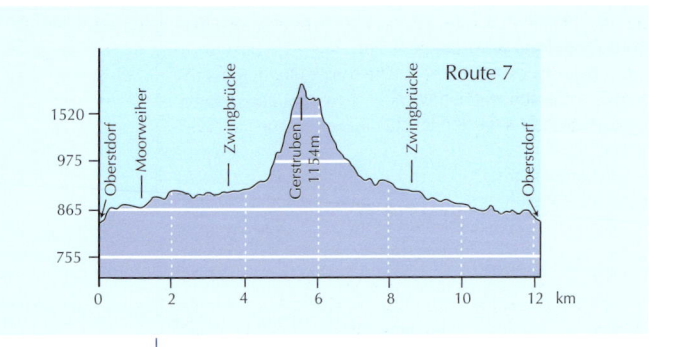

continue on the signposted route to the **Moorweiher**. In about 5mins you will reach this pond, situated idyllically on the edge of an upland moor.

The onward trail to Gerstruben leads through woods, along the edge of Oberstdorf's golf course, to a small asphalt road. Turn left and follow the road uphill to a fork. Here take the road branching left to a bridge (Zwingbrücke) over the Trettach. ▸ The route continues right towards Gerstruben and soon reaches another fork. The road to the left climbs directly to Gerstruben, but the more interesting alternative is to continue right along the trail to the picturesque Hölltobel (Hell Gully).

What was at first a paved road soon deteriorates to gravel as it threads its way through pastures with a wonderful view to the mountains further south. After some 15mins a narrow trail turns sharp left off the road and brings you to the wooded slopes concealing the **Hölltobel**. Accompanied by the sound of rushing water, as the Dietersbach stream squeezes its way through a narrow corset of rock, you climb steeply alongside the gorge. At one place a platform allows a bird's-eye view over the narrow chasm, and a little higher, you can clamber over a rock to view an impressive waterfall. After ½hr climbing the track reaches the asphalt road again and it is only a few minutes' walk to **Gerstruben**.

> On the other side the trail going left runs back to Oberstdorf in 1hr.

This walk can be extended by continuing over the Hahnenkopf to the Oytal (see Route 8). A shorter alternative would be to continue along the Dietersbachtal (Gerstrubental) to Gerstrubner Alpe (20mins) or further to Dietersbach Alpe (1hr).

In Gerstruben walk towards the church, then turn right along a signposted trail to Christlessee. After crossing pastures the trail starts to descend more steeply, and the Dietersbach stream is crossed on a small wooden bridge. The trail now enters open forest on its way down to the valley. At the bottom go right, pass the **Christlessee** (a lake), and the turn-off to the Hölltobel, to reach the Zwingbrücke over the Trettach. Instead of returning the same way over the bridge follow the trail along the right bank of the river. Oberstdorf is reached after 1hr walk with cafés Gruben and **Jägerstand** offering refreshments on the way.

ROUTE 8
From the Gerstrubental to the Oytal

Start	Oberstdorf
Parking	Car park (parking fee) next to Nebelhornbahn
Transport	Local buses
Distance	10.3km/6.5 miles (from Gerstruben), 16km/10 miles (from Oberstdorf)
Height gain	581m (1906ft)
Height loss	909m (2982ft)
Time	6hrs
Grade	2
Refreshments	Gasthof Gerstruben, Oytal Haus, Café Jägerstand
Map	Kompass-Wanderkarte No 3: Allgäuer Alpen – Kleinwalsertal

This varied route links the valleys of the Gerstrubental and Oytal in a circular walk from Oberstdorf. The first section is a picturesque stroll past a beautiful pond in an area of upland moor, followed by a steep climb up a wild and romantic gorge. After leaving the tiny village of Gerstruben it is another steep climb up to the Hahnenkopf for some fine views, then a long, steep descent begins to the Oytal. From there it is an easy, mostly level walk back to Oberstdorf.

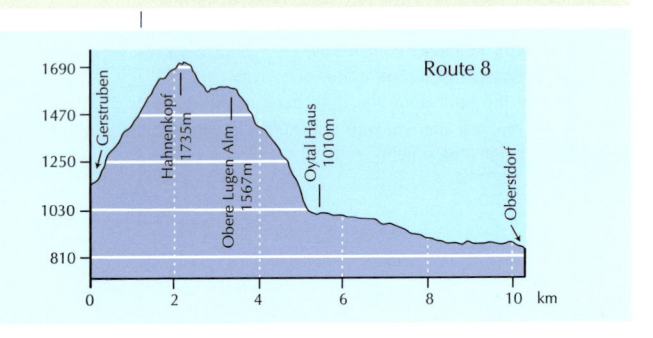

ROUTE 8 – FROM THE GERSTRUBENTAL TO THE OYTAL

The Hahnenkopf summit

The first section of the walk up to **Gerstruben** is the same as described in Route 7.

In Gerstruben walk to the rear of the *Gasthof* to find a track which climbs steeply up a grassy slope before entering woods. After about 1hr of strenuous climbing you reach the ridge between the **Riffenkopf** (1749m) and **Hahnenkopf** (1736m). Continue right in the direction of the Hahnenkopf. The trail runs first below and past the summit, then swings back along a ridge and over a patch of rock to the summit cross. Apart from the view over Oberstdorf and the tiny Christlessee the panorama takes in the Nebelhorn massif, together with the Laufbachereckweg (see Route 5), the peaks of the Kleinwalsertal and the Illertal.

Return to the point where the track forked left to climb up to the summit. An unmarked but obvious trail runs down from here, over grass slopes in a northeasterly direction towards Obere Lugen Alm. From the alm hut continue downhill to Untere Lugen Alm – the track is not very clear along this section, with only a few faded red dots on rocks at irregular intervals to mark the way. After passing the alm – be careful not to miss the track – the trail descends more steeply and brings you through woods to **Oytal Haus**.

Follow the small asphalt road west from Oytal Haus in the direction of Oberstdorf. After about 25mins level walking

WALKING IN THE BAVARIAN ALPS

you will reach a signposted track (Dr. Hohenadelweg) on the left. This pleasant trail will take you along the Oybach stream, past **Café Jägerstand** on the banks of the Trettach, and back to Oberstdorf (1hr).

KLEINWALSERTAL: AROUND RIEZLERN AND MITTELBERG

Tourist office: Kleinwalsertal Tourismus (main office), Walserhaus, Walserstrasse 64, D-87568 Hirschegg. Tel: +43 (0)5517 5114-0, fax: +43 (0)5517 5114-21; www.kleinwalsertal.com, e-mail: info@kleinwalsertal.com

Riezlern is the largest settlement in the valley and is densely packed with hotels, restaurants, sports and souvenir shops. Probably the most interesting fact for walkers is that the Kanzelwand cable railway begins here. There are three campsites in the near vicinity.

Mittelberg is the oldest parish in the Kleinwalsertal with a parish church that dates from 1463. Plenty of walks start in or near the town, and there is a nicely situated campsite only a few kilometres further south in the direction of Baad.

ROUTE 9
Kanzelwandbahn to Fellhorn (2038m) and Söllereck (1706m)

Start	Riezlern
Parking	Car park next to Kanzelwandbahn
Transport	Local buses
Distance	13km/8 miles
Height gain	70m (295ft)
Height loss	967m (3172ft)
Time	4–5hrs
Grade	1–2
Refreshments	Fellhorn Bergstation, Schrattenwang Alpe, Mittel Alpe
Maps	Kleinwalsertal (Zumstein Verlag) 1:25,000; Kompass-Wanderkarte No 3: Allgäuer Alpen – Kleinwalsertal

ROUTE 9 – KANZELWANDBAHN TO FELLHORN AND SÖLLERECK

This popular ridge walk allows some magnificent views over the Kleinwalsertal and Allgäu Alps. The track, which runs directly along the German–Austrian border, offers virtually no shade so it is wise to bring a hat and plenty to drink.

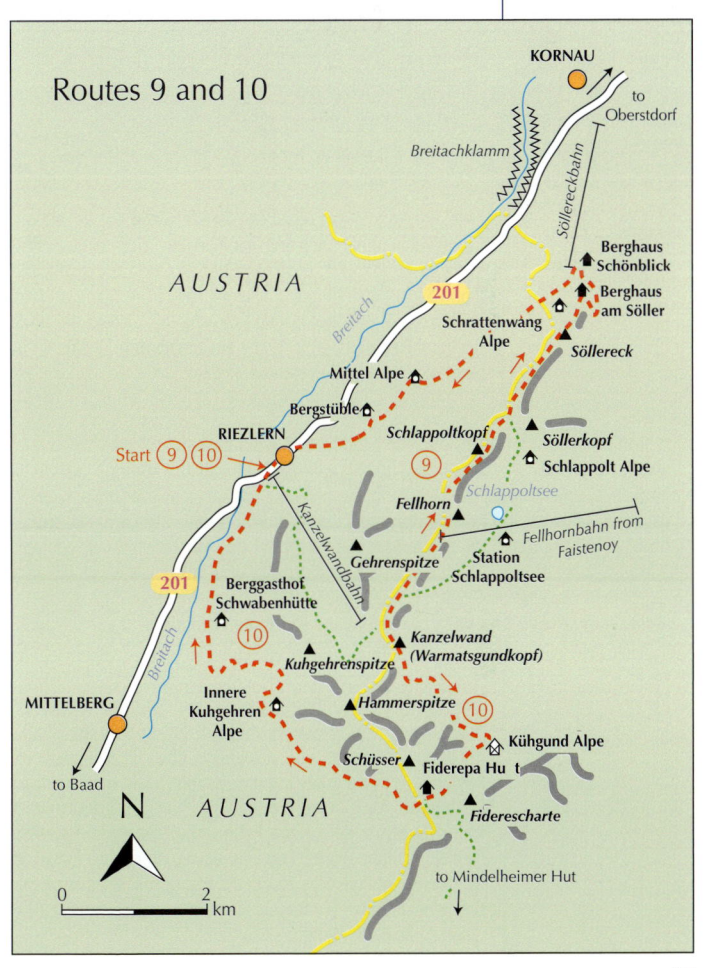

WALKING IN THE BAVARIAN ALPS

Route 9 — elevation profile: Bergstation Kanzelwandbahn; Fellhorn 2038m; Mittel Alpe 1300m; Riezlern. Axes: 560–1840 m vs 0–12 km.

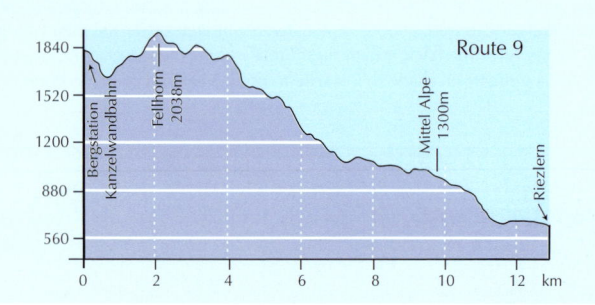

From the upper station of the **Kanzelwand** cable railway (1968m) walk a short distance in the direction of the Warmatsgundkopf then turn northeast and descend to the Gund Saddle (1800m). It is a steep climb from here up to the **Fellhorn** (2038m), but before reaching the summit the track passes the upper station of the **Fellhornbahn**, and those in need of a drink and a rest can stop here.

Unfortunately, this is also where the track starts getting really crowded, as just about everybody who rides up with the Fellhornbahn has the summit as their goal. Accompanied by dozens of fellow walkers the cross at the top is soon reached. Here, as if choreographed by some hidden hand, the cameras and binoculars are pulled out of a multitude of bags, groups form for photos, while admiring cries of 'Ach, wie schön!' ('Oh, how lovely!') are only slightly more frequent than requests of 'Could I get past, please?' But the views make it all worthwhile as the Allgäu Alps open out before you in all their splendour.

The crowd thins out (slightly) as you continue along the ridge over the **Schlappoltkopf** (1968m) to Schlappolteck. Excellent views in all directions the whole way. At Schlappolteck the path going downhill to the right leads to **Schlappolt Alpe** (*refreshments*) and the Schlappoltsee, a small lake just below the Fellhornbahn's middle station (Station Schlappoltsee). This very easy path can be followed by those who wish to return to the upper station of the Kanzelwandbahn via the Gund Saddle – alternative to the direct route back along the ridge.

Route 9 – Kanzelwandbahn to Fellhorn and Söllereck

Ridge trail to Söllereck

WALKING IN THE BAVARIAN ALPS

The Söllereck cable car takes you down to Kornau from where a bus runs to Riezlern and Oberstdorf.

The ridge walk continues downhill to the left in the direction of **Söllereck** (1706m) and the Söllereckbahn. ◄ Near the cable car station are a couple of mountain inns (*refreshments and accommodation*). Before reaching the cable car, however, turn left towards **Schrattenwang Alpe**. Now follow an easy path southwest via Amans Alpe and **Mittel Alpe** (1300m) to **Riezlern**.

ROUTE 10
Fiderepaß Hut

Start	Riezlern
Parking	Car park next to Kanzelwandbahn station
Transport	Local buses
Distance	12.6km/8 miles
Height gain	481m (1578ft)
Height loss	994m (3261ft)
Time	4½hrs
Grade	2
Refreshments	Fiderepaß Hut, Innere Kuhgehren Alpe, Berggasthof Schwabenhütte
Accommodation	Fiderepaß Hut
Maps	Kleinwalsertal 1:25,000 (Zumstein Verlag); Kompass-Wanderkarte No 3: Allgäuer Alpen – Kleinwalsertal

In comparison to the very popular walk to the Fellhorn and Söllereck (Route 9), this beautiful walk is much less frequented and more alpine in character. Those who wish to dispense with the cable railway can follow the Zwerenbach stream southeast from town (the track starts near the valley station of the Kanzelwandbahn) and then ascend steeply via Adlerhorst Hut (*refreshments*) to the ridge which leads to the Warmatsgundkopf (add about 2hrs).

ROUTE 10 – FIDEREPAß HUT

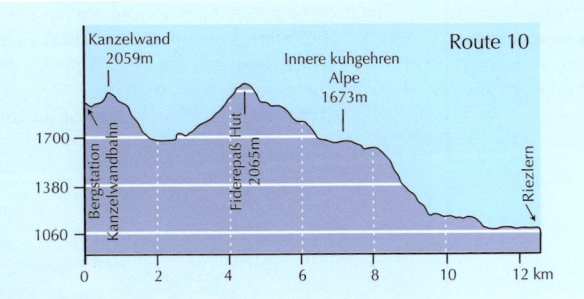

From the upper station of the **Kanzelwandbahn** the short but steepish walk to the summit of the **Kanzelwand** (Warmatsgundkopf) (2059m) is clearly signposted. After admiring the views descend southeast (path 446) towards the abandoned **Kühgund Alpe**. In summer red-flowering alpenrose add a splash of colour to this section of the route. The alp is marked by two small huts and this is where the trail forks: the left-hand track heads along the Krumbacher Höhenweg to Mindelheimer Hut, but our route continues right and uphill to **Fiderepaß Hut**, which is already visible from the alp. At first it is relatively easy walking through mountain pastures but then the track climbs more steeply up a rocky slope to the pass. Alpenrose are also common around here and you will probably hear the high-pitched warning cries of marmots during the ascent. Easier to see than the shy marmots are ibex, which seem to have grown accustomed to the presence of walkers in this area.

Fiderepaß Hut is a friendly place with a cosy atmosphere, and they usually have some home-baked treats to tempt the appetites of hungry walkers. The disadvantage of the place – at least if you want to sleep here – is that it is very crowded in summer due to the fact that it serves as the starting, or end, point for the well-known Mindelheimer Klettersteig (Via Ferrata). Though only suitable for the experienced, this ridge walk to **Mindelheimer Hut** (4hrs) is extremely popular – you may even have to queue for certain sections! To avoid the worst crowds those who are able to tackle it should pick early or late summer.

Alpenrose enliven the scenery en route to Fiderepaß Hut

Extension to the Großer Widderstein and Baad

An interesting possibility for extending this tour from Fiderepaß Hut would be to continue to Baad. Climb in an easterly direction to Fiderscharte, then descend to the Krumbacher Höhenweg – also on the route of the Via Alpina. This relatively level trail continues southwest to Mindelheimer Hut (2½hrs, *accommodation*). From here the trail runs along the Schwabengrat, past the Geißhornjoch, to Gemstelpass and Obere Widderstein Hut (2½hrs). Either continue down from the pass through the Gemsteltal to Bödmen or go around the Großer Widderstein and descend via the Bärgundtal to Baad (from Kanzelwand 8½–10hrs or 2 days; see also Route 12).

From **Fiderepaß Hut** the path winds steeply downhill to a fork, where you turn right in the direction of Wanne Alpe (1821m). It is now fairly easy walking across the rocky slopes below the Hochgehrenspitze and Hammerspitze to the abandoned alp, with good views all the way. From the alp hut the track starts descending more steeply across dawrf-pine-covered slopes before levelling out again on the way to Innere Kuhgehren Alpe (*light refreshments available in summer*). Pass through the gate in front of the hut and continue downhill in the direction of Hirschegg/Riezlern (signposted). Äussere Kuhgehren Alpe is passed en route and then it is more or less directly downhill all the way to Brand Alpe (1306m). Once you are right down in the valley it is just a matter of following the signs back to Riezlern. A place where you can stop for a meal on the way is Berggasthof Schwabenhütte. Shortly before arriving in town the trail (a road now) passes the Zwerwald campsite.

ROUTE 11
Gottesacker Plateau

Start	Auen Hut, southwest of Riezlern
Parking	At Auen Hut (parking fee)
Transport	Bus connection (Linie 5) from Riezlern to Auen Hut/Ifen
Distance	10.4km/6.5 miles
Height gain	569m (1867ft)
Height loss	877m (2877ft)
Time	5–5½hrs
Grade	2
Refreshments	Only at or near start (Auen Hut, Ifen Hut, Bergadler Hut); take your own supplies and plenty to drink
Maps	Kleinwalsertal, 1:25,000 (Zumstein Verlag); Kompass-Wanderkarte No 3: Allgäuer Alpen – Kleinwalsertal

WALKING IN THE BAVARIAN ALPS

Though the best views are from the top of the Hoher Ifen the real attraction of the area is the Gottesacker Plateau with its bizarre-looking karst formations. For this reason the much more modest summit of the Hahnenköpfle is chosen as a goal, as it lies right in the midst of this almost other-worldly landscape.

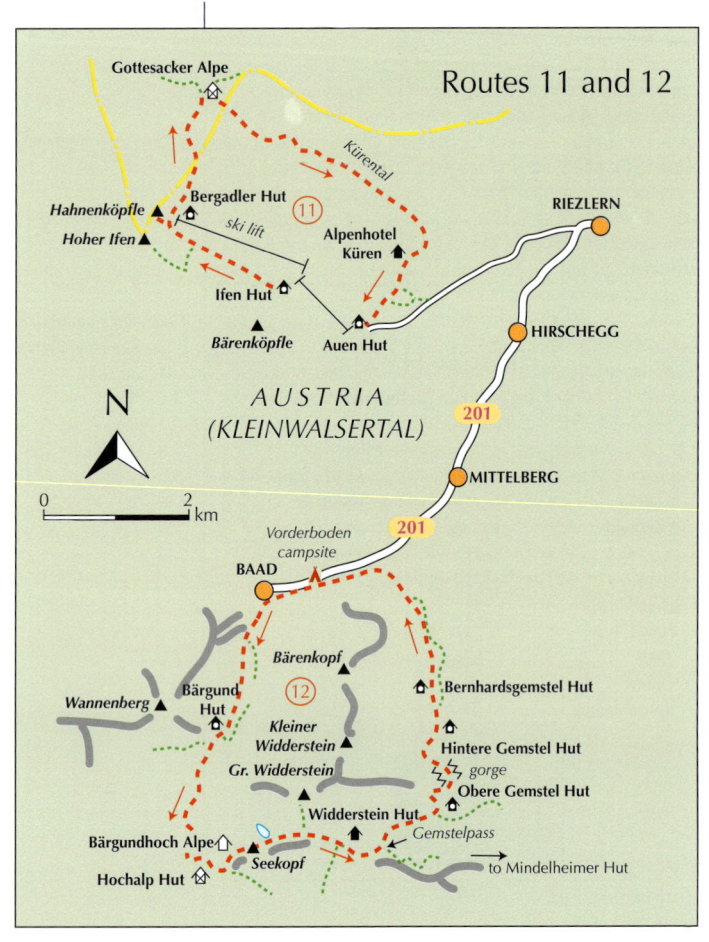

ROUTE 11 – GOTTESACKER PLATEAU

A bizarre saw-tooth ridge near the Hahnenköpfle

To get to Auen Hut from Riezlern by car turn off at the sign to Ifen 2000. From **Auen Hut** either walk along a road up to Ifen Hut (1hr) or, if you want to save yourself this stretch, take the chairlift (Sesselbahn–Ifenhütte). From **Ifen Hut** the trail climbs at first steeply uphill, but the ascent becomes a bit more gradual once the trail enters the so-called Ifenmulde, a long depression directly below the Ifen ridge which rises above you on the left. After climbing for just over 1hr (from Ifen Hut) the **Bergadler Hut** (*self-service restaurant, closed Wed and in bad weather*) at the top of the ski lift is passed, and you are soon standing atop the **Hahnenköpfle** (2143m).

Note Although this route is relatively easy it should not be attempted in misty conditions as the many deep holes and crevices in the limestone rock are difficult to see.

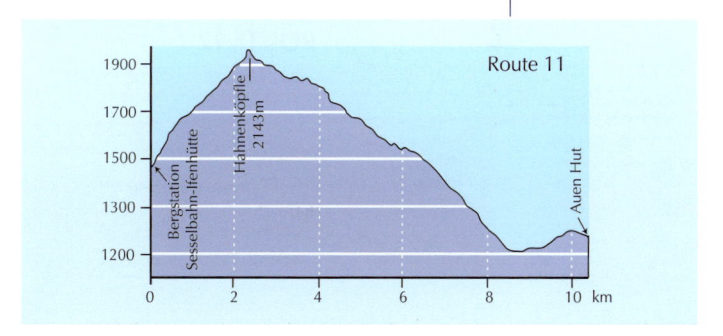

WALKING IN THE BAVARIAN ALPS

> Rising hardly more than 50m above the rocky wasteland that surrounds it, the summit of the Hahnenköpfle nevertheless provides a good vantage point. It's not hard to imagine this rocky, barren plateau as a kind of petrified sea, its elevations as huge waves forever frozen at precisely the moment they were about to break.

In order to continue onwards through this desolate, yet fascinating sea of limestone it is necessary to retrace your steps as far as Bergadler Hut. The yellow waymarks (easier to see when it is misty) are followed from here in the direction of the now-abandoned **Gottesacker Alpe** (1832m). Except for a few ups and downs as you get closer to the alm it is easy walking along an almost level track. With a little luck you might spot ptarmigan on the way. In late autumn they are already moulting their drab grey feathers for the snow-white plumage of winter.

At the alm, which is marked by a ruined stone building, the track turns right and leads downhill through the narrow rocky gorge of the **Kürental**. The yellow waymark is now exchanged for the usual red one, and after 1hr walking you pass a small hut used by hunters. A bit further on the path enters the woods. If it has been a hot, sunny day the shade is a welcome relief. After about 10mins a gravel road is crossed, and in another 10mins you arrive at a second gravel road, which is now followed down to a tar-sealed road. Go right, pass **Alpenhotel Küren**, and come to a sign which points the way to **Auen Hut** and the car park.

ROUTE 12
Around the Großer Widderstein (2533m)

Start	Baad
Parking	Car park at entrance to village
Transport	Buses to Baad from other settlements in the Kleinwalsertal and from Oberstdorf with the 'Walserbus'

ROUTE 12 – AROUND THE GROßER WIDDERSTEIN

Distance	14.3km/9 miles
Height gain	883m (2897ft)
Height loss	883m (2897ft)
Time	5½hrs
Grade	2
Refreshments	Bärgund Hut, Widderstein Hut, Obere and Hintere Gemstel Huts, Bernhardsgemstel Hut
Accommodation	Widderstein Hut
Maps	Kleinwalsertal (Zumstein Verlag), 1:25,000 or Kompass-Wanderkarte No 3: Allgäuer Alpen – Kleinwalsertal

The Großer Widderstein is the highest peak in the Kleinwalsertal, its bare dolomite summit soaring some 1300m above the tiny settlement of Baad at the valley's end. The name is derived from the German word for thunderstorm (*Gewitter*), and storm clouds often cross this isolated massif (it is separated from the main chain of the Allgäu Alps by the saddle at Haldenwanger Eck) before bursting over the valley. Though the climb to the summit is certainly worthwhile it should only be attempted by the fit and experienced. It was, incidentally, first climbed by a parson in 1669.

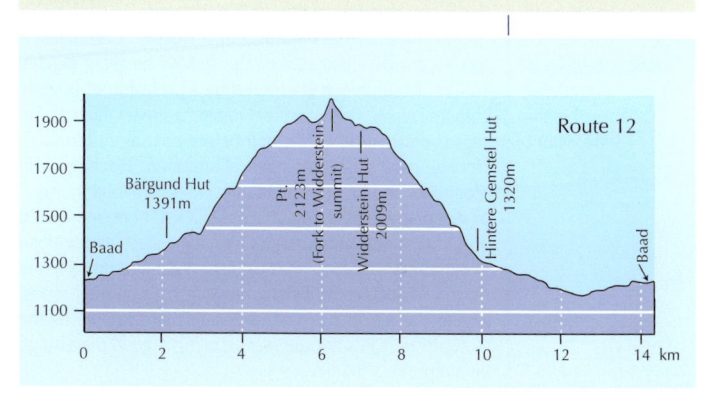

Bärgund Hut provides a welcome first stop before the steep climb to the Hochalp Pass

The name Bärgund refers to the fact that bears once lived in this area; the last one was bagged in the 19th century.

From the car park (the 'Walserbus' from Oberstdorf also stops here) at the entrance to the village head to the wooden bridge over the River Breitach. At this point the onward route is signposted 'Bärgundhütte' (**Bärgund Hut**). The Bärgundbach stream is followed along a gently climbing access road to the hut, which is reached in around 45mins. Over a century old the hut (which now caters to walkers) was originally built for the men who tended the cows here during the summer months. ◄ From the hut what is now a simple track starts climbing more steeply. Eventually it reaches a small alpine pasture situated at a height of roughly 1650m. In summer it is covered by a profusion of brightly coloured alpine flowers. After crossing a stream the trail zigzags even more steeply uphill before bearing left towards Hochalppaß. Pass the now abandoned **Hochalp Hut** (Zollhütte) and in a few minutes you will arrive at the signposted pass (1938m) – the track is marked here by wooden pegs. At the pass follow the trail left, up a steep grassy slope to Bärgundhoch Alpe – the trail right continues down to the Austrian settlement of Hochkrumbach (1hr). Further along, and to the left of the trail, is a small tarn known as the Hochalpsee. On a hot summer's day it is a good place to go for a dip.

ROUTE 12 – AROUND THE GROßER WIDDERSTEIN

> Near this spot experienced alpinists can branch left along the track to the Widderstein summit. **Note** The ascent should only be attempted in stable weather conditions. The route, as described, together with the climb to the summit, would take 8–9hrs.

Continuing eastwards, along steep grass slopes, it is not long before **Widderstein Hut** comes into view. The trail to the hut is virtually level, offers good views and passes through alpine meadows dotted, once again, with wildflowers. There are also plenty of marmots around here. Even if you do not actually see them you will at least hear their high-pitched warning signals as you walk.

From the hut the trail continues through meadows to **Gemstelpass** (1972m). Here you turn left (north) and begin your descent back down to the main valley via the Gemsteltal. The path crosses an area of scree, and it pays to watch your step on the loose rocks. At **Obere Gemstel Hut** it might be worth taking a break to try the Zirbenschnaps (cembral pine schnapps – a kind of brandy with a distinctive resinous taste), a speciality of the hut. After passing through a deep, narrow gorge or *Klamm*, where the path is secured on both sides by ropes, **Hintere Gemstel Hut** is reached.

After Gemstel and **Bernhardsgemstel** Huts it is not much more than 40mins along a minor road to the road between Mittelberg and Baad. Those who want to save themselves the last stretch of the walk can catch the bus from Bödmen, which runs every 10–20 mins. Otherwise, after crossing a bridge over the Breitach at Gemstelboden, follow the Breitachweg left along the river, past the Vorderboden campsite, to the starting point in **Baad** (½hr).

Extension

This tour could be extended from Gemstelpass by following the trail to the right to Mindelheimer Hut (accommodation). From there continue along the Krumbacher Höhenweg to Fiderepaß Hut (see Route 10) and then via Flucht Alpe to Mittelberg. Much of this walk is at an altitude of around 2000m and combined with the tour from Baad it would require 9½hrs.

WALKING IN THE BAVARIAN ALPS

The Großer Widderstein

TANNHEIM (AUSTRIA)

Tourist office: Tourismusverband Tannheimer Tal, Oberhöfen 110, A-6675 Tannheim, Austria. Tel: (05675) 62200, fax: (05675) 622060;
www.tannheimertal.com

Tannheim enjoys a picturesque situation in the idyllic Tannheim Valley (Tannheimer Tal). In the vicinity are numerous lakes (swimming is permitted in Haldensee and Vilsalpsee) and some of the most beautiful mountain scenery to be found anywhere in the Allgäu Alps (the Tannheimer Berge are considered a part of this group). The town is quickly reached from Sonthofen (north of Oberstdorf) on the B308. There is a regular bus service between Sonthofen (Germany) and Reutte (Austria) which runs through the valley. The campsite is located directly on the shores of Haldensee.

ROUTE 13
Tannheim to Vilsalpsee

Start	Tannheim
Parking	Car park next to Vogelhornbahn
Transport	Bus from the Vilsalpsee to Tannheim only runs in summer
Distance	20km/12.5 miles
Height gain	284m (932ft)
Height loss	877m (2877ft)
Time	4–7hrs (comfortable 2-day walk if night spent at Landsberger Hut)
Grade	2
Refreshments	Gappenfeld Alpe, Landsberger Hut, Vils Alpe and restaurants by car park at north end of the Vilsalpsee
Accommodation	Landsberger Hut
Map	Kompass-Wanderkarte No 4: Füssen – Ausserfern

WALKING IN THE BAVARIAN ALPS

Five mountain lakes, a rich variety of alpine flora and magnificent scenery make this route irresistible for photographers, hobby botanists and any connoisseur of the picturesque. The first half of the route up to Landsberger Hut is quite easy going, but the second half is more alpine in character and involves a few passages where sure-footedness is necessary. The crowds are usually left behind at the hut, and those who press on towards the Kugelhorn and the Vilsalpsee will find they can enjoy the views for the most part in 'splendid isolation'.

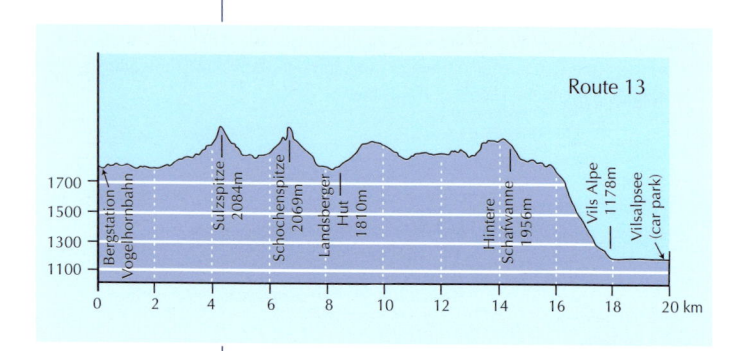

Route 13 elevation profile: Bergstation Vogelhornbahn – Sulzspitze 2084m – Schochenspitze 2069m – Landsberger Hut 1810m – Hintere Schafwanne 1956m – Vils Alpe 1178m – Vilsalpsee (car park), 0 to 20 km.

Though the fit can complete this route in a day it is wise to remember that in autumn it is already getting dark by 18.00. At this time of year an early start is essential.

From the upper station of the gondola-lift (1800m) walk to the nearby **Neunerköpfle** (1864m). The summit is marked by an elaborately carved wooden cross, usually surrounded by swarms of people who wish to have their photos taken in front of it. Apart from the cross it is the panorama that claims most attention. To the northeast is the Vilser Group, while directly below is the Haldensee with the jagged peaks of the Tannheim Group rising behind it. Also close at hand is the Lailachspitze (southeast) and the peaks surrounding the Vilsalpsee – the lake itself is not visible from here.

The track now runs south, keeping at first fairly close to the crest of the ridge, but then crossing it to traverse its eastern slopes in the direction (southeast) of the Strindenscharte (1870m). Dominating the view ahead is the formidable rock face of the Litnisschrofen. At the Strindenscharte the trail joins briefly with a gravel access road, which first climbs a bit, but soon levels out on its way to the **Gappenfelder Scharte**.

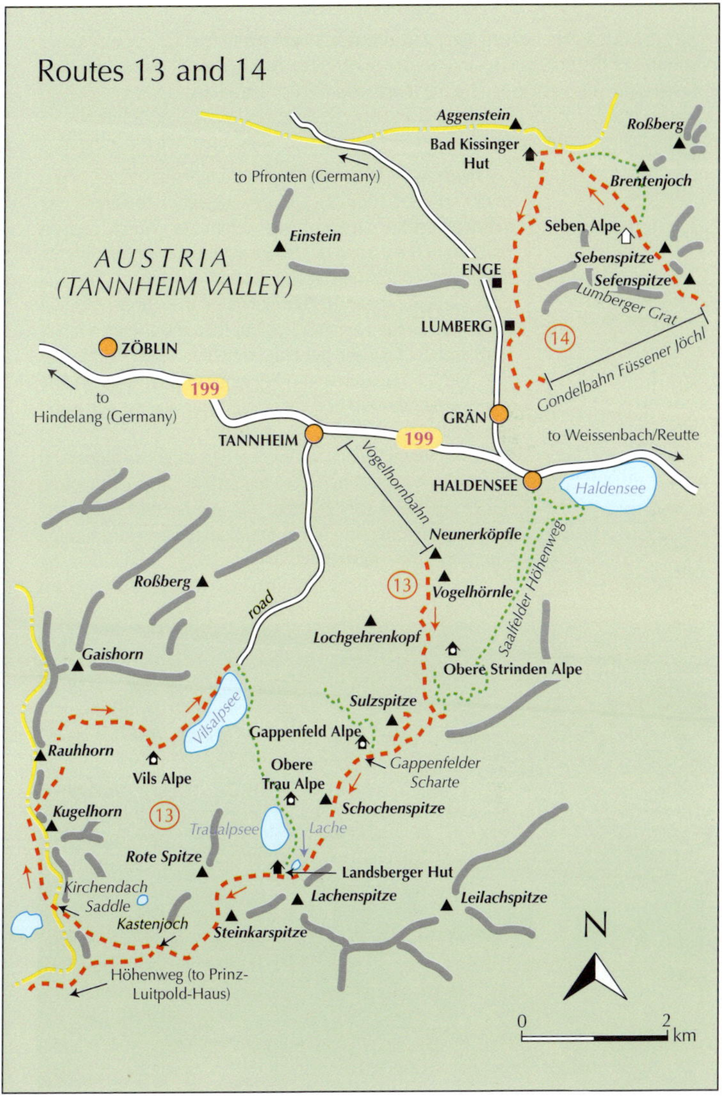
Routes 13 and 14
Aggenstein
Bad Kissinger Hut
Roßberg
Brentenjoch
to Pfronten (Germany)
Einstein
Seben Alpe
Sebenspitze
Sefenspitze
Lumberger Grat
AUSTRIA (TANNHEIM VALLEY)
ENGE
LUMBERG
14
ZÖBLIN
Gondelbahn Füssener Jöchl
199
to Hindelang (Germany)
GRÄN
TANNHEIM
199
to Weissenbach/Reutte
Vogelhornbahn
HALDENSEE
Haldensee
Neunerköpfle
Saalfelder Höhenweg
13
Vogelhörnle
Roßberg
road
Lochgehrenkopf
Gaishorn
Obere Strinden Alpe
Vilsalpsee
Sulzspitze
Gappenfeld Alpe
Rauhhorn
Vils Alpe
Gappenfelder Scharte
Obere Trau Alpe
Schochenspitze
Kugelhorn
13
Lache
Rote Spitze
Landsberger Hut
Kirchendach Saddle
Lachenspitze
Leilachspitze
Kastenjoch
Steinkarspitze
N
Höhenweg (to Prinz-Luitpold-Haus)
0
2
km

> Before reaching the *Scharte* (col) a worthwhile 35min detour can be made to the summit of the **Sulzspitze** (2084m) for unobstructed views in all directions. A book is provided at the summit for those who wish to record their visit.

The road is left behind at the Gappenfeldscharte, and a track starts climbing fairly steeply towards the **Schochenspitze** (2069m), the summit of which can be reached in the course of a short detour. Continuing on the track levels out briefly then starts descending. At first the view directly ahead is dominated by the almost vertical north face of the Lachenspitze but then the Lache, a small tarn, and the Landsberger Hut come into view. A little further and the Traualpsee also becomes visible. After a fairly steep drop the track curves around the Lache and soon reaches the hut (1810m).

Next morning continue in a westerly direction along path 421. It is an easy climb up to the saddle between the Rote Spitze and Steinkarspitze. Here you turn left and walk a few paces in the direction of the **Steinkarspitze** before turning right to the **Kastenjoch** (signposted 'Saalfelderweg/ Schrecksee') where the trail forks. Go right here along path

Kugelhorn, Rauhhorn and Geißhorn from Neunerköpfle (the Vilsalpsee is hidden from view by Lochgehrenkopf)

ROUTE 13 – TANNHEIM TO VILSALPSEE

> The **Landsberger Hut** occupies a magnificent position on an elevation above the two lakes. The Traualpsee, the larger of the two, lies nearly 180m below. If you wish you could shorten the route here by descending directly to Vilsalpsee via Traualpsee (path 425). Otherwise, the routecould be extended into a very comfortable two-day tour by spending the night at the hut. There is certainly plenty to explore in the vicinity; apart from the two small lakes there are also three peaks within easy reach: Rote Spitze (2129m), Steinkarspitze (2066m) and Lachenspitze (2125m).

54. ▶ On the way up to the **Kirchendach Saddle** you have good views down onto the tiny Alpelsee in a grassy basin below and also get a first glimpse of the Vilsalpsee. As the slopes are steep and the track is rather narrow in places some care is necessary if it is wet.

At the saddle you are rewarded with a wonderful view onto the beautiful Schrecksee with its tiny island. This is where path 54 meets up with the Jubiläumsweg from Prinz-Luitpold-Haus. Follow the trail north, across the grassy west flank of the **Kugelhorn**, towards the rock precipices that mark the western face of the **Rauhhorn**. Just when you are starting to wonder how on earth you are going to cross to the other side of the ridge the trail swings right, climbs, and then descends to the Hintere Schafwanne (1956m). From the saddle it descends steeply to **Vils Alpe** and the Vilsalpsee. ▶

Follow the path north along the lake's western shore. It brings you in around 20mins to a car park, restaurants and, if you have not arrived too late, the bus to **Tannheim** – last bus departs around 18.00, but please check beforehand!

The Saalfelderweg (path 421), which has been followed since Strindenscharte, continues left to Prinz-Luitpold-Haus (see also Route 6).

The Jubiläumsweg branches left before reaching Vils Alpe and continues on to Willers Alpe on the German side of the border.

ROUTE 14
*Füssener Jöchl to Bad Kissinger Hut
(Tannheimer Höhenweg)*

Start	Grän
Parking	At gondola lift
Transport	Local buses
Distance	9km/5.5 miles
Height gain	100m (328ft)
Height loss	700m (2296ft)
Time	3–3½hrs
Grade	1
Refreshments	Upper station (Bergstation) of gondola lift, Bad Kissinger Hut
Accommodation	Bad Kissinger Hut (Pfrontner Hut)
Maps	Kompass-Wanderkarte No 4: Füssen – Ausserfern or No 6: Alpenwelt Karwendel

This easy walk is made even easier in that the hard work of the ascent is taken care of by the modern Füssener Jöchl Gondelbahn. It covers the 616m of altitude from the valley station to the top in only 9mins. This fact is, however, of only secondary nature when compared to the beautiful mountain scenery that the Tannheimer Höhenweg (Tannheim High Level Walk) reveals to the growing number of people who walk it.

From the lift station go left in the direction of Aggenstein – Bad Kissinger Hut (path 414). The path climbs steadily until it reaches the saddle between **Sefenspitze** and Lumberger Grat (a ridge to the west of the Sefenspitze). In the distance it is already possible to see both the hut and the Aggenstein. The path now drops considerably in altitude as it zigzags down to the huts of **Seben Alpe**, the lowest point on the route (1620m). ◄

*From Seben Alpe a 50min (ascent only) detour could be made to the scarcely visited **Brentenjoch** (2000m).)*

Continue from the alm pastures towards the beautifully situated **Bad Kissinger Hut** (1800m), which is reached after a gradual climb, partly through woods, along the

ROUTE 14 – FÜSSENER JÖCHL TO BAD KISSINGER HUT (TANNHEIMER HÖHENWEG)

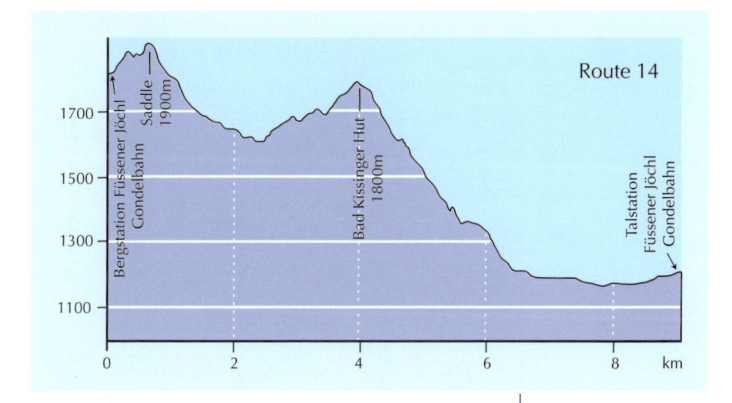

Brentenjoch's western slopes. The view over the Tannheim Valley, which had been hidden by the wall of the Lumberger Grat, is now all the more enjoyable. However, if that is not enough then the energetic can always ascend the **Aggenstein** (1981m), which rises directly behind the hut.

For the return route take the path that descends south from the hut to **Enge** and **Lumberg**. From here it is roughly 20mins back to the car park next to the gondola lift or to **Grän**.

Bad Kissinger Hut

WALKING IN THE BAVARIAN ALPS

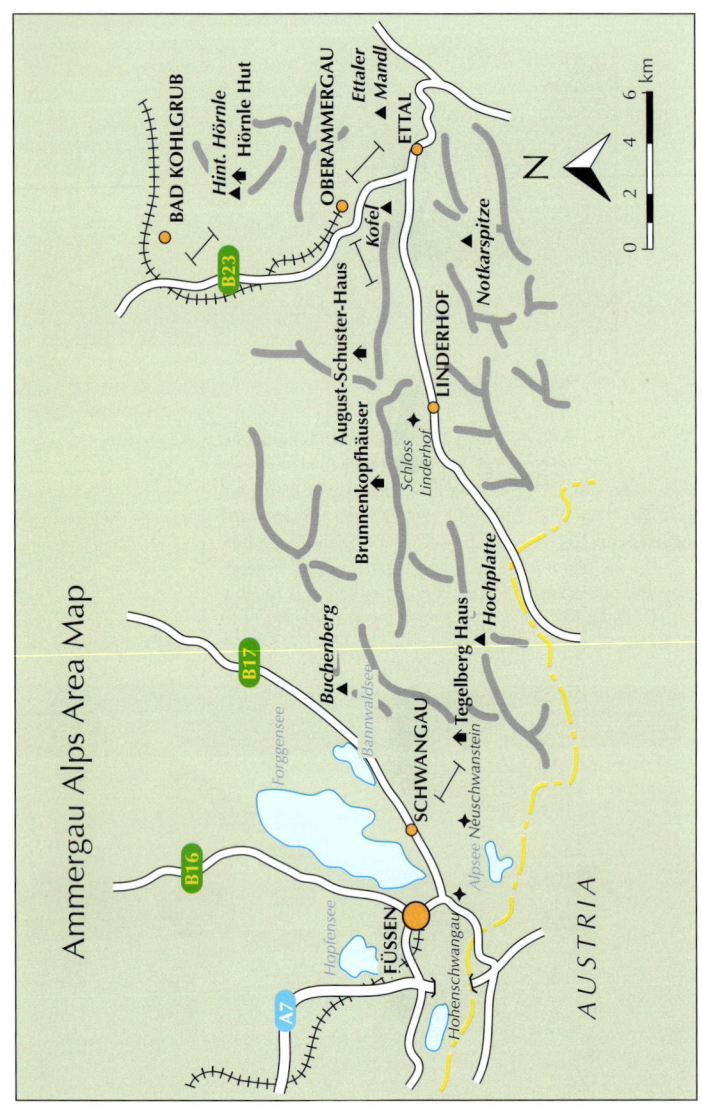

Ammergau Alps Area Map

View down to Ettal from Notkarspitze (Route 21)

PART II
THE AMMERGAU ALPS

PART II
THE AMMERGAU ALPS

Oberammergau is famed for its painted house façades: Pilatushaus

The Ammergauer Alpen – or Ammergebirge as they are also known in German – are bounded to the west by the River Lech and to the east by the River Loisach. The towns of Trauchgau and Bad Kohlgrub mark the group's northernmost limits, and Lermoos in Austria the southernmost. Among the highest peaks in the group are Hochplatte (2082m), Kreuzspitze (2185m) and Daniel (2342m).

In the 19th century the forests of the Ammergau Alps were the exclusive hunting domain of Bavarian royalty. Following the motto 'Commoners keep out!' the area was never developed to any great extent and was able to preserve much of its natural beauty. A large section is now protected as the Naturschutzgebiet Ammergebirge (**Ammergebirge** Nature Reserve), which is in large part due to the efforts of the German Alpine Club. Covering an area of 276 sq km it is the largest reserve of its type in Bavaria and ranks as the third largest in Germany. Only the western and eastern fringes of the range have been made easily accessible by cable railway, which means that even in mid-summer it is not hard to find less heavily used trails, away from the main crowds.

PART II – THE AMMERGAU ALPS

FÜSSEN
Tourist office: Tourist Information, Kaiser-Maximilian-Platz 1, D-87629 Füssen. Tel: (08362) 9385-0, fax: (08362) 9385-20; ***www.fuessen.de****, e-mail: tourismus@fuessen.de. 24hr Room Reservation Service (English): tel: (08362) 9385-34.*

Füssen has centuries of history behind it as the castle, the local museum and a few beautifully decorated churches can prove. However, even more of a tourist attraction than the town and its sights are the castles near Hohenschwangau. Above all it is Schloss Neuschwanstein that captures the imagination of visitors. Built for King Ludwig II of Bavaria (1845–86) in the 19th century this fairy-tale castle occupies a magnificent site above the Schwansee and can be visited in the course of a walk from Füssen, or shorter, from Hohenschwangau.

Füssen can be quickly reached from the north (Munich) by either road or rail. Those driving from the Allgäu need to follow the German Alpine Road (B310) east. There are a couple of campsites on the shores of the Forggensee, directly north of the town.

Late afternoon on the Altherrenweg (Route 17)

WALKING IN THE BAVARIAN ALPS

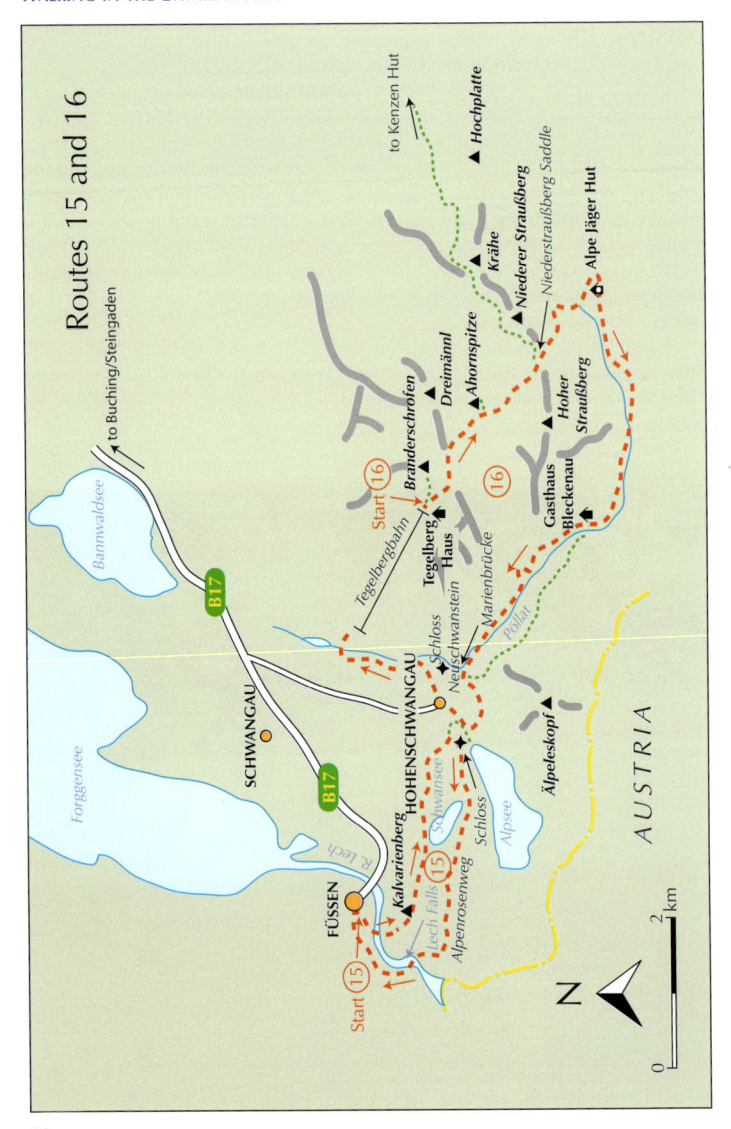

ROUTE 15
Kalvarienberg (Mount Calvary)

Start	Füssen
Parking	In Füssen (no free parking)
Transport	Local buses
Distance	9.9km/6 miles
Height gain	159m (521ft)
Height loss	159m (521ft)
Time	2½–3hrs
Grade	1
Refreshments	Cafés and restaurants in Füssen and Hohenschwangau
Map	Kompass-Wanderkarte No 4: Füssen – Ausserfern

A swim in Swan Lake (Schwansee), great views over Füssen, an edifying, if all too brief, tour of Schloss Hohenschwangau and a waterfall are the highlights of this short but varied walk.

Starting point is downtown **Füssen**, at the upper end of a street known as Reichenstrasse. Even if you have not equipped yourself with a town plan (available from the tourist office) you should not have too much trouble finding your way down to the large bridge across the River Lech.

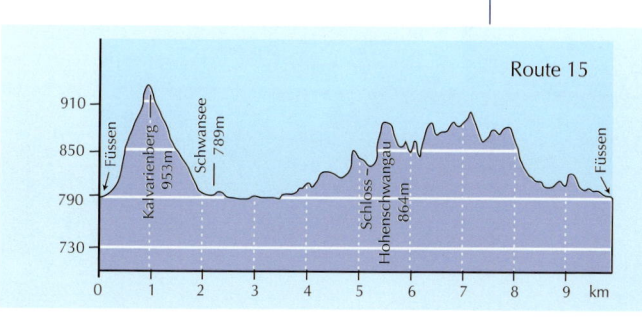

Before reaching the bridge it is worth pausing for a look at the brightly painted façade of the Spitalkirche (a small church). After crossing the river go right along the road to another church. From here steps lead up past the various stations of the Cross to the three crosses atop the **Kalvarienberg**'s modest summit (953m). For the relatively minor effort of the ascent the panorama is quite good. Looking east you can see the Schwansee and Schloss Hohenschwangau.

From the summit the path zigzags down the other side of the hill to the lake. In summer you can enjoy a refreshing dip in its cool waters, but bear in mind that swimming is restricted to certain areas of the lake (observe the signs) in order to protect shore vegetation and wildlife. Afterwards a leisurely stroll through a beautifully laid-out park leads to **Hohenschwangau** and up to the castle of the same name. As the guided tour through the castle lasts only 30mins there should be no problem including it on the itinerary.

Bavaria's 'Mad King Ludwig' spent his childhood at Schloss Hohenschwangau

> It was at Schloss Hohenschwangau that King Ludwig II of Bavaria spent his childhood. **Note** Tickets must be purchased beforehand from the Ticket-Center in Hohenschwangau. Open: May–Sept from 09.00, Oct–Mar from 10.00.

After this brief cultural interlude continue west, around the Perzenkopf, and along the Alpenrosenweg (Alpenroses Trail) to Ziegelwies. Turning right in the direction of **Füssen** it is not far to the impressive Lechfall (Lech Falls). A small bridge crosses the river and in 15mins you are back in the centre of town.

ROUTE 16
A Walk above Hohenschwangau

Start	Hohenschwangau
Parking	Car park next to Tegelbergbahn
Transport	Bus 78 from Füssen to Tegelbergbahn, Schwangau. Using bus connections at the end (private bus Bleckenau – Hohenschwangau and bus 78 Hohenschwangau – Tegelbergbahn) shortens the walk by 1½hrs
Distance	16.6km/10 miles
Height loss	888m (2913ft)
Time	4½hrs (using buses only 3hrs)
Grade	1
Refreshments	Tegelberg Haus, Alpe Jäger Hut, Gasthaus Bleckenau
Accommodation	Tegelberg Haus, Gasthaus Bleckenau, (Kenzen Hut)
Maps	Kompass-Wanderkarte No 4: Füssen – Ausserfern or No 5: Wettersteingebirge – Zugspitzgebiet

WALKING IN THE BAVARIAN ALPS

> The cable railway to the top of the Tegelberg starts operating at 09.00 and those who want to avoid the crowds should make sure that they are among the first to arrive at **Tegelberg Haus** (1707m). The views from here are already superb, but those with sufficient experience and a head for heights can make a ½hr detour northeast to the summit of the Branderschrofen (1880m) for what some claim is an even more breathtaking outlook – wire ropes aid the last 20m or so of the ascent to the summit cross.

From the cable railway station follow the Alpenlehrpfad (alpine nature trail) east in the direction of the Branderfleck Saddle. At the saddle a path on the right leads down to Bleckenau (1½hrs). However, this route continues southeast and after a steepish climb comes to another path which branches left. This leads to the summit of the **Ahornspitze** (1780m; not signposted), which is reached in the course of an easy 20min scramble. The views at the top are not as impressive as those from the Tegelberg, but it has the advantage of being a lot more peaceful. To the south the bare rock peak of the Hoher Straußberg (1934m) is plainly visible. No waymarked paths disturb the tranquillity of this mountain and it is said that the few golden eagles that have managed to survive in the Bavarian Alps still favour it as a place to build their eyries.

The main path continues southeast around the Straußbergköpfl down to the alm pastures of the pretty Niederstraußberg-Alm (1610m) and then up to the **Niederstraußberg Saddle** (1650m). From here it descends to

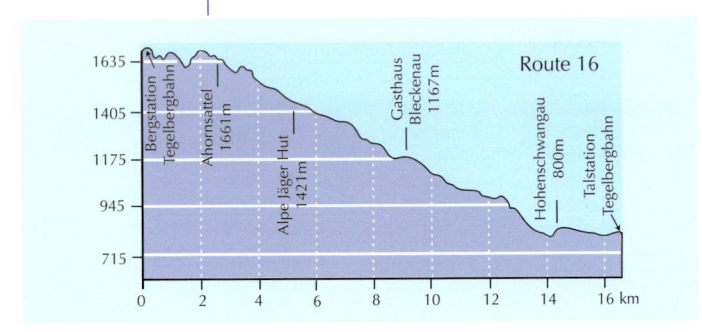

ROUTE 16 – A WALK ABOVE HOHENSCHWANGAU

View along the trail to the Branderschrofen

the Köllebach stream, passes through the meadows of Ochsenängerle and then curves right to **Alpe Jäger Hut** in the Pöllat Valley. The hut marks the beginning of the pleasant forest road which can be followed all the way back to Hohenschwangau. However, there is a minibus from Gasthaus Bleckenau (about halfway along the road) to Hohenschwangau for those who want to shorten this section of the walk by an hour or so. Departure times are written up on a blackboard at the hut – last bus usually goes at 17.30. From the village follow first the Pöllatweg and then a signposted path along the banks of the Pöllat stream to the car park at the Tegelberg cable railway (½hr).

Those who choose to walk, rather than take the minibus, can make a 5min detour to the Marienbrücke (bridge) before descending to Hohenschwangau. From here there is an impressive view of Neuschwanstein Castle.

The best views of Neuschwanstein Castle are from the Marienbrücke in the Pöllat Valley

Two-day tour

The following extension of the above route follows a section of the Via Alpina long-distance walk. The Via Alpina continues from Kenzen Hut to Schloss Linderhof.

From the Niederstraußberg Saddle walk in a northeasterly direction to the Gabelschrofen Saddle (1916m). An excursion can be made from here to the summit of the Krähe (2012m). Return the same way and then descend into a rock basin known as the Gumpenkar, where you have a good chance of seeing marmots. Continue on from here to the Kenzen Saddle (1650m) and Kenzen Hut (1285m, 3½hrs from Niederstraußberg Saddle). After spending the night at Kenzen Hut continue northwest over the Leiterau (1103m) to Buching (3hrs). Catch the bus back to Schwangau.

ROUTE 17 – BAD KOHLGRUB TO OBERAMMERGAU

OBERAMMERGAU

*Tourist office: Oberammergau Tourismus, Eugen-Papst-Strasse 9a, D-82487 Oberammergau. Tel: (08822) 92 310, fax: (08822) 923 190; website: **www.oberammergau.de**, e-mail: info@oberammergau.de*

Woodcarvers, frescoed house fronts (known locally as *Lüftlmalerei*) and performances of the famous Passion Play are what most people associate with Oberammergau. In festival years (the passion plays are only held every 10 years) the town is packed with tourists, in which case it is probably better to seek accommodation elsewhere. To the west of the town Schloss Linderhof is another of King Ludwig II's famous castles. It is well worth visiting because of the lavish interior and its beautiful park setting. Oberammergau has a railway station, and both the youth hostel and campsite are close to the centre of town.

ROUTE 17
Bad Kohlgrub to Oberammergau

Start	Bad Kohlgrub
Parking	At chairlift
Transport	Train from Oberammergau to Bad Kohlgrub
Distance	9.9km/6 miles
Height gain	145m (476ft)
Height loss	701m (2300ft)
Time	4hrs
Grade	1
Refreshments	Hörnle Hut, Berggasthaus Romanshöhe
Accommodation	Hörnle Hut
Maps	Kompass-Wanderkarte No 6: Alpenwelt Karwendel or No 7: Murnau – Kochel

On a sunny day in autumn this walk is hard to beat. When a river of mist obscures the valley below the gentle grass peaks of the Hörnle Group are invariably bathed in sunshine under a bright blue sky. The locals are obviously well aware of this and on a Sunday morning after church there is often quite a queue at the chairlift station. Though some find it enough to walk just as far as the Stierkopf it is rewarding to extend the walk to Oberammergau. The last section along the so-called Altherrenweg is particularly beautiful in the soft light of late afternoon.

From **Bad Kohlgrub** take the chairlift to **Hörnle Hut** (1390m) at the foot of the Vorderes Hörnle. ◀ The following route via the Vorderes (1484m), Mittleres (1496m) and Hinteres Hörnle (1548m) to the Stierkopf (1520m) does not take much more than 1hr, but offers wonderful views the whole way. As the main trail goes around the individual peaks it is not necessary to climb each one, but it is worth going to the top of the **Vorderes Hörnle** as it gives a good overview of the onward route. Descending from here continue around the base of **Mittleres Hörnle** past Hörnle Alm and then veer east to **Hinteres Hörnle**. The **Stierkopf** lies directly ahead, and though it is the only one of these grassy peaks which is not marked by a cross it is nevertheless worth climbing so as to enjoy the panorama one last time before beginning the descent.

The descent to the Drei-Marken Saddle (1263m) is steep and requires a good ½hr. Continue on a short distance until you come to a fork. Take path 19a downhill in the direction of Berggasthaus Romanshöhe. In about 15mins you will pass a hut from where you start following a forest road. At the next fork turn left. The route is not so clearly

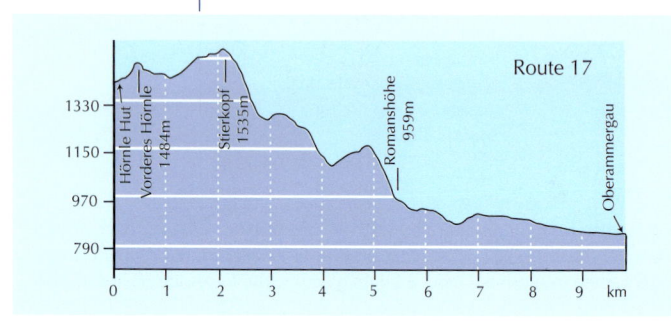

> Those who do without the chairlift will need about 2hrs to reach the hut.

Route 17 – Bad Kohlgrub to Oberammergau

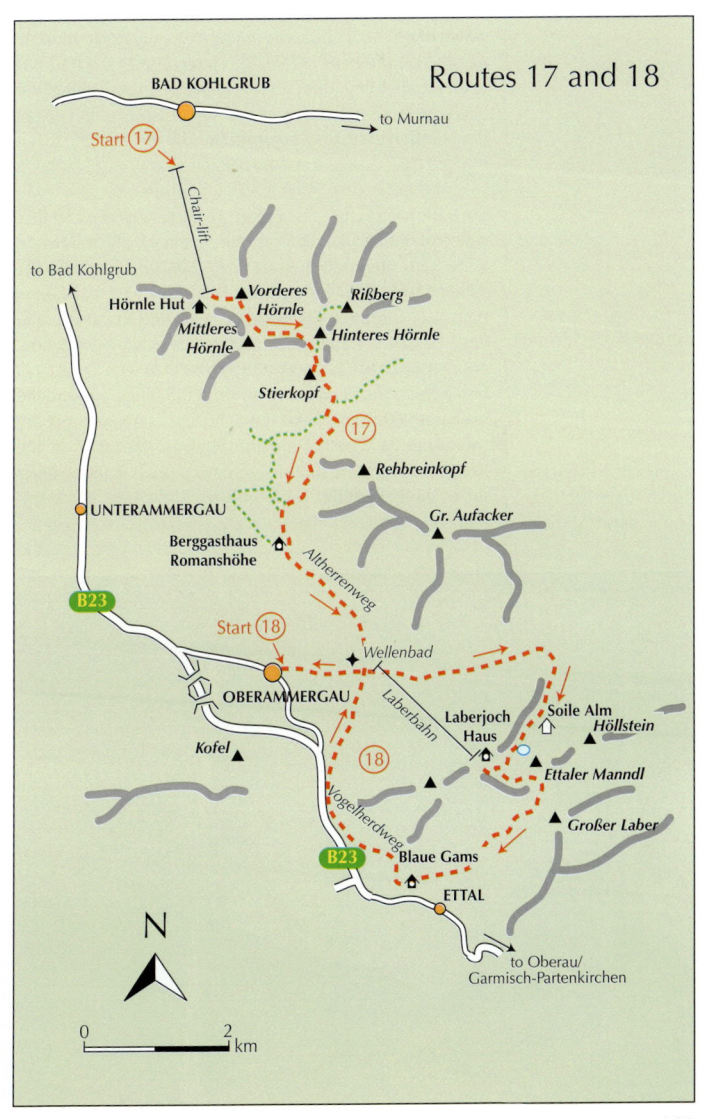

waymarked here, but you should see a green triangle painted on the trees at irregular intervals. As the trail has been descending through the woods since leaving the Stierkopf there is not a lot in the way of views until you get close to **Berggasthaus Romanshöhe** – by this time the green triangle has become a yellow one.

At the *Gasthaus* (*closed Mon*) there are nice views over the valley and Oberammergau. From here you can either descend directly to town or, more interestingly, follow the wide path downhill a short way, then turn left onto the Altherrenweg (Old Gentlemen's Path). This well-maintained path keeps to the grass slopes just above Oberammergau and passes through an almost park-like landscape. Numerous benches are provided for those who want to sit and admire the scenery. In autumn the fields are studded with purple crocus. Near the Schnitzel Graben (a gully) a footbridge is crossed and the *Fußweg* (footpath) to the Wellenbad (a large indoor swimming-pool) is followed as far as the **Laberbahn** cable railway. The centre of town is reached in about 15mins.

Loisach Valley and Walchenseegebirge from Stierkopf

ROUTE 18
Over the Laberjoch (1685m) to Ettal

Start	Oberammergau
Parking	Next to cable railway
Transport	Bus 9622 or 9606 between Ettal and Oberammergau (bus stop opposite Kloster Gasthof)
Distance	13km/8 miles
Height gain	786m (2579ft)
Height loss	850m (2789ft)
Time	5hrs (with cable railway 3hrs)
Grade	1
Refreshments	Laberjoch Haus, restaurants in Ettal
Maps	Kompass-Wanderkarte No 5: Wettersteingebirge – Zugspitzgebiet or No 6 Alpenwelt Karwendel

If possible try to avoid doing this route on weekends – large crowds on the Laberjoch and queues at the Ettaler Manndl! Apart from the ascent of the Ettaler Manndl it is a fairly easy route, though it is a longish climb up to the Laber. A highlight near the end is the famous *Klosterkirche* (monastery church) in Ettal. Of even more interest to some is the Kloster Gasthof where they serve beer that is brewed at the monastery – see also Route 21.

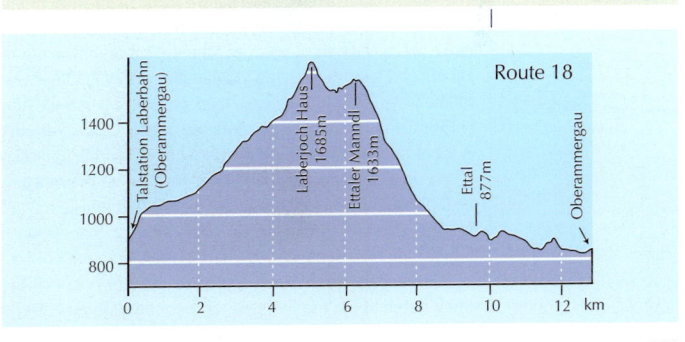

The rocky outcrop of the Ettaler Manndl

The valley station of the **Laberbahn** can be reached from the centre of **Oberammergau** in about ¼hr. If you really want to make an easy day of it you can take the cable railway up to Laberjoch Haus, thus saving roughly 2hrs walking. Otherwise follow waymark 246 northeast, then southwest past **Soile Alm** (1150m) and up to the pretty Soilesee (a tarn; 1¼hrs; 1400m). A lot of people stop and picnic here before starting the steep climb up to the Laberjoch and Laberjoch Haus. The magnificent panorama from the restaurant terrace is adequate reward for the effort of the walk up and the fact that most of Oberammergau seems to be sharing the view with you! ◄

From **Laberjoch Haus** return to the point where the track descends to the Soilesee, and continue in an easterly

This is also a favourite starting point for hang-gliding pilots.

direction around the Manndlköpfe towards the **Ettaler Manndl** (1633m). Shortly before the peak is reached a path branches to the right and down to Kloster Ettal (path 245). It brings you in about 1hr to the monastery. If, however, you do not get nervous at the sight of sheer drops, you can first go left for the ascent of the **Ettaler Manndl**.

The detour to the summit and back adds another 30mins to the walk. The route is secured with chains and apart from any possible psychological problems (do not attempt it if you are uncertain of yourself) there are no real technical difficulties involved – Grade 2–3.

Path 245 (Manndlweg) to Ettal zigzags down through the woods and is rather dull. In **Ettal** it is well worth having a look at the impressive baroque interior of the monastery church before following the Vogelherdweg back to **Oberammergau** (1½hrs). This path starts near the **Blaue Gams** restaurant, which is behind the monastery complex. Note that there is also a bus connection between Ettal and Oberammergau (hourly – check timetable).

ROUTE 19
The Kofel (1341m)

Start	Oberammergau
Parking	Car park in Eugen-Papst-Strasse
Transport	Local buses
Distance	7.5km/4.5 miles
Height gain	511m (1676ft)
Height loss	511m (1676ft)
Time	3½hrs
Grade	2
Refreshments	Kolben Alm
Accommodation	Kolben Alm
Maps	Kompass-Wanderkarte No 5: Wettersteingebirge – Zugspitzgebiet or No 6: Alpenwelt Karwendel

WALKING IN THE BAVARIAN ALPS

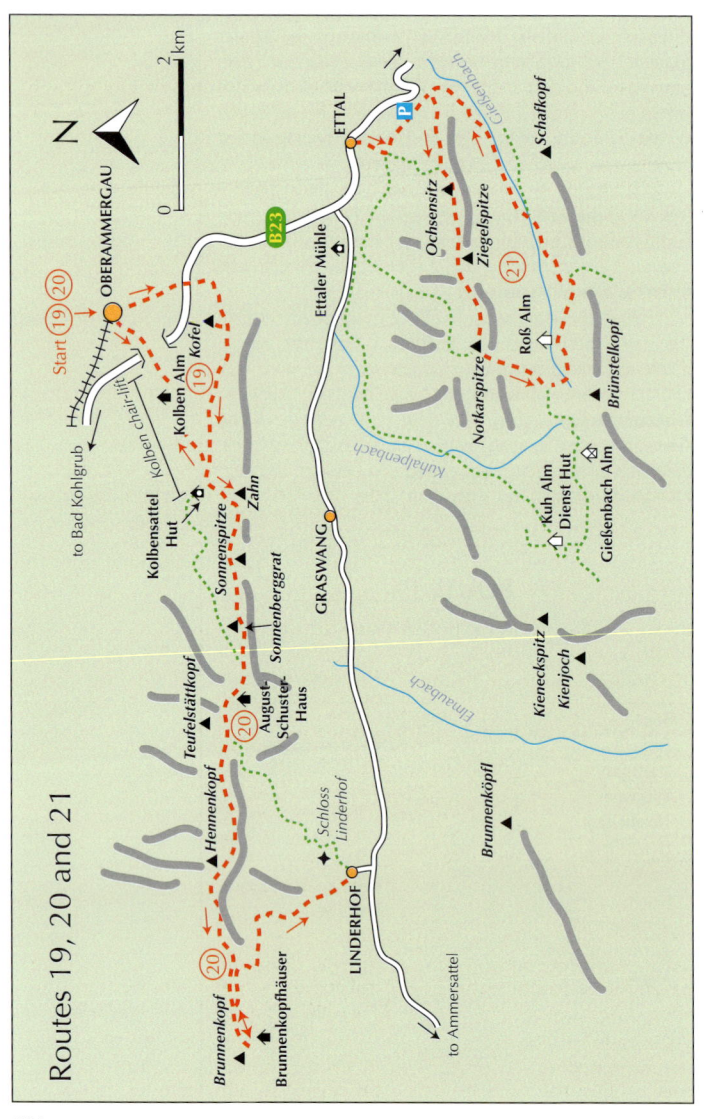

Routes 19, 20 and 21

ROUTE 19 – THE KOFEL

Oberammergau's landmark, the Kofel, is situated at the southern end of town and is a good alternative for those who shy away from the crowds associated with the more popular route to the Laberjoch and Ettaler Manndl (Route 18). Though this stubby finger of rock looks almost unclimbable from town it does not present any particular problems, at least when approached from the south. If the climb to the top of the Kofel is left out then the route can be done by anybody, the only strenuous section being the slog up to the Kofel Saddle.

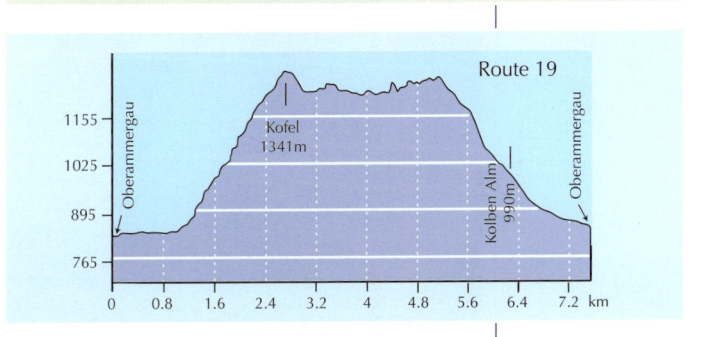

Route 19 elevation profile: Oberammergau – Kofel 1341m – Kolben Alm 990m – Oberammergau, distances 0 to 7.2 km, elevations 765m to 1155m.

The start of the track is easily reached on foot from the centre of town (837m): from Eugen-Papst-Strasse (car park) cross the River Ammer along König-Ludwig-Strasse, then turn left along Malensteinweg and follow the river south. After passing below the bypass road you come to a sign. This directs you to the Kofel along the Grottenweg. First walk past the cemetery, then follow the track left to where the climb up to the Kofel Saddle begins.

At first the track ascends gradually through a field, but as soon as it enters the woods it starts zigzagging its way steeply uphill to a saddle (1200m) just below the peak. The 10–15mins climb up to the summit of **Kofel** is not too difficult (wire ropes along the tricky bits) but it requires sure-footedness at the very least. At the top there is a large cross and a wonderful bird's-eye view of Oberammergau. The panorama also encompasses the Sonnenberggrat, Hörnle Group, Laberjoch and Notkarspitze, all of which are locations of walks in this section. ▶

Those who wish to commemorate their ascent can do so in the visitor's book.

The Königssteig begins at the saddle and is a pleasant walk but does not offer much in the way of views, as the

The Kofel

path goes through the woods. In the morning there is a good chance of seeing chamois grazing near the track. In about 40mins it brings you to a fork, where you have the choice of either continuing to August Schuster Haus (1¼hrs; Route 20), or descending to Oberammergau via **Kolben Alm** (990m). From the alm restaurant it does not take much more than 30mins back to the centre of town.

ROUTE 20
Along the Sonnenberggrat to August-Schuster-Haus and Linderhof

Start	Oberammergau
Parking	Car park in Eugen-Papst-Strasse
Transport	Bus 9622 between Linderhof and Oberammergau
Distance	16.6km/10.5 miles
Height gain	772m (2533ft)
Height loss	661m (2168ft)
Time	6½hrs (alternative route 4½hrs)
Grade	2
Refreshments	Kolben Alm, August-Schuster-Haus, Brunnenkopfhäuser, restaurant at Schloss Linderhof, (Kolbensattel Hut)
Accommodation	Kolben Alm, August-Schuster-Haus (Pürschling Haus), Brunnenkopfhäuser
Map	Kompass-Wanderkarte No 5: Wettersteingebirge – Zugspitzgebiet

This enjoyable ridge walk offers plenty of fine views and rustic mountain huts in which to relax. It is also an area that was popular with Bavaria's nature-loving kings: King Maximilian II and King Ludwig II. With this in mind it is perhaps appropriate that the tour ends at Schloss Linderhof, one of King Ludwig's fairy-tale castles.

From the large car park in Eugen-Papst-Strasse turn right, along the River Ammer, and cross a footbridge. On the other side a signpost directs you to the *Kreuziggungsgruppe* (Crucifixion group). The path passes through a lightly wooded area until it reaches a paved street (König-Ludwig-Strasse) where you turn right and uphill. Within a few minutes you reach the stone Crucifixion group. It was donated

If a visit to Schloss Linderhof is to be included on your itinerary an early start is essential.

to the people of Oberammergau by King Ludwig in remembrance of the Passion Play which he attended (private performance of course!) on 27 September 1871.

The path continues on through pastures and soon arrives at an asphalted road. Ahead the jagged crest of the Sonnenberggrat is already visible and to the left, like an exclamation mark at the end of the ridge, is the Kofel. Turn right and follow the road up to **Kolben Alm** (990m).

After a brief rest at the alm continue on uphill a short distance through the woods, then turn left along the signposted track to Kolben Saddle. After a steepish climb the track arrives at a signposted fork. Walk a few minutes in the direction of Pürschling via **Kolbensattel Hut** (the easy route) then turn left at the sign 'Zahn'. A bit further on another sign confirms that you are walking in the right direction: 'Zahn, Sonnenspitze, Pürschling'. The 'Nur für Geübte' ('only for the experienced') should not worry you unduly unless narrow tracks and steep slopes are a problem. Just over 30mins is required to reach the point where the track levels out below the appropriately named *Zahn* = tooth. The trail which is now followed does not run directly over the bare, rocky ridge but just below it. It is clearly defined, fairly level, and apart from a few short stretches where you might need to make use of your hands it does not present any major difficulties. In another 30mins or so the turn-off to the **Sonnenspitze** is reached. The short detour to the top is well worth it because of the fine views. The huts comprising August-Schuster-Haus (Pürschling Haus) are clearly visible ahead.

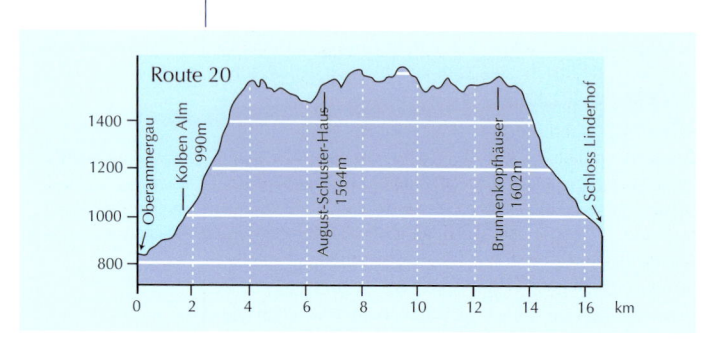

ROUTE 20 – ALONG THE SONNENBERGGRAT TO AUGUST-SCHUSTER-HAUS

On the Sonnenberggrat (Sonnenspitz)

Back on the main track you continue awhile along the north side of the ridge, then the track crosses over to the south side. A bit of care is needed here if the track is slippery as it is somewhat exposed. However it is not long before a road is reached and from here it is not far to the hut. Situated on a saddle between the Pürschling and Teufelstättkopf, **August Schuster Haus** offers fine views over the Graswang Valley and further south to the higher peaks of the Ammergau Alps. Considering the fact that Schloss Linderhof is not too far distant it is not surprising to hear that these huts were originally built as hunting lodges for Bavarian royalty.

The quickest and easiest way down to Schloss Linderhof (943m) is to proceed west towards the Latschenkopf, then turn left along path 232 (1½hrs). It is more interesting, however, to continue straight ahead towards the **Brunnenkopfhäuser** (2hrs). This route runs along the south side of the ridge linking **Teufelstättkopf** to **Hennenkopf** and though not as 'exciting' as the more difficult route (not for beginners!) directly over the ridge it offers views that are almost as good. The descent along the bridle path to the Schloss takes about 1hr. ▶

Make sure you check the time of the last bus back to Oberammergau from the Schloss before starting out.

WALKING IN THE BAVARIAN ALPS

In the latter half of the 19th century King Ludwig II of Bavaria transformed a simple hunting lodge into what is now Schloss Linderhof. Opulently furnished in rococo style, it is set in a beautiful park with fountains, ponds, an artificial grotto and more besides. Open: daily Apr–Sept 09.00–18.00, Oct–Mar 10.00–16.00; www.linderhof.de

Alternative route

Instead of continuing to Schloss Linderhof you could walk back to Oberammergau via the Kolben Saddle. From August-Schuster-Haus descend along the road until you reach a trail that enters the woods on your right (path 233, signposted). The track is quite level most of the way and brings you to **Kolbensattel Hut** in less than 1hr. Either take the chairlift down to **Oberammergau** or enter the woods just above the hut and return along the route you took from town.

ROUTE 21
The Notkarspitze (1889m)

Start	Ettal
Parking	In Ettal
Transport	Bus 9622 or 9606 from Oberammergau to Ettal
Distance	15km/9 miles
Height gain	1020m (3346ft)
Height loss	1020m (3346ft)
Time	6hrs (5hrs for direct descent to Ettaler Mühle)
Grade	2
Refreshments	Take your own
Maps	Kompass-Wanderkarte No 5: Wettersteingebirge – Zugspitzgebiet or No 6: Alpenwelt Karwendel

ROUTE 21 – THE NOTKARSPITZE

> The panorama from the summit of the Notkarspitze is even better than that from the top of the Laberjoch (Route 18). In spite of a long, strenuous climb at the beginning this route promises plenty of variety with alpine scenery *par excellence* on the tops and a picturesque river valley at the end.
>
> The village of Ettal is famed for its large *Kloster* (monastery; www.kloster-ettal.de). It was founded in the 14th century, and the monastery church is an important attraction. Originally Gothic in style it was later rebuilt in baroque fashion and received a domed roof. The interior is splendidly decorated with frescoes and stuccowork. Attached to the monastery is a brewery that has been quenching thirsty throats for some 400 years. The final product can be sampled at the Klosterbräustüberl.

From **Ettal** a path goes south through fields to the woods at the foot of the Notkarspitze. Here you go left, skirting the woods to the point where the path joins a gravel road (near a car park on the Ettaler Sattel). Continue along it to a sharp curve. Whereas the road descends into the Gießenbach Valley you go right and uphill along a steeply climbing track. For close to 1hr there is not much to be seen, but in the vicinity of the **Ochsensitz** the breaks in the trees become more frequent. Here it is worth pausing to take in the magnificent view of Kloster Ettal, nestled like a child's playhouse at the foot of the Laberberg.

The views get better and better as you climb up to the **Ziegelspitze**. A ridge covered by dwarf pines leads on from the summit cross to the **Notkarspitze** which is clearly visible ahead. One last steep climb brings you to the top. Though

As there are no huts offering refreshments en route (fewer huts, fewer people!) remember to take your own food and drink.

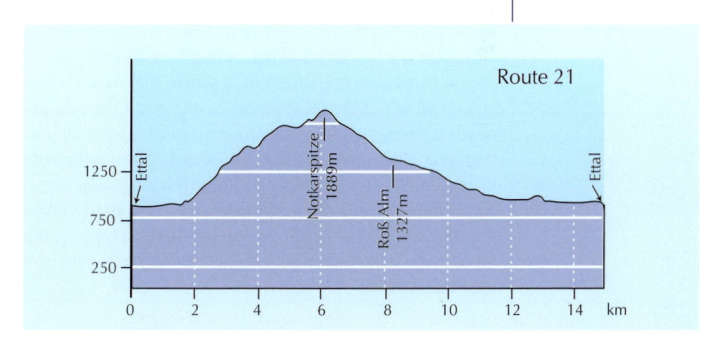

Estergebirge from Notkarspitze

you will probably have to share the grassy summit with other walkers there is plenty of room if you want to picnic here. Fantastic panorama with impressive views of the nearby Wettersteingebirge (including Zugspitze), Ammergebirge and Estergebirge. The route of the ridge walk to August Schuster Haus (northwest) is also easy to make out.

There is a rather steep track leading down the mountain's north slopes to Ettaler *Mühle* (mill) and from there directly to Ettal. A more comfortable, if somewhat longer, alternative is to descend along the south ridge. At a fork (point 1600m on map) you are presented with the choice of either turning right to the Kühalpenbach Valley or left to the Gießenbach Valley. Both possibilities have their individual charm but the latter is the shorter route (2hrs to Ettal). It takes you down to **Roß Alm** where a gravel road is followed into the woods. At a signposted fork turn left along path 265 to Ettal. You are still descending through the woods but the road is eventually exchanged for a simple trail which brings you down to a stream (Gießenbach). If it is not carrying too much water walk along the stream bed for about 15mins until you come to a road. This is followed up and away from the stream. It is quite a pleasant stroll with nice views down into what is now a deep, narrow gorge. The road climbs steadily up to the point where the long ascent to the Ochsensitz and Notkarspitze began. In about 20mins you are back in **Ettal**.

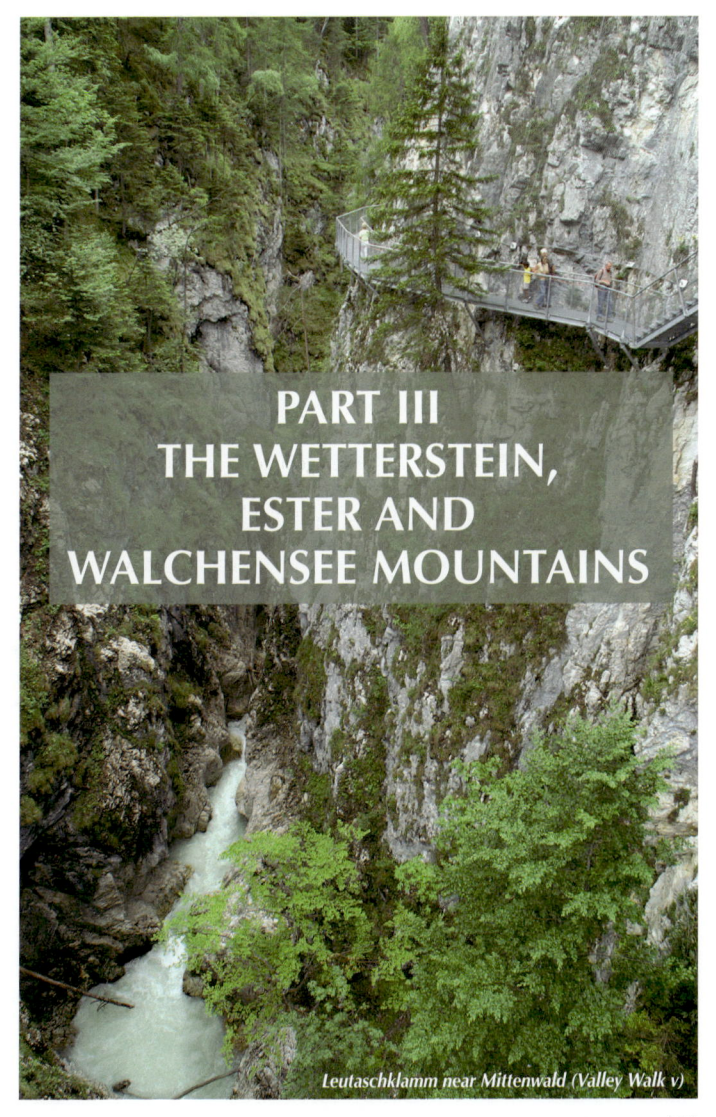

PART III
THE WETTERSTEIN, ESTER AND WALCHENSEE MOUNTAINS

Leutaschklamm near Mittenwald (Valley Walk v)

WALKING IN THE BAVARIAN ALPS

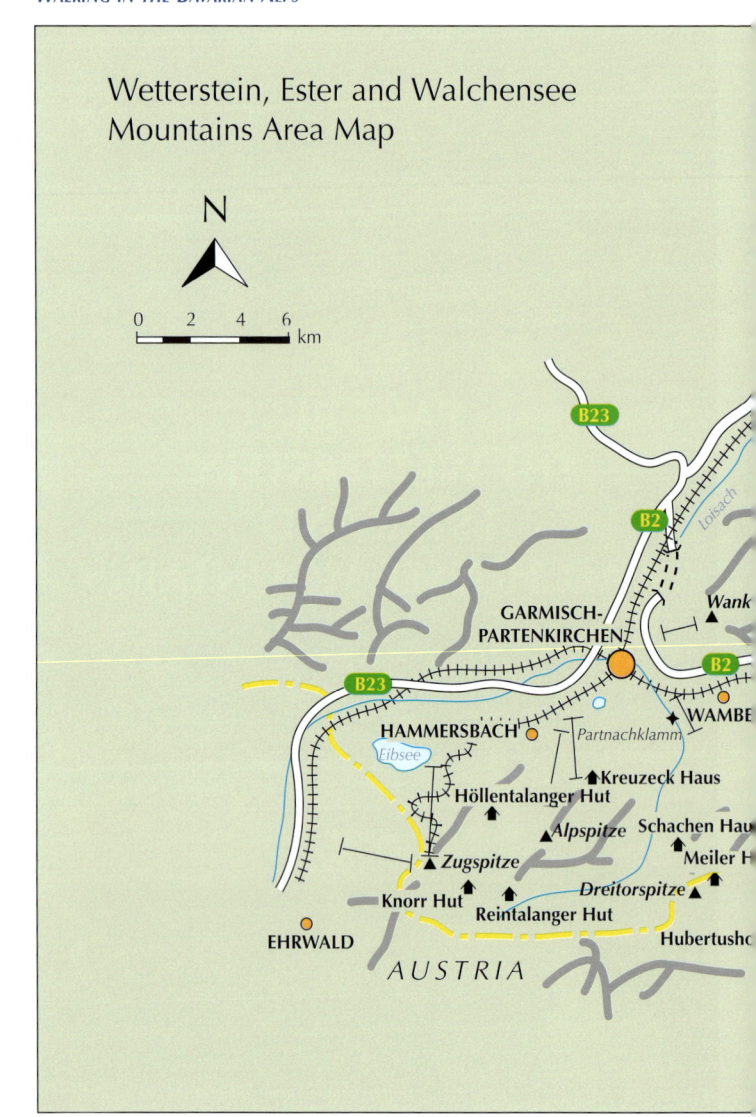

Wetterstein, Ester and Walchensee Mountains Area Map

PART III – THE WETTERSTEIN, ESTER AND WALCHENSEE MOUNTAINS

PART III
THE WETTERSTEIN, ESTER AND WALCHENSEE MOUNTAINS

In German these mountain groups are referred to as the Wettersteingebirge, Estergebirge and Walchenseegebirge. The German Alpine Club groups them under the overall heading Bayerische Voralpen/West.

The Wetterstein massif is bounded by the Isar Valley to the east, the Leutasch and Gais valleys to the south and the Loisach Valley to the west. The northern boundary is marked by the River Loisach and the River Kanker. The most famous peak in this massif is undoubtedly the Zugspitze (2962m), the highest mountain in Germany.

Estergebirge is the name given to the chain of mountains between the Loisach, Eschenlaine, Obernach and Kanker valleys. They lie to the north of the Wettersteingebirge. The highest peaks are the Hoher Fricken (1940m), the Krottenkopf (2086m) and the Hoher Kisten (1922m).

The Walchenseegebirge lie directly north of the Estergebirge and are conveniently separated from the Benediktenwandgebirge by the B11 (*Bundestrasse* [federal highway] No 11). They are named after Bavaria's deepest lake (192m), the Walchensee. As far as walking is concerned the two most popular peaks in this range are the Herzogstand (1731m) and Heimgarten (1790m).

Also included within this section are the northwestern fringes of the Karwendel, in particular the Soiern Group.

A picturesque corner of Garmisch-Partenkirchen with the Wank forming a backdrop

PART III – THE WETTERSTEIN, ESTER AND WALCHENSEE MOUNTAINS

Eibsee near Garmisch (Valley Walk iii)

GARMISCH-PARTENKIRCHEN
Tourist office: Tourist Information (main office), Richard-Strauss-Platz 2, D-82467 Garmisch-Partenkirchen. Tel: (08821) 180-700, fax: (08821) 180-755;
***www.garmisch-partenkirchen.de**, e-mail: tourist-info@gapa.de.*
Tourist Information Partenkirchen, Rathaus, Rathausplatz 1. 24hr Accommodation Service: tel: (08821) 19 412.

Garmisch-Partenkirchen is a large, sprawling town, its few picturesque corners being largely swallowed up by all the trappings associated with a world-famous centre for winter sports. Originally two separate villages, Garmisch and Partenkirchen were joined in 1936, the year the Winter Olympics were held here. What it lacks in 'cosiness' it makes up for in terms of its excellent tourist facilities (for example, eight cable railways), and the splendid mountain scenery on its doorstep. Whether north, south, east or west, there are mountains everywhere beckoning you to pull on your boots and head for the hills.

WALKING IN THE BAVARIAN ALPS

Garmisch-Partenkirchen is quickly reached by road from Oberammergau (bus connection, see previous section), and also has good rail connections, for instance to Mittenwald, the second base town in this section. There is a youth hostel near the railway station, but the campsite (Camping Zugspitze) is located southwest of the town centre at Grainau.

VALLEY WALKS
Maps: Kompass-Wanderkarte Nos 5 or 6.

iii THE EIBSEE (1½–2hrs) One of the prettiest of the shorter walks in the vicinity of Garmisch-Partenkirchen is the stroll around the Eibsee (6½km). The lake is beautifully situated at the foot of the Zugspitze massif and can be reached either by road (Eibsee bus) or railway (Zugspitzbahn) from Garmisch. As the path is not only very well marked but also keeps close to the lake shore there is hardly any need for a more detailed description. However, those who would like a bit more exercise can start the walk in Obergrainau: follow the Törlenweg (waymark G3) to the Eibsee road, and then continue along a pleasant forest path (waymark E) uphill to the lake (2hrs return).

The walk around the Eibsee could also be combined with a cable railway or rack railway ride up to the top of the Zugspitze, the highest peak in the Bavarian Alps.

Meadow near Graseck (Route 24)

ROUTE 22
Wank (1780m), Esterberg Alm and Gams Hut

Start	Garmisch-Partenkirchen
Parking	Car park next to Wankbahn
Transport	Local buses to Wankbahn
Distance	12.7km/8 miles
Height loss	1055m (3461ft)
Time	3½–4hrs
Grade	1
Refreshments	Wank Haus, Esterberg Alm, Gams Hut
Accommodation	Wank Haus
Maps	Kompass-Wanderkarte No 5: Wettersteingebirge – Zugspitzgebiet or No 6: Alpenwelt Karwendel

Esterberg Alm and the Wank are both popular destinations, especially in summer when the tourists descend upon Garmisch-Partenkirchen in their thousands. However, in early summer and especially in late autumn the crowds are noticeably thinner and the walking all the more enjoyable. The advantages inherent in the area's popularity are, of course, the excellent facilities and the many well-marked paths.

The ride up to the Wank summit in the small four-seater gondola takes about 20mins. At the top there is a restaurant (**Wank Haus**), an observatory and, if the weather is fine, swarms of people. ▶

From **Wank Haus** continue northwest, and you will soon come to a signpost directing you down to **Esterberg Alm**. The trail zigzags its way slowly downhill and eventually comes to a fork at which you turn right. It then continues through the woods for a short distance before entering the alm pastures. The track is level here and the alm buildings are quickly reached (*simple but hearty meals served in the rustic restaurant*) – a pleasant spot for a brief stop.

The Wank is a favourite place to soak up the sun as it offers not only spacious meadows to lie on but also a fantastic panorama encompassing some 400 alpine peaks.

WALKING IN THE BAVARIAN ALPS

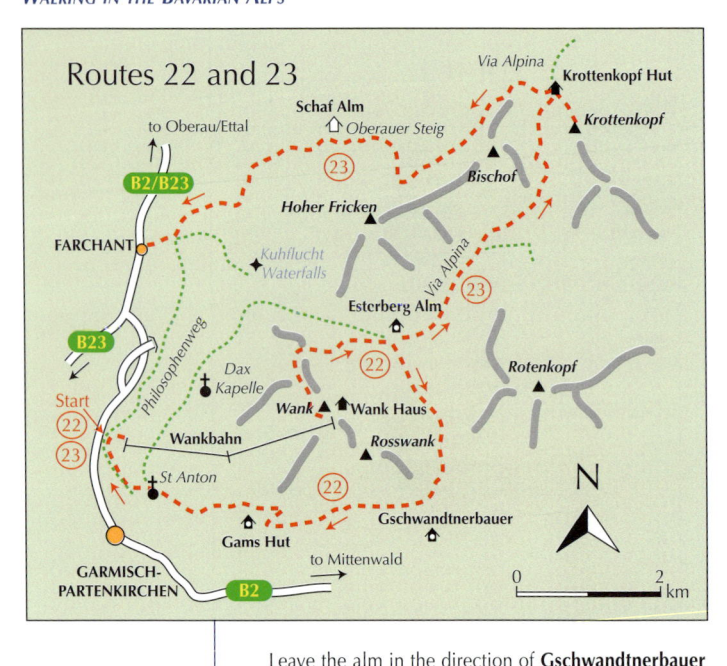

> The path straight ahead leads to Gschwandtnerbauer.

Leave the alm in the direction of **Gschwandtnerbauer** (south). At first the trail goes through fields, then shortly after passing the Esterberg ski lift it enters a valley and follows a stream – quite pretty along here. After walking a short while along the stream it is crossed on a wooden footbridge and the track climbs up into the woods. Once the fork to the Rosswank is passed the trail starts descending again, and there are some good views towards the Wetterstein Mountains behind Garmisch. At the next fork turn right to Gams Hut. ◄ The track climbs again through the woods (mainly conifers here), then it is fairly easy walking with only a few minor ups and downs. At one point you go past a large grassy clearing, where the trail widens to a rough forest road. Eventually it brings you to a fork, the left branch of which continues along the Adamweg to Partenkirchen and the right (which this route follows) to **Gams Hut**. The Gams Hut is quite a cosy place with good views over Garmisch and the mountains behind.

ROUTE 22 – WANK, ESTERBERG ALM AND GAMS HUT

Wank summit

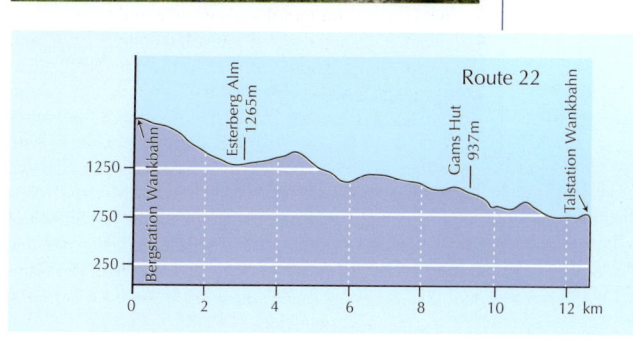

Continue downhill from the hut in the direction of the cable railway (signposted 'Wankbahn Talstation'). Where the trail forks turn right, cross a footbridge, and enter a pretty gorge. The path soon brings you to Josefsbichl, a spot marked by a large cross. Turn right here along a path (K6) that leads to the pilgrimage church of **St Anton**. Near the church entrance a dirt footpath (signposted 'Philosophenweg') is followed to a fork, where you turn right in the direction of Farchant. At the next fork turn right again. It is now not far to the car park at the cable railway station.

ROUTE 23
Partenkirchen to the Krottenkopf (2086m)

Start	Garmisch-Partenkirchen
Parking	Car park next to Wankbahn
Transport	Local buses to Wankbahn and from Farchant to Garmisch
Distance	16.5km/10 miles
Height gain	326m (1069ft)
Height loss	1416m (4645ft)
Time	7–8hrs (or 2 days)
Grade	2
Refreshments	(Wank Haus), Esterberg Alm, Krottenkopf Hut
Accommodation	(Wank Haus), Krottenkopf Hut
Maps	Kompass-Wanderkarte No 5: Wettersteingebirge – Zugspitzgebiet or No 6: Alpenwelt Karwendel

This walk takes you to the Krottenkopf, the highest peak in the Estergebirge. As it is rather long some may prefer to break it up by spending the night at Krottenkopf Hut. Those who do overnight at the hut will enjoy the advantage of either a spectacular sunrise or sunset from the nearby Krottenkopf summit (20mins from the hut). The hut is also a stop on the Via Alpina long-distance route. It continues

ROUTE 23 – PARTENKIRCHEN TO THE KROTTENKOPF

north from the hut to Eschenlohe, from where it swings northeast to eventually cross the ridge to the Herzogstand (see Route 33) en route to Walchensee.

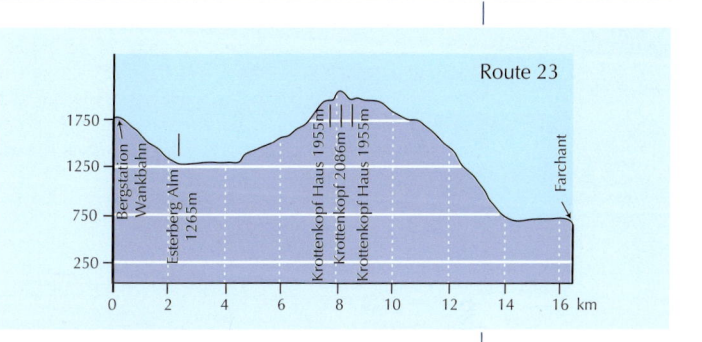

Either take the Wankbahn up to the summit of the **Wank** and then walk to **Esterberg Alm** as described in Route 22 or – if you would prefer not to use the cable railway – start from the pilgrimage church of **St Anton** (Wallfahrtskirche St Anton) and follow a gently climbing road past the Dax-Kapelle to the alm. However, if the weather is good the first alternative is probably preferable as the views from the Wank are superb. St Anton lies to the southeast of the Wankbahn and can be reached from the centre of town in about 20mins – a free town plan of Garmisch-Partenkirchen is available from the tourist office.

The route to the Krottenkopf is clearly signposted from Esterberg Alm. Follow the trail in a northeasterly direction through meadows and woods up to **Krottenkopf Hut** (Weilheimer Hut, 1955m). From here it is not far to the summit (4hrs from starting point). Tremendous views: the entire Karwendel chain, the Wetterstein massif, the Ammergau Alps and in the blue haze of the distance the snow-capped peaks of the Central Alps.

Starting from the hut the descent route follows a narrow path to a saddle between the **Bischof** (2033m) and Henneneck (1964m) – great views from here! Continue along steeply falling slopes covered by dwarf pines and pass a turn-off on the left (trail WG on map). A short distance further on

The trail to the Krottenkopf passes through the meadows of Esterberg Alm, then turns left (out of picture) to climb up to the summit and hut

the path takes a sharp turn to the right (on to the Oberauer Steig) and zigzags its way down to **Schaf Alm Hut** from where there is a magnificent view of the Zugspitze and over the Loisach Valley to the Kramerspitz. Still descending steeply the winding trail eventually arrives at a small lake (Ursprungsee), where it turns left in the direction of Farchant (3hrs from Krottenkopf). Here it is possible to catch the train back to **Garmisch-Partenkirchen**, or the Philosophenweg (Philosopher's Trail) could be followed south through the woods to the car park next to the Wankbahn (add 1hr).

Farchant (www.farchant.de) is an attractive village with numerous farmhouses dating from the 17th and 18th centuries. From town a trail (F1, 'Walderlebnispfad') leads in 45mins to the Kuhfluchtwasserfälle (waterfalls): the Kuhflucht stream makes for an impressive sight as it bursts in a torrent of water from the middle of a rock face.

ROUTE 24
Wamberg, Berggasthof Eckbauer and the Partnachklamm

Start	Garmisch-Partenkirchen
Parking	Car park between the public baths (Kainzenbad) and district hospital (Kreiskrankenhaus/Klinikum)
Transport	Local buses to the Klinikum
Distance	9.5km/6 miles
Height gain	508m (1666ft)
Height loss	508m (1666ft)
Time	3½–4hrs
Grade	1
Refreshments	Gasthof Wamberg, Gasthof Eckbauer, Forsthaus (Alpenhotel) Graseck, Lenz'n Hut
Acommodation	Forsthaus (Alpenhotel) Graseck
Maps	Kompass-Wanderkarte No 5: Wettersteingebirge – Zugspitzgebiet or No 6: Alpenwelt Karwendel

Fine views and the romantic Partnachklamm as a finale are the main attractions of this pleasant hill walk from Garmisch. The *Klamm* is a small but pretty riverfilled gorge roughly 700m long and 70m deep. It was made accessible to the general public back in 1912. Due to its popularity it is wise to avoid walking it either on weekends or public holidays. Those who do this walk in spring will find it particularly beautiful, as the alm meadows around Wamberg are covered by a luxuriant carpet of wildflowers.

The walk begins at the southern end of the large car park between the district hospital and Kainzenbad. A sign directs you uphill in the direction of Wamberg. After passing a group of houses the sealed road ends and it becomes more like a gravel track – cars may not drive along here. For the

WALKING IN THE BAVARIAN ALPS

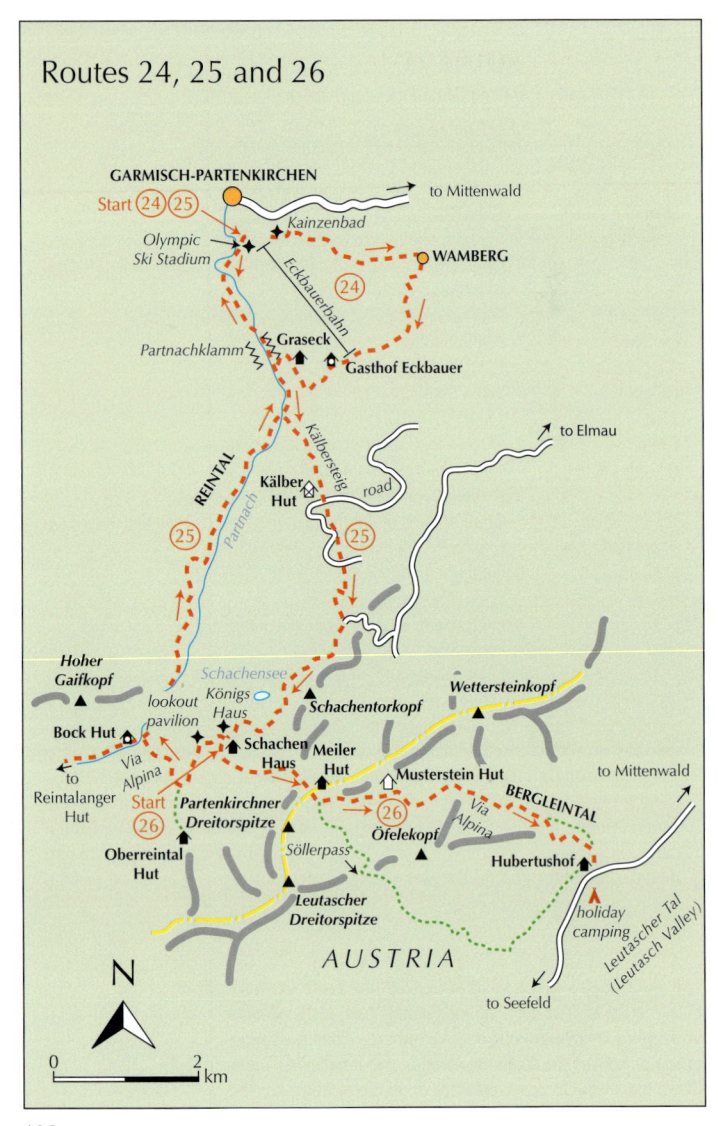

Routes 24, 25 and 26

Route 24 – Wamberg, Berggasthof Eckbauer and the Partnachklamm

most part the route is shaded as it winds its way steeply uphill through woods and meadows. **Wamberg** is an idyllic little village consisting of not much more than a church and a few houses. Accommodation is available here; it would make a nice out of the way place to stay.

From Wamberg follow the sign uphill in the direction of Eckbauer. The narrow farm road climbs very steeply in places but the going gets easier once it is left behind and you turn right (west) along a grassy ridge. A fairly level path now leads past the cable railway station to **Gasthof Eckbauer** (1238m). ▸

An alternative for those who want to avoid any climbing whatsoever is the Eckbauerbahn cable railway, which starts near the Olympic ski stadium.

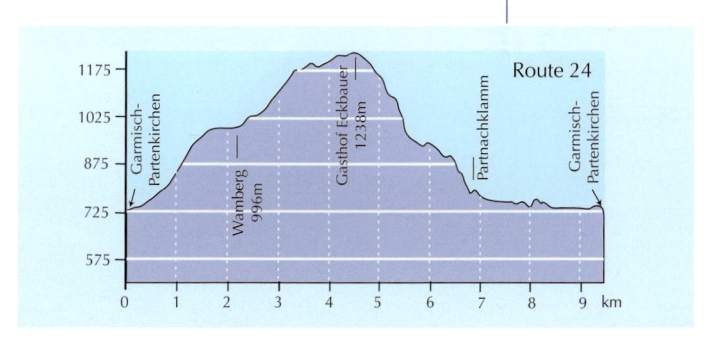

From the terrace of the *Gasthof* continue in a south-westerly direction downhill through the woods (signposted). Steps and well-maintained paths make the descent quite easy and it is not long before a gravel road is reached. Now turn right towards the Graseckbahn. Turn left here and follow the signs in the direction of the **Partnachklamm**. There are a number of places offering refreshments along this section of the route but you probably have the nicest outdoor setting at the alm restaurant that is passed prior to descending to the *Klamm*. The *Klamm* proper is entered through a tunnel that has been carved through the rock. More tunnels and a narrow but safe path guide visitors through this spectacular and at times claustrophobically narrow gorge. A modest entrance fee has to be paid at the other end.

After passing through the gorge follow the road past the ski stadium and back to the starting point. Instead of walking it is also possible to travel by horse and carriage as far as the ski stadium.

WALKING IN THE BAVARIAN ALPS

In the Partnachklamm

ROUTE 25
Schachen Haus and the Königs Haus

Start	Garmisch-Partenkirchen
Parking	Car park next to Olympic Ski Stadium and Eckbauerbahn
Transport	Local buses to Eckbauerbahn
Distance	20.8km/13 miles
Height gain	1136m (3727ft)
Height loss	1136m (3727ft)
Time	7½–8hrs (2-day walk, with an overnight stop at Schachen Haus)
Grade	2–3
Refreshments	Schachen Haus, Bock Hut
Accommodation	Schachen Haus
Maps	Kompass-Wanderkarte No 5: Wettersteingebirge – Zugspitzgebiet or No 6: Alpenwelt Karwendel

Though the very fit can do this walk in a day, it would be more enjoyable to give yourself more time and to spend the night at Schachen Haus. This allows you to visit the Königs Haus (see below) and to explore the Alpengarten at leisure, as well as more time to explore the vicinity of the hut. Those who want to continue to Leutasch (see Route 26) in Austria could instead spend the night at Meiler Hut, another 1½hrs away.

Apart from the dramatic scenery of the Partnachklamm at the start of the walk, and the panorama from the pavilion near Schachen Haus, a highlight of this tour is the so-called Königs Haus. It was built as a mountain refuge in Swiss-chalet style for King Ludwig II of Bavaria in 1870. Every year he spent close to two weeks here, as an escape from the duties of his court in Munich. Though the exterior of the building is comparatively plain, the interior reveals a room worthy of the extravagant tastes of the man who built the fairy-tale Neuschwanstein Castle near Füssen. The Turkish Hall occupies the entire upper floor and appears to have sprung directly from the pages of the Arabian Nights. In the middle of the room is an oriental fountain, while stained-glass windows bathe opulent fabrics and golden candelabras in a magical light. Anything more different from the wild mountain scenery outside is hard to imagine.

Just below the Königs Haus is the Botanischer Alpengarten (Botanical Alpine Garden). For over 100 years it has been under the care of the Botanical Garden in Munich. At an altitude of 1850m it is possible to cultivate native alpine flora, along with rarities from the distant Himalayas and other high mountain regions.

The Königs Haus is open 1 June–3 Oct. Daily guided tours at 11.00, 13.00, 14.00 and 15.00. Entrance fee. Website: www.schloesser.bayern.de. The Botanischer Alpengarten is open July–mid-Sept, 08.00–17.00. Entrance fee. Website: www.botmuc.de

Königs Haus on the Schachen

From the Olympic ski stadium follow the road south to the **Partnachklamm** (see also Route 24). After roughly 30mins the picturesque gorge is left behind, and the Ferchenbach stream is crossed over a footbridge near the point where it joins the Partnach. At a junction after the bridge, follow the signposted trail along the Kälbersteig to **Schachen Haus** (3½hrs). ◄

► The right-hand trail leads along the Partnach towards Reintalanger Hut and requires 5hrs (see Route 27).

ROUTE 25 – SCHACHEN HAUS AND THE KÖNIGS HAUS

Evening on the Schachen: the sheer cliffs of the Frauenalplspitz rise abruptly behind Schachen Haus

The Kälbersteig trail climbs immediately into the woods. It is steep going for much of the way, though trees provide merciful shelter from the sun. In 1hr a clearing is reached at the site of the former Kälber Hut (1234m). From here cross a gravel road, then continue on up wooded slopes, touching on the road a couple more times until, after one more steep stretch, the Schachenweg is reached. This road is now followed right, past the tiny Schachensee to the **Königs Haus** with **Schachen Haus** directly below it.

After resting at Schachen Haus climb a short distance from the hut to where the trail forks left for the climb to Meiler Hut. Now follow the right branch along a comfortable trail to a lookout pavilion. Enjoy the magnificent views over the Reintal (Rein Valley) and Zugspitze massif before beginning the very steep, zigzag descent to the Oberreintal (Upper Rein Valley) some 800m below.

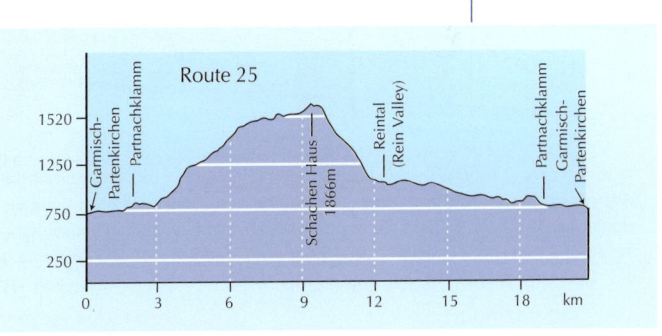

Walking in the Bavarian Alps

Those who wish could turn left and walk the short distance to the hut for refreshments.

At the end of this descent you will arrive at the junction with the track to **Oberreintal Hut**. Turn right here, then continue through the woods to where the trail meets up with the route from **Bock Hut**. ◀ Continue right along the Partnach. This trail leads past the Hinterklamm, a narrow gorge of the Partnach, after which the track widens to a gravel road. It is now about 1hr easy downhill walking back to the **Partnachklamm** and from there another 30mins to the starting point.

ROUTE 26
Schachen Haus/Meiler Hut to Leutasch

Start	Schachen Haus (Meiler Hut)
Parking	In Garmisch-Partenkirchen
Transport	Local bus
Distance	8km/5 miles
Height gain	506m (1660ft)
Height loss	1291m (4239ft)
Time	4hrs
Grade	2–3
Refreshments	Apart from huts at start, only Hubertushof in Leutasch
Accommodation	Schachen Haus, Meiler Hut, Hubertushof
Maps	Kompass-Wanderkarte No 5: Wettersteingebirge – Zugspitzgebiet or No 6: Alpenwelt Karwendel

With the ascent route to Schachen Haus (see Route 25) this crossing of the Wetterstein range to Austria forms a wonderful two-day walk amidst dramatic alpine scenery. Those who decide to press on to Meiler Hut, instead of overnighting at Schachen Haus, will have saved themselves around 1½hrs walking the next day. Certainly, Meiler Hut has a gloriously lonely location at the foot of the

ROUTE 26 – SCHACHEN HAUS/MEILER HUT TO LEUTASCH

Dreitorspitzen. The more westerly of these three peaks is the goal of experienced rock climbers, who follow the Hermann-von-Barth Weg from the hut.

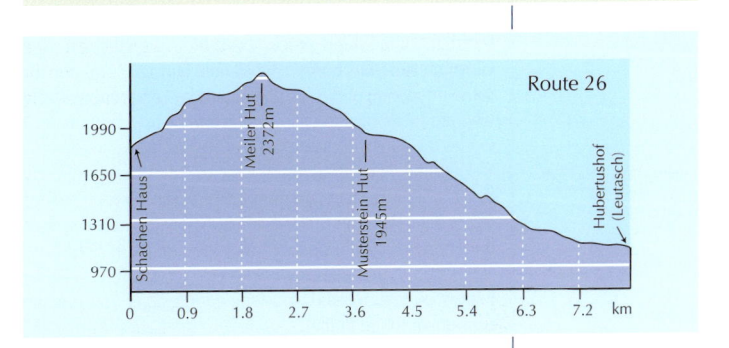

The route to Meiler Hut is clearly signposted from **Schachen Haus** (1866m). At first the trail climbs along a grassy ridge, then snakes its way more steeply uphill along a narrow, rocky path. To the left the mountain slope falls almost vertically to the basin below Schachen Haus. ▶ Once the grassy hollow of Frauenalpl is reached you will have left the more

The trail is relatively safe when it is dry, though extreme care should be taken in misty, wet or icy conditions.

Descent from Meiler Hut below the Törlspitzen

exposed section of track to the hut behind you. On the slopes around here it is often possible to glimpse chamois.

From Frauenalpl the hut is already visible on the narrow saddle between the Törlspitzen and Dreitorspitze. It takes about 40mins to reach the saddle after climbing steeply through scree and rock. Located directly on the German–Austrian border the **Meiler Hut** (2372m) affords some fine views of the surrounding mountain scenery. Those who are lucky might even a spot a rare bearded vulture as it circles the surrounding peaks in search of food.

For the descent to Leutasch the trail first zigzags directly downhill along steep, slippery scree slopes. It then swings left to descend at an easier gradient below the naked rock of the Törlspitzen. In around 15mins the turn-off to Söllerpass is reached. It branches right, and runs across the Leutascher Platt (a plateau formed by a long-gone glacier) to cross the pass down to the Puittal.

> The somewhat exposed route via the **Söllerpass** (2211m) and Söllerrinne, down to the Puittal and Leutasch, is very steep and requires a good head for heights – accidents have occurred here! The route is best avoided when the track is wet.

The trail via the Bergleintal to Leutasch continues past the turn-off and eventually reaches **Musterstein Hut** next to a boulder with a cross. Shortly after the Berglbach is crossed. The scenery here is dominated by the sheer rock walls of the Wettersteinwand on the left and the massive bulk of the **Öfelekopf** (2478m) to the right. Continue on the right of the stream, along steep slopes covered by low shrubs and dwarf pines offering little in the way of shade. If snow is still lying on parts of the sometimes very narrow track (possible even in late June) extra care is required. On the final section of this steep knee-jarring descent the trail runs down through woods towards Reindlau and **Hubertushof**. Here it is possible to arrange a taxi to Mittenwald.

ROUTE 27
The Zugspitze (2963m)

Start	Garmisch-Partenkirchen
Parking	Car park at Olympic Ski Stadium/Eckbauerbahn
Transport	Local buses to Eckbauerbahn
Distance	20.7km/13 miles
Height gain	2232m (7324ft)
Time	10½–11hrs (2-day walk, overnight stop at either Reintalanger or Knorr huts)
Grade	2–3
Refreshments	Bock Hut, Reintalanger Hut, Knorr Hut, Münchner Haus
Accommodation	Reintalanger Hut, Knorr Hut, Münchner Haus
Maps	Kompass-Wanderkarte No 5: Wettersteingebirge – Zugspitzgebiet or No 6: Alpenwelt Karwendel

In 1820 Lieutenant Josef Naus, his assistant Maier and a local guide became the first men to climb the Zugspitze. This route up Germany's highest mountain follows the one they probably took. It is the easiest of the three classic ascent routes and can be undertaken by anyone who possesses the necessary fitness. The other routes, via the Höllental and Wiener-Neustädter Hut in Austria, require climbing experience in high alpine regions.

The first section of this route is the same as that described in Route 25 as far as the junction that is reached on leaving the Partnachklamm. Instead of following the Kälbersteig up to Schachen Haus go right over the Partnach, which is now followed south into the Reintal along a forest road. After about 1hr walking the road climbs above the Mitterklamm (Middle Gorge) before finally petering out prior to reaching the narrow gorge of the Hinterklamm. Descend on what is now a

WALKING IN THE BAVARIAN ALPS

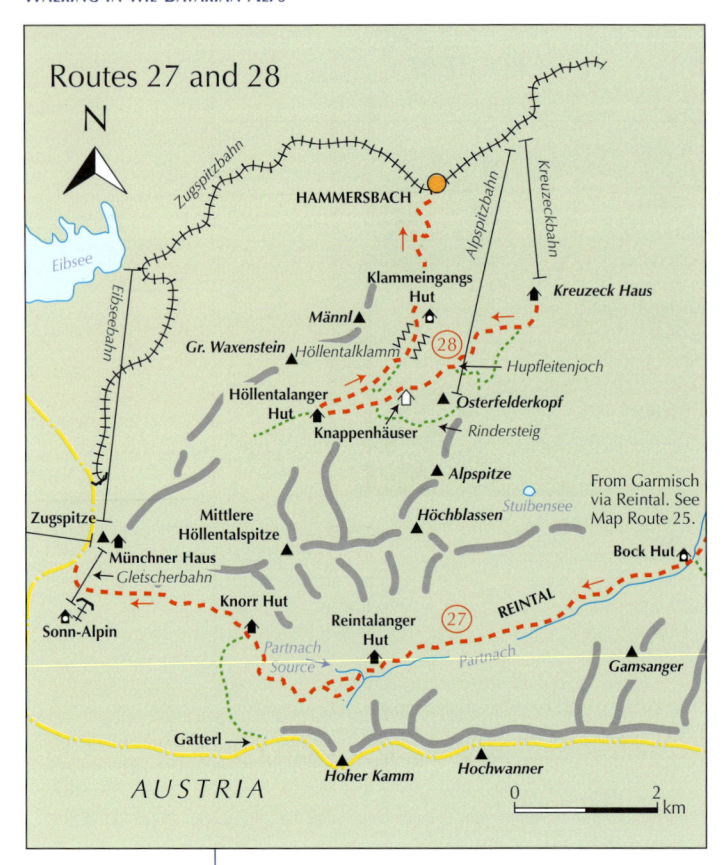

Routes 27 and 28

simple track above the gorge to a footbridge over the Partnach. A little further on the trail passes a turn-off on the left to Schachen Haus and Meiler Hut. From here **Bock Hut** is reached in a few minutes over a bridge that takes you once again across the Partnach (2¾hrs from the ski stadium).

After taking a break at the hut continue in what is now a westerly direction through the Reintal. The track climbs at a moderate gradient on now more lightly wooded slopes along the Partnach. Here the valley widens again, having

ROUTE 27 – THE ZUGSPITZE

View back down to Knorr Hut at the head of the Reintal

narrowed before reaching Bock Hut. In around 35mins the spot marked on the map as being the location of the Vordere Blaue Gumpe is reached. ▶ The scenery has already taken on a more alpine character on this section of track, an impression that is reinforced the deeper the trail penetrates into the valley.

Once you pass the Partnach waterfall the track climbs a short distance before reaching **Reintalanger Hut** (1½hrs from Bock Hut). Set above the broad, rocky river bed of the Partnach the hut enjoys a glorious location. Tibetan prayer

This small lake was destroyed by a flood in August 2005 and marked the point where the Partnach disappeared underground to re-emerge 1km further on by the Hintere Blaue Gumpe.

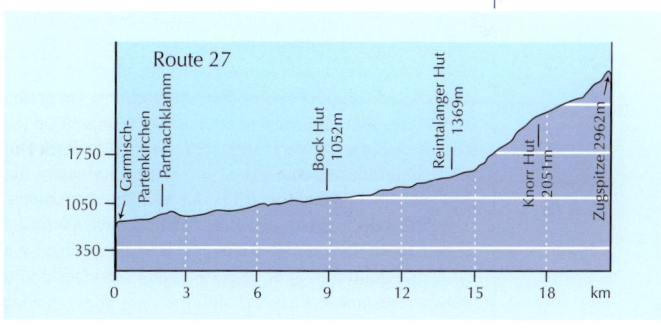

flags flutter over the river, and there are magnificent views towards such peaks as the Gatterlköpfe, Plattspitzen and Kleinwanner. If you are planning an overnight stop (recommended) this hut is a good choice, as you can save the steep climb up to Knorr Hut for when you are refreshed the next day. Don't be surprised by a musical wake-up call early in the morning – it's a hut tradition!

From the hut the trail crosses the Partnach on a footbridge. Here one has the choice of either continuing directly to Knorr Hut, or a slight detour could be made via the **Partnachursprung** (Source of the Partnach), where the river gushes forth from a rock cavity. Both tracks meet again at the wide, rock strewn meadows of the Obere Anger. Once the meadows are crossed the trail begins a steep, sweaty climb towards Knorr Hut. During pauses on the way up you can enjoy splendid views back towards the Reintal; clearly visible now is the trough-like form of the valley, which was carved out by a glacier. After passing the Veitelbrünnl (a spring) in the narrow little valley of the Brunntal there is one last steep climb to the hut.

Before reaching – and just below – Knorr Hut, a signposted trail branches left towards the Gatterl (2023m), a saddle between the Gatterlköpfe and Kleinwanner. From here it is possible to follow an interesting trail via Rotmoosalm and Wangalm to Leutasch (7hrs). For the most part it keeps to an altitude of 1900–2000m as it runs east along the Austrian side of the Wetterstein massif. From the saddle you can also descend to Ehrwald in about 3hrs.

Knorr Hut is situated on the lower edge of the Zugspitzplatt, a broad rock slope shaped by a glacier. The trail climbs at first quite steeply from the hut, then at a more moderate gradient with numerous minor ups and downs towards the Zugspitze. Poles and red dots mark the route, which runs along the edge of the Platt often crossing small snowfields along the way. After 1¼hrs walking from the hut the trail arrives at **Sonn-Alpin**, the upper terminus of the Zugspitzbahn rack railway. There is a restaurant here, and a little further away, a chapel. Rising behind Sonn-Alpin is the Zugspitze summit, crowned not only by a cross but also a variety of buildings. They include Münchner Haus and a meteorological station.

ROUTE 27 – THE ZUGSPITZE

The quickest way to the top from here is with the Gletscherbahn cable railway to the summit. Otherwise, climb up to the ridge from the Schneeferner (remnant of a glacier), passing the former hotel Schneefernerhaus (now an environmental research station) on the way. On the ridge follow the secured route past the junction with the ascent route from the Austrian side to **Münchner Haus** (2959m) on the west summit. The short crossing to the east summit and the cross is also secured with wire ropes (1½hrs from Sonn-Alpin). Assuming the weather is fine the view is absolutely fantastic.

For the return journey to Garmisch-Partenkirchen either take the cable railway down to the **Eibsee** and then catch the Eibsee Bus or take the Zugspitzbahn from Sonn-Alpin. ▶

On the last stretch of the trail before Sonn Alpin and the summit

Remember to check timetables in Garmisch beforehand!

ROUTE 28
Kreuzeck, Knappenhäuser and the Höllentalklamm

Start	Garmisch-Partenkirchen
Parking	At Kreuzeckbahn
Transport	Local buses to Kreuzeckbahn, or with Zugspitzbahn
Distance	9.5km/6 miles
Height gain	103m (338ft)
Height loss	986m (3235ft)
Time	4hrs
Grade	2–3
Refreshments	Kreuzeck Haus, Höllentalanger Hut, Klammeingangs Hut (Gorge Entrance Hut)
Accommodation	Kreuzeck Haus, Höllentalanger Hut
Maps	Kompass-Wanderkarte No 5:Wettersteingebirge – Zugspitzgebiet or No 6 Alpenwelt Karwendel

This route promises some grandiose alpine scenery in the region of the Alpspitze and should be saved for a day when you can be certain of fine weather. With its characteristic, pyramid-like form, the Alpspitze is one of the most photographed peaks in this part of the alps. Remember to take waterproof clothing for the spectacular Hell Valley Gorge (Höllentalklamm; entrance fee).

From the centre of Garmisch drive first in the direction of Griesen and then turn left at the signpost to the Kreuzeckbahn. This cable railway is very popular, so it pays to get an early start if you want to be among the first at the top. From the upper station (1651m) and **Kreuzeck Haus** the route to the **Hupfleitenjoch** (1754m) is clearly signposted. The modest 100m of the ascent are hardly noticed as they

ROUTE 28 – KREUZECK, KNAPPENHÄUSER AND THE HÖLLENTALKLAMM

are spread over a longish, gently rising path. Once you reach the top of the Joch it is easy to understand the cable railway's popularity: a spectacular view of the Höllental and the Zugspitze for a minimum of effort!

The **Knappenhäuser** (1526m) are reached along a narrow, winding track that leads down from the Hupfleitenjoch. ▶ Some of the more exposed sections of the route down to the huts are secured with wire ropes but present no real difficulties. Nevertheless, those without a head for heights are warned! The track continues its scenic

Höllentalanger Hut

These huts were once used by miners (*Knappe* = miner), who were working the iron and zinc deposits below the Kreuzeck.

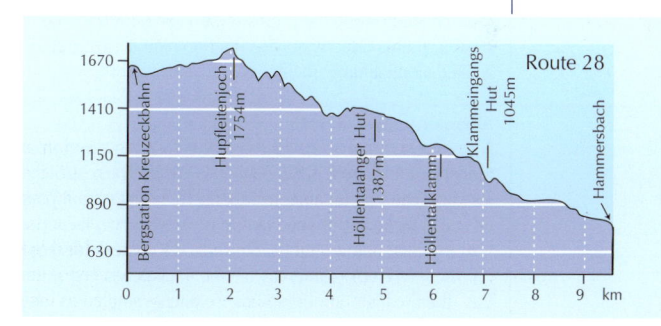

Route 28

descent to the Höllental behind the buildings and should be no problem if you mastered the first stretch down.

Once down in the valley **Höllentalanger Hut** (1387m) offers an opportunity for refreshments. With such magnificent mountain scenery as a backdrop it is indeed hard not to relax here awhile before continuing northeast through the **Höllentalklamm** (Hell Valley Gorge) towards Hammersbach. **Note** The routes going southwest from the hut (over the Zugspitze and Riffelscharte) are difficult and only suitable for those with sufficient mountaineering experience and the proper equipment.

The walk through the spectacular Höllentalklamm is one of the highlights of this tour. This wild, rocky gorge was made accessible to the general public around 1900 and has been one of the most popular attractions in the area ever since. The gorge is navigated through a series of sparsely illuminated tunnels and narrow paths hewn from the valley walls. All the while one is accompanied by the almost deafening roar of water as the stream tumbles and squeezes its way through its corset of rock. In some places huge piles of snow (remnants of spring avalanches) clog the gorge's upper reaches.

Not a few walkers are relieved when the **Klammeingangs Hut** (1045m) at the end of the gorge is reached. Perched at the edge of a precipice its tiny terrace is a great place to pause and toast the efforts of the day – those who want to use the toilets will find them located in a nearby rock face! From the hut follow the Hammersbach stream through woods to **Hammersbach**. Here it is possible to catch the Zugspitzbahn (rack railway) or a bus back to the starting point. Otherwise, the final few kilometres can be walked along a flat path through the fields (c.½hr).

Alternative route (4½hrs)
A less frequented route to the Höllental is to go via the Rindersteig (cattle path). Although it would also be possible to start from the top of the Kreuzeckbahn 1hr or so's walking can be saved by taking the nearby Osterfelderbahn to its upper station, just below the summit of the **Osterfelderkopf** (2030m). From the cable railway the track heads first south but then, after about 250m, branches right to the

ROUTE 28 – KREUZECK, KNAPPENHÄUSER AND THE HÖLLENTALKLAMM

In the Höllentalklamm

WALKING IN THE BAVARIAN ALPS

Rinderscharte (2000m). The Rindersteig now threads its way steeply downhill between the Höllentorkopf (2150m) and the **Alpspitze** (2628m). Magnificent views over the Höllental and towards the Zugspitze massif. The **Höllentalanger Hut** is reached in about 2hrs. For route to Hammersbach see above.

MITTENWALD

*Tourist office: Tourist-Information, Dammkarstrasse 3, D-82481 Mittenwald. Tel: (08823) 33981, fax: (08823) 2701; website: **www.mittenwald.de**, e-mail: touristinfo@markt-mittenwald.de*

Beautifully situated at the foot of the Karwendel massif Mittenwald is, like Garmisch, an important tourist resort, but is much smaller and has a 'cosier' feel to it. The old town centre has retained many of its picturesque qualities, especially in the vicinity of the parish church. Lining the Obermarkt are some particularly fine old buildings with frescoes dating from as far back as the 18th century. Just around the corner from the church is the Geigenbaumuseum (Violin-Making Museum). Mathias Klotz (1653–1743) was the first and most famous violin-maker the town ever produced, and the tradition he started continues to this day.

As far as accommodation is concerned Mittenwald should present no problems. There is a youth hostel in town and a campsite to the north on the road to Krün. The railway station is conveniently located close to the town centre.

VALLEY WALKS
Map: Kompass-Wanderkarte No 5.

iv GRUBSEE AND BARMSEE (2–3hrs) Among the more interesting of the many short valley walks in the vicinity of Mittenwald is that from Klais to the Grubsee and Barmsee. As swimming is possible in both these lakes this walk is an ideal way to take it easy on a hot summer afternoon. Starting point is the railway station at Klais, northwest of Mittenwald. From here go left along Bahnhofstrasse, cross the tracks, use the subway under the main road and follow the path to the Grubsee. At the north end of the lake follow the Barmsee-Rundgang (a circular walk) around the much larger Barmsee. This will bring you via Alpengasthof Barmsee (restaurant) back to the Grubsee and Klais.

v LEUTASCHKLAMM (1–2hrs) Opened in 2006 the Leutasch Gorge Walk is a major new attraction for visitors to Mittenwald. In an impressive feat of

ROUTE 28 – KREUZECK, KNAPPENHÄUSER AND THE HÖLLENTALKLAMM

Mittenwald hugs the foot of the Karwendel

construction work an 800m-section of walkway was created high above the gorge along vertical cliffs. The result is a unique and exciting trail that offers fabulous bird's-eye views over the roaring torrent below. Prior to construction the gorge was only accessible from Mittenwald on a short trail that ended at an impressive waterfall. Since completion the gorge is now also accessible from the Leutasch Valley in Austria.

The gorge can be explored along three trails: the Klammgeistweg (Mountain Spirit Trail), at 3km the longest; the Koboldpfad (Goblin Trail, 1.9km) and the original Waterfall Trail, for which there is an entrance fee. The first two trails offer information about the geology and natural history of the gorge at various stations along the way. Brochures with a map of the three trails are available from information kiosks at both the Austrian and Mittenwald ends of the gorge – to get to the Mittenwald end head to the Isarbrücke (bridge) at the southern end of town, from where it is a short walk to the entrance.

ROUTE 29
Soiern Haus, Schöttelkarspitze (2050m) and Seinskopf (1961m)

Start	Krün
Parking	Car park near tourist office
Transport	Bus 9608 from Mittenwald to Krün
Distance	18.5km/11.5 miles
Height gain	1177m (3861ft)
Height loss	1177m (3861ft)
Time	6½hrs
Grade	2
Refreshments	Fischbach Alm, Soiern Haus
Accommodation	Soiern Haus
Map	Kompass-Wanderkarte No 6: Alpenwelt Karwendel

The Soiern group lies to the north of the Karwendel chain in the midst of a large nature preserve. It was once the exclusive hunting domain of King Ludwig II, who used Soiern Haus as a hunting lodge.

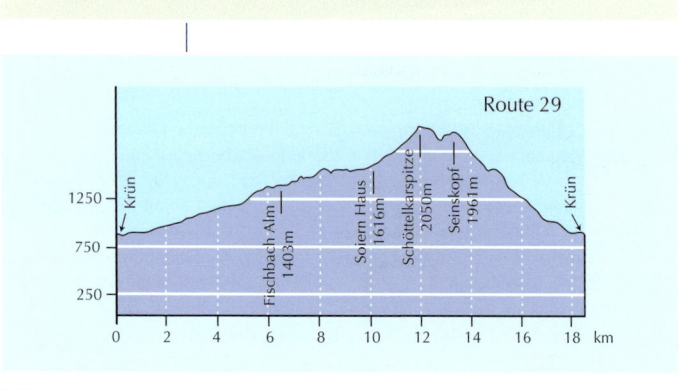

Route 29 – Soiern Haus, Schöttelkarspitze and Seinskopf

From the tourist office (*Verkehrsamt*, 874m) cross a canal and a little bit further down the road, on the left, is a large car park next to a timber yard. Continue in an easterly direction, cross the Isar bridge, and turn left along a gravel road (signposted 'Fischbachalm – Soiernhütte'). This road is followed as far as **Fischbach Alm** (1403m), and because it climbs rather steeply in places it can be a rather sweaty

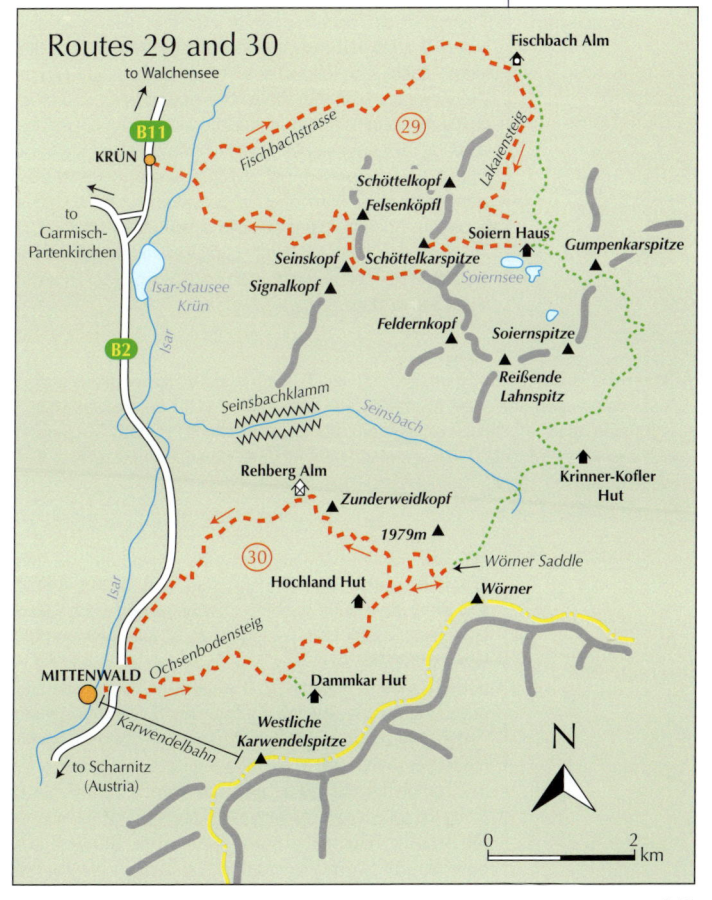

WALKING IN THE BAVARIAN ALPS

> Though the sign warns that the Lakaiensteig is only for *Trittsichere* (the sure-footed) it does not present any real difficulties. It is a very pretty trail and thoroughly recommended.

exercise on a hot day (1½–2hrs to alm). Such being the case the inviting alm hut is a good excuse to stop for a drink and a rest. The easiest route from here to Soiern Haus is to continue along the road (1½hrs). A much more interesting alternative is to follow the Lakaiensteig (Lackeys' Path). ◄

From the alm the track forks right, through a meadow, and then enters a patch of forest. After walking only a short while Soiern Haus with the pyramid-like peak of the Soiernspitze as a backdrop comes into view. Below the hut a waterfall adds that extra touch of picturesqueness to the scene – those who follow the route by road go right past it. The views are beautiful the whole way to the hut, and in spring the route is further enhanced by dark blue gentians covering the grassy slopes. Roughly halfway along the track there are a few very narrow stretches where it cuts its way along some cliffs. Wire ropes are provided, but some care is necessary. Apart from this one can devote one's attention to the landscape; the track hardly climbs at all, though it does get a little steeper (and narrower once again) prior to arriving at **Soiern Haus**.

Soiern Haus is beautifully situated above a basin framed by rocky peaks and looks down upon one of the two pretty little lakes known as the Soiernseen. This is a world apart, a peaceful refuge from the hustle and bustle of daily life, and one can well understand that a romantically inclined potentate like Ludwig II wanted it all to himself.

The route continues in the direction of the **Schöttelkarspitze** which is signposted from the hut. A little way along the steadily climbing track the second of the Soiern lakes reveals itself from behind the trees, and the views get better with every ascending step. At the top the panorama is not just good, it is fantastic! It extends to Mittenwald and beyond to Austria. The Walchensee and Sylvensteinsee are visible to the north and northeast respectively, and the Soiern basin now shows itself to full advantage.

For the descent it is necessary to return a short distance along the ascent route to where a signpost points the way to the nearby Feldernkreuz and Krün. The short stretch between the two peaks is rather exposed in places and

ROUTE 29 – SOIERN HAUS, SCHÖTTELKARSPITZE AND SEINSKOPF

The Soiernseen

requires some care – if there is still snow lying on the track it can be quite tricky going and a head for heights is not out of place! Once this moderately difficult section is overcome it is relatively plain sailing along a ridge to the Seinskopf. Great views en route towards Mittenwald and the Karwendel.

At the **Seinskopf** fork right and downhill – the summit cross visible further on from the fork belongs to the Signalkopf. On the way down the Schöttelkarspitze displays its precipitous western flanks but is eventually lost to view as the track curves away into the woods to arrive at a fork. The track to the right follows the Herzogsteig back to Fischbach Alm, but this route turns left to Krün via the Schwarzkopf. From now on the track is quite well shaded and not too steep.

Am Schwarzkopf (1100m) is a good viewpoint from where one can look down onto Mittenwald and the Barmsee. Turn left at the fork and the track soon comes to a forest road. Here it is possible to either turn right along the road or keep to the track and go left. This route turns left where yet another fork is reached. Those with excess energy could walk along the pretty Hüttlebachklamm (left) to **Krün** but it is shorter to turn right. This path brings one directly down to the Isar bridge and the starting point.

ROUTE 30
Dammkar Hut, Hochland Hut and Wörnersattel

Start	Mittenwald
Parking	Car park next to bypass (road to Innsbrück)
Transport	Local buses
Distance	16km/10 miles
Height gain	1052m (3451ft)
Height loss	1052m (3451ft)
Time	6hrs
Grade	2–3
Refreshments	Dammkar Hut, Hochland Hut
Accommodation	Dammkar Hut, Hochland Hut
Maps	Kompass-Wanderkarte No 5: Wettersteingebirge – Zugspitzgebiet or No 6: Alpenwelt Karwendel

This route takes you into the high alpine scenery directly on Mittenwald's doorstep. Apart from the towering peaks of the Karwendel, which rise immediately above the trail to Hochland Hut, there are impressive views of the Wetterstein mountains south of Garmisch-Partenkirchen and the Soiern massif to the north. If this distant

ROUTE 30 – DAMMKAR HUT, HOCHLAND HUT AND WÖRNERSATTEL

> view of the Soiern peaks is not enough it is possible to reach them from the Wörnersattel (see the note at the end of the route description).

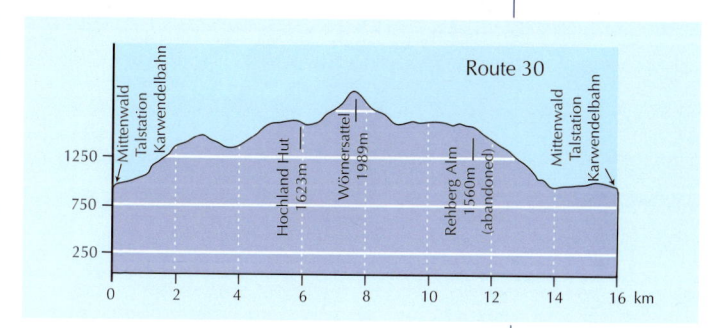

To get to the start of the track by car or on foot it is easiest to start from **Mittenwald** railway station and to follow the signs to the Karwendelbahn (cable railway). If you are walking go through the Karwendelbahn car park and turn left along Alpenkorpsstrasse. The route to Dammkar, Hochland and Mittenwälder Huts is signposted. After passing Gebirgsjägerstrasse cross under a road bridge (B2 Garmisch – Innsbrück), then a few metres further on turn right, along what is at first a paved path, in the direction of Mittenwälder Hut and Ochsenboden – this is the start of the walk proper.

If you have a car drive past the Karwendelbahn along Alpenkorpsstrasse, and after crossing under the road bridge continue a little further on to a parking area on the left side of the road.

Continue walking in the direction of Mittenwälder Hut until you come to a small footbridge. Do not cross the bridge but turn left and follow the Ochsenbodensteig (as this section of the track is named) towards Dammkar Hut. The trail zigzags its way up through forest and allows some great views over Mittenwald and surroundings along the way. Benches are provided at convenient intervals if you need a rest.

After about 1hr climbing the track levels out before it swings southeast and drops down to the impressive

En route to Dammkar Hut (screefield below the Kreuzwand)

ROUTE 30 – DAMMKAR HUT, HOCHLAND HUT AND WÖRNERSATTEL

Dammkar, a glacially eroded rock basin or cirque. From the bend where the track starts descending there is a wonderful view towards the Dammkar and Dammkar Hut. After crossing a large screefield at the base of the Kreuzwand the trail arrives at a fork. Those who wish could follow the right fork up to **Dammkar Hut** (1650m; 25mins), otherwise descend a short way downhill and then head in a northeasterly direction – the route is clearly signposted – towards Hochland Hut. It is very easy walking at first along scree slopes covered by dwarf pines, but after a while the track starts climbing again through open forest. Once the Hochland Hut becomes visible the track levels out again and allows some magnificent views of the Tiefkarspitze and Predigtstuhl. Walking at a steady pace the stretch of track between Dammkar and **Hochland Hut** requires about 1hr.

> Situated at the edge of the Wörner massif, Hochland Hut (1623m) can provide its guests with clear views of the Wetterstein, Tannheim, Ammergau and Ester mountains. The hut itself is small and cosy looking, with a personal touch being added by the flower boxes decorating the window ledges.

The route to the **Wörnersattel** is signposted from Hochland Hut. A short distance further on the trail forks. Those who want to avoid the climb to the saddle can turn left to Rehberg-Alm, otherwise the trail bears right towards the saddle and Ferein Alm. Though it has been fairly easy going so far, the track soon gets much steeper as it approaches and climbs up to the saddle (1989m). There are great views at the top towards Mittenwald and the Soiern massif. In fact this splendid panorama is only 'marred' by the great bulks of the Wörner (2476m) and Westliche Karwendelspitze (2385m). Directly below the Soiernspitze, to the northeast, it is possible to make out a small lake with the huts at Ferein Alm (Krinner-Kofler Hut) just to the right of it.

From the saddle turn return to where the trail forked just after Hochland Hut and follow the path towards **Rehberg Alm**. It runs along the steep slopes below the Wörnerkopf (1979m) and Zunderweidkopf (1810m) to reach a large grassy clearing – the meadows of what used to be Rehberg

On the Wörner Saddle looking towards the Soiern massif

Alm. If it is time for an afternoon tea break then there could be no better spot.

Following the signs to **Mittenwald** leave the alm meadows and enter the woods. As you get closer to Mittenwald you will see and hear the traffic on the *Bundesstrasse*. Eventually the track arrives at a gravel road above a military barracks. Turn left along the road and then at the sign 'Mittenwald, Krün, Kasernen' turn right, off the road, and go downhill along a track. After crossing a wooden footbridge come to another gravel road. Turn left, cross a bridge, and follow the signs back to the Karwendelbahn. This last stretch of the walk is very easy going and runs parallel to the *Bundesstrasse*.

Three-day tour

An interesting possibility for those who want to turn this route into a three-day tour would be to continue on from Hochland Hut to the Wörner Saddle and then on to Ferein Alm (6hrs from Mittenwald). Spend the night at Krinner-Kofler Hut and then walk around the east flank of the Soiernspitze to Soiern Haus (second night). On the final day either cross the Schöttelkarspitze and Seinsköpfe directly to

Krün or take the forestry road via Fischbach Alm (see Route 29). Note that some care needs to be taken on the Wörner Saddle in those places still covered by snow. As the route down to Ferein Alm is not clearly waymarked it is a good idea to try and make out the general direction from the top of the saddle.

ROUTE 31
Kranzberg (1391m), Grünkopf (1588m) and Ederkanzel (1181m)

Start	Mittenwald
Parking	Car park next to chairlift (Kranzbergbahn)
Transport	Local buses
Distance	12.3km/7.5 miles
Height gain	707m (2319ft)
Height loss	948m (3110ft)
Time	3½hrs
Grade	2
Refreshments	St Anton Haus, Kranzberg Haus, Gasthaus Ferchensee, Hotel Lautersee, Lautersee Alm, Berggasthaus Ederkanzel
Accommodation	Kranzberg Haus, Gasthaus Ferchensee, Hotel Lautersee
Maps	Kompass-Wanderkarte No 5: Wettersteingebirge – Zugspitzgebiet or No 6: Alpenwelt Karwendel

This relatively easy walk is particularly attractive in autumn, but the two lakes en route (bathing permitted) also make it a pleasant excursion on a hot summer's day. At the Lautersee there are rowboats for hire.

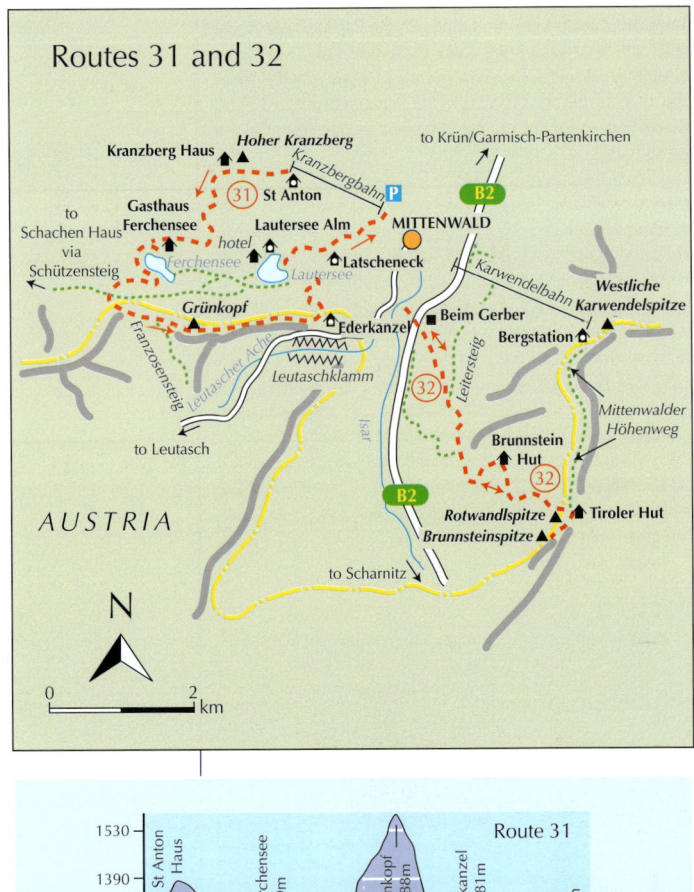

WALKING IN THE BAVARIAN ALPS

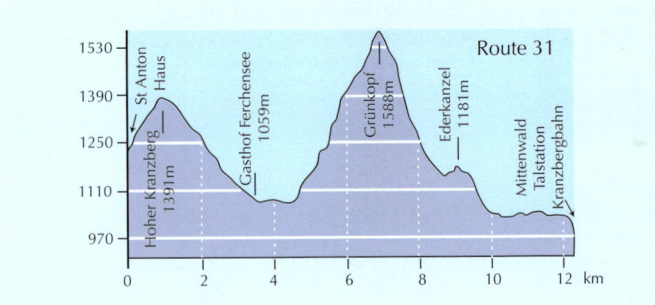

Routes 31 and 32

Route 31

ROUTE 31 – KRANZBERG, GRÜNKOPF AND EDERKANZEL

Take the chairlift up the slopes of the Hoher Kranzberg (1391m) as far as **St Anton Haus** (1140m). Though there are already great views from the restaurant terrace (5mins from top of chairlift) most people will continue uphill to the Kranzberg summit and Kranzberg Haus – another ¾hr (at the most).

From the summit walk briefly through meadows, then start descending through the woods. The route is well marked and eventually the track arrives at a gravel road. Follow a signposted track to the left off the road. This brings you to another gravel road down in the valley. It is now no more than a couple of minutes to **Gasthaus Ferchensee**, which is nicely situated directly on the lake shore. One of the first things that you will notice here are the large fat carp that swim in the lake's clear waters. Near the restaurant is a fish food dispenser, and if you are travelling with children make sure you have some small change handy – they will have great fun feeding the fish as well as the odd passing duck! The Ferchensee is perhaps the prettier of the two lakes, with mountains and forest providing a very picturesque setting.

View over Mittenwald from the Kranzberg

Continue around the lake's southern shore (closest to the Grünkopf) until you come to a large grassy area where there is a wooden hut – bathing is permitted here. A little further on look out for a track (not signposted) through the meadow which branches right and up to a ridge. It leads into the woods and a sign which points the way to the Grünkopf.

> After a swim near the hut those who wish to make a really lazy day of it could just walk directly to the Lautersee and from there to **Latscheneck**. This shortened version of the walk (2½hrs) is very easy and quite suitable for families with small children.

The track climbs steeply uphill to another fork. The right fork leads to the Obere Wettersteinspitze (only for the experienced) but we turn left and then a bit further on right, all the time following the signs 'Franzosensteig – Grünkopf'. At the next fork the right branch goes down to Leutasch in Austria along the Franzosensteig. Our route continues straight ahead, along the Austrian border to the **Grünkopf**. The summit is marked by a cross dedicated to the 'goat breeders and herders of Mittenwald' and there are a couple of benches where you can sit and admire the view.

From the summit walk downhill (sometimes steeply) through the woods to the **Ederkanzel** (1181m). There are good views from the *Gasthaus* into the Leutasch Valley in Austria. Return the same way a short distance and then turn right at the sign to Mittenwald. Continue downhill and follow the signs to the Lautersee, which is reached in about 20mins along a nature trail. Before reaching the bathing area and restaurant turn right, away from the lake, and cross a wooden footbridge over some swampy land.

Continue along a level path until you reach a signposted fork. Those who do not have to return to the car park can take the right-hand path to Mittenwald via Mittereck. Otherwise turn left in the direction of Latscheneck – Laintal. At yet another fork turn left along the Höhenweg which brings you to the lower terminus (*Talstation*) of the Kranzberg chairlift. For much of this section of the route you are walking through attractive pine forest. Shortly before Café Latscheneck there is a fine view over **Mittenwald** with the Karwendel as an imposing backdrop. It is not far from here to the chairlift and car park.

ROUTE 32
The Brunnsteinspitze (2179m)

Start	Mittenwald
Parking	Car park P3 near footpath to Karwendelbahn
Transport	Local buses
Distance	7.5km/4.5 miles (one way)
Height gain	1265m (4150ft)
Height loss	1265m (4150ft)
Time	6hrs
Grade	2–3
Refreshments	Brunnstein Hut, Tiroler Hut (even in summer, not always open)
Accommodation	Brunnstein Hut
Map	Kompass-Wanderkarte No 5: Wettersteingebirge – Zugspitzgebiet

True, it's a steep climb, but this route enables even the average mountain walker to get a whiff of high alpine air. Even those who only go as far as Brunnstein Hut will be amply rewarded for their efforts: from the hut's terrace there is a fantastic view across to the Arnspitzen and beyond them to the Wetterstein range. Of course, at the top the views are even more dramatic. Here the panorama encompasses the entire Wetterstein massif, the peaks and valleys of the Karwendel and the snow-capped mountain chains of the Austrian Alps.

From the railway station in **Mittenwald** first follow the signposted route towards the Karwendelbahn (cable railway). Go right into Dammkar-Strasse, cross the tracks, turn into Mühlen-Weg and then left into Weiden-Weg. This street brings you over the River Isar and to some steps that lead up to the Karwendelbahn – car park near here. At the steps

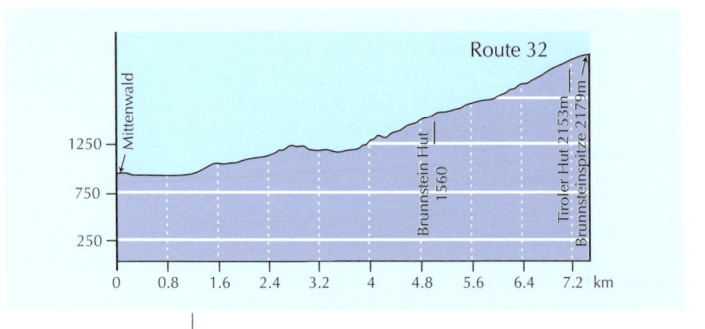

Route 32

Elevation profile: Mittenwald — Brunnstein Hut 1560 — Tiroler Hut 2153m — Brunnsteinspitze 2179m; distance 0 to 7.2 km

continue right until you come to a street bearing the name Im Schwarzenfeld. Follow this street over the railway tracks again and into Lindlahner-Strasse. At the end of the street turn left, then sharp left again. The route to the hut is now signposted.

From '**Beim Gerber**' (a small cluster of buildings, with Gasthaus Karwendelschanze as an identifying feature) the track starts climbing and eventually joins up with the Leitersteig trail from Mittenwald. Now the ascent gets

Brunnstein Hut, with the Große Ahrnspitze on the left

steeper but the pretty mixed forest through which the trail winds its way up to **Brunnstein Hut** (1560m) is some consolation for the extra perspiration. After resting at the hut continue even more steeply uphill to the Brunnsteinanger (2100m; 1½hrs), an alpine meadow. From here it is not far to **Tiroler Hut** and the summits of the **Rotwandlspitze** (2190m) and **Brunnsteinspitze** (2179m). Magnificent views!

> Near 'Beim Gerber' another path runs south, through the flat meadows of the Hoffeld. It runs parallel to the road and railway tracks then, after about 1km, swings left (signposted) and climbs to eventually meet up with the track that climbed directly from the Gerber. The meadows of the Hoffeld are dotted with numerous old, weathered wooden hay sheds, which are typical of the area.

Return the same way until you get to the point where the Leitersteig turns right and away from the ascent route. Those who are sure-footed enough can follow this interesting trail back to **Mittenwald**. Otherwise keep left and retrace your steps to the starting point.

Mittenwalder Höhenweg (14km via Brunnstein Hut)

The Tiroler Hut is at the southern end of the Mittenwalder Höhenweg, a magnificent Via Ferrata for those with the necessary experience in high alpine regions. Fixed cables, ladders and bridges aid walkers across eight peaks above the 2000m mark. From Tiroler Hut it follows the ridge to the upper station of the Karwendelbahn below the **Westliche Karwendelspitze** (2385m), at the northern end of the trail. Including the ascent from Mittenwald it would take up to 9hrs to reach the cable car station – starting at the other end, with the descent via **Brunnstein Hut**, up to 8hrs are required.

Absolute freedom from dizziness and sure-footedness are prerequisites for this route. It is also wise to carry the proper equipment such as a harness and so forth. Those who would like to tackle the *Steig*, but are uncertain of their ability, should enlist the help of a professional mountain guide (*Bergführer*). The tourist information in Mittenwald can supply addresses.

Walking in the Bavarian Alps

WALCHENSEE

*Tourist office: Tourist Info Walchensee, Ringstrasse 1, D-82432 Walchensee.
Tel: (08858) 411, fax: (08858) 275; website: **www.walchensee.de**,
e-mail: info@walchensee*

For centuries the forested shores of the Walchensee were frequented only by a few fishermen from neighbouring monasteries. A road built in 1492 eventually made the lake more accessible – though in the days of horse and cart a gradient of 21 percent did not make it one of the more popular routes to the south. Today the villages of Einsiedl, Walchensee and Urfeld provide starting points for numerous walks in the area and activities on the lake itself. At the lake's southern end a very scenic toll road leads to Jachenau, in the Jachenau Valley. Worth visiting on a rainy day is the Walchensee Kraftwerk (hydroelectric power station), at the southern end of the Kochelsee. It is fed by water from the Walchensee, which lies 200m above it.

Accommodation is available in all three of the above-mentioned villages (youth hostel in Urfeld), and there is a beautifully situated campsite at Lobesau, just south of Walchensee. Walchensee can be reached by bus from Mittenwald or Kochel.

ROUTE 33
Herzogstand (1731m) and Heimgarten (1790m)

Start	Walchensee
Parking	Next to cable railway (parking fee)
Transport	Bus 9608 between Garmisch-Partenkirchen, Mittenwald and Kochel
Distance	9km/5.5 miles
Height gain	163m (535ft)
Height loss	981m (3218ft)
Time	4–6hrs
Grade	2–3
Refreshments	Herzogstandhäuser, Heimgarten Hut
Accommodation	Herzogstandhäuser

ROUTE 33 – HERZOGSTAND AND HEIMGARTEN

Maps	Kompass-Wanderkarte No 5: Wettersteingebirge – Zugspitzgebiet or No 6: Alpenwelt Karwendel or No 7: Murnau – Kochel

Both peaks on this beautiful walk offer fabulous views, but it was the Herzogstand that held the greatest attraction for Bavaria's royalty. The mountain owes its name to Herzog (Duke) Wilhelm IV of Bavaria (16th century) who used to go hunting in the area. In the 19th century it was also a popular refuge for King Max II and his son King Ludwig II. Ludwig's hunting lodge, the so-called Königshaus, was destroyed by fire in 1990.

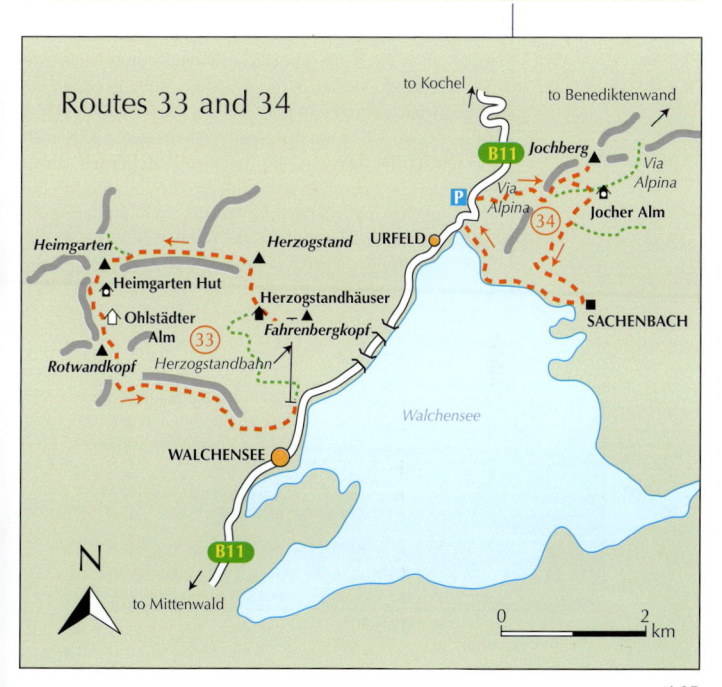

The quickest route to the top of the Herzogstand is, of course, the cable railway, but those who would prefer to save their money for other pursuits can walk up the steep path that begins at the northern end of town. As it is shaded by trees (mixed forest and not boring pine monoculture) for the entire ascent and allows some fine views back over the lake, it it is an altogether pleasant, if somewhat longer, alternative (2½hrs).

The cable railway whisks the great majority of hikers to the top of the Fahrenbergkopf (1627m) from where they walk to **Herzogstandhauser** (Berggasthof Herzogstand), and from there to the pavilion on the summit of the **Herzogstand**. The views from here are tremendous and almost make you forget that you are sharing them, in summer at least, with dozens of other alpine enthusiasts.

The ridge walk over to the Heimgarten starts at the pavilion and also promises wonderful, unobstructed alpine views. ◄ Though it is made reasonably secure with wire ropes along the more exposed sections it still requires care and a head for heights. In roughly 1½hrs it brings you to the **Heimgarten** summit and hut. This is a nice place to relax a while before following the clearly waymarked, shady path via **Ohlstädter Alm** (1423m) back to **Walchensee** (2hrs).

Not far from the car park at the bottom of the Herzogstandbahn is a pleasant lakeside café. Bordering the café a section of lakeshore has been set aside for swimming and sunbathing – a great opportunity to cool off after the walk!

> There is virtually no shade along here, so don't forget a hat.

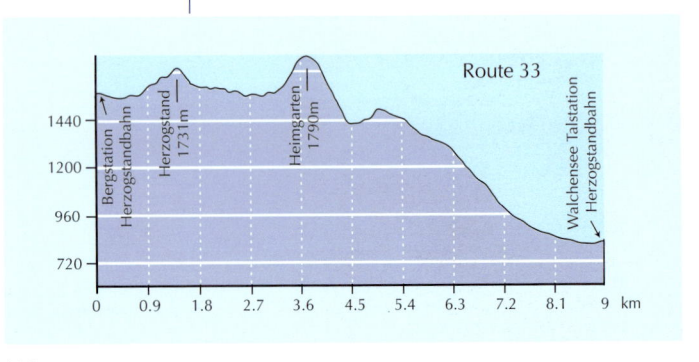

ROUTE 33 – HERZOGSTAND AND HEIMGARTEN

Ridge trail to the Heimgarten

ROUTE 34
The Jochberg (1567m)

Start	Urfeld, north of Walchensee
Parking	Car park on B11, north of village
Transport	Bus 9608 from Walchensee
Distance	9.1km/5.5 miles
Height gain	703m (2306ft)
Height loss	703m (2306ft)
Time	4½hrs
Grade	1
Refreshments	Jocher Alm
Maps	Kompass-Wanderkarte No 6: Alpenwelt Karwendel or No 7: Murnau – Kochel

The panorama from the Jochberg summit is hardly less impressive than that from the far more popular Herzogstand (Route 33). An extra attraction of this walk is that it can be finished off with a swim or row on the lake.

The ascent of the Jochberg begins from the parking area (858m) on the Kesselberg Pass road, just north of **Urfeld** at the northern end of the Walchensee. Note that as parking spaces tend to be rare in the walking season it is a good idea to get an early start.

The path starts climbing immediately from the road, and though trees provide some welcome shade in summer those who have managed an early morning start will certainly have the better of it. About halfway up there is a clearing which allows unobstructed views over the Kochelsee and therefore serves as a good excuse for a brief rest. Further on the track divides: the left fork brings you along a ridge to the **Jochberg** summit, whereas the right fork goes direct to **Jocher Alm**. On the ridge walk a bit of extra care should be taken – especially with small children – as the path runs very close to the mountain's precipitous north face. Just below

ROUTE 34 – THE JOCHBERG

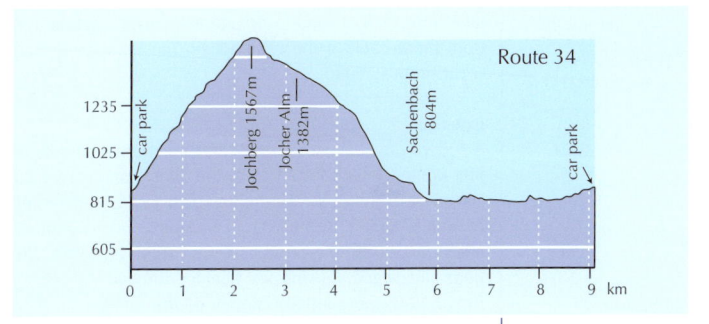

the summit cross the grassy south-facing slope is the perfect spot for a long, leisurely picnic lunch. Directly below is the shimmering expanse of the Walchensee, while further south the Wetterstein and Karwendel groups hold one's gaze. In the far distance, if it is not too hazy, you can make out the snow-capped Stubai Alps.

For the descent follow the path to Jocher Alm (1382m) and then path 482 down to **Sachenbach** (804m), on the northeast shore of the Walchensee. Continue along the

The magnificently situated Walchensee serves as a starting point for the ascent of the Jochberg and Herzogstand

lakeshore road (closed to private vehicles) to **Urfeld** and from there back to the car park on the Kesselberg road (2½hrs from summit).

Extension

A superb possibilty for a long-distance route would be to link Route 34 with Route 35 to the Benediktenwand near Lenggries. From Jocher Alm follow path 451 (also the route of the Via Alpina) northeast past Kot Alm. A short distance after the alm the trail swings right towards the Benediktenwand. It leads past Kochler Alm and Staffel Alm, runs below the southern slopes of the Glaswand, then climbs to the Glaswandscharte from where it goes right to a fork. Take the trail left to Tutzinger Hut (*accommodation*; 5hrs from Walchensee). From the hut either continue below the Benediktenwand towards the Achselköpfe and descend to Lenggries via Hintere Längental Alm or continue to the Brauneck (3–4hrs).

The meadows of Kessel Alm (Route 43)

PART IV
THE TEGERNSEE AND SCHLIERSEE MOUNTAINS

Tegernsee & Schliersee Mountains Area Map

Part IV – The Tegernsee and Schliersee Mountains

PART IV
THE TEGERNSEE AND SCHLIERSEE MOUNTAINS

Magnificent views over the Tegernseegebirge from the track below the Lempersberg (Route 44)

The Tegernseer Berge are those mountains between Tegernsee and the rivers Rottach and Weißer Valepp in the east, the River Isar in the west and the Sylvensteinsee, Achenbach, Ampelsbach, Sattelbach and Bayrachbach in the south. The Schlierseer Berge are situated between the River Leitzach in the east, Tegernsee in the west, the rivers Rottach and Weißer Valepp in the southwest and Elendgraben in the south. We have exhibited a certain amount of generosity as far as these boundaries are concerned and have also included the Benediktenwandgebirge (Brauneck, Benediktenwand, Rabenkopf) to the west of Lenggries and those mountains to the east as far as the River Inn.

Among the more important peaks in this region are the Benediktenwand (1801m), Wallberg (1722m), Rotwand (1885m) and the Wendelstein (1838m). Of these it is the Wendelstein that is most popular. It can be 'climbed' by cable railway from Bayrischzell or rack railway from Brannenburg. The views at the top are justly famous. Most popular of the many lakes in the area is the Tegernsee (which is also the largest) but the Schliersee, Sylvensteinsee and Spitzingsee are all very attractive in their own ways.

PART IV – THE TEGERNSEE AND SCHLIERSEE MOUNTAINS

LENGGRIES
Tourist office: Gästeinformation Lenggries, Rathausplatz 2, D-83661 Lenggries.
*Tel: (08042) 50 180, fax: (08042) 50 1810; website: **www.lenggries.de**,*
e-mail: info@lenggries.de

Halfway between Bad Tölz and the Sylvensteinsee the winter and summer resort of Lenggries makes a good base for walks in the lovely Isar Valley. To the west it is the Brauneck and the Benediktenwand that draw most walkers, while the peaks to the east are lesser known but also less visited, making them ideal destinations for those who prefer to steer clear of crowds. Lenggries has a railway station, a youth hostel and there is a campsite (Isar Campingplatz) further south near Winkel.

VALLEY WALKS
Map: Kompass-Wanderkarte No 8.

vi **MÜHLBACH – LAßELN – HOLZ – MÜHLBACH (1½hrs)** This easy walk takes you through a very pretty section of the Isar Valley. Those with a car can park in the farming village of Mühlbach, which is just south of Lenggries (see also Route 36). From the village follow the road south (path 624/625), past the hamlet of Laßeln, until you come to a fork in the woods. Turn right here and then right again at the Almbach stream. Follow the stream a short while, then where the road forks left to Fleck turn right in the direction of Holz. From here it is not far (path 5) to Mühlbach.

Wallberg chapel (Route 38)

WALKING IN THE BAVARIAN ALPS

ROUTE 35
*Brauneck (1555m), Achselköpfe (1707m)
and Benediktenwand (1801m)*

Start	Lenggries
Parking	Car park next to cable railway
Transport	Local buses
Distance	15.5km/9.5 miles
Height gain	301m (987ft)
Height loss	1105m (3625ft)
Time	6½hrs
Grade	2–3
Refreshments	Brauneck Hut, Hintere Längental Alm, Reiser Alm
Accommodation	Brauneck Hut, Freisinger Hut
Maps	Kompass-Wanderkarte No 6: Alpenwelt Karwendel or No 7: Murnau – Kochel

The trail to the Achselköpfe and Benediktenwand summit is a magnificent high-level route that promises fine views all the way. Though it is quite easy walking as far as the Latschenkopf it gets somewhat more difficult when the path crosses the narrow ridge of the Achselköpfe. It is possible to turn off onto an easier trail before this, however, and so the route is suitable for anybody who is reasonably fit.

From the upper station of the Brauneck cable railway follow the signposted path up to **Brauneck Hut** (5mins) and to the **Brauneck** summit. The panorama is spectacular! Those who want to linger and enjoy the view over a coffee can do so from the hut terrace, just a short way down from the summit. Otherwise continue along a broad gravel path along a ridge. Ignore the fork to Tölzer Hut, which follows the gravel path to the left, and continue straight ahead along a narrow track. This soon brings you to a sign pointing the way to the Latschenkopf, a confirmation that you are heading in the

ROUTE 35 – BRAUNECK, ACHSELKÖPFE AND BENEDIKTENWAND

right direction – the route is also signposted as 'Großer Höhenwanderung' (High Level Walk – long route).

So far the ridge walk has been quite easy, without any significant ups and downs, but a bit further on from the point where the track passes the tops of the ski lifts that climb up from Tölzer Hut the trail starts climbing. ▶ From the vicinity of the **Latschenkopf** the trail descends steeply through a corridor of dwarf pines to arrive at the fork to Probst Alm and the Benediktenwand. Here a choice has to be made: those with a head for heights continue straight ahead over the Achselköpfe, the rest turn right and follow the easier route down to Probst Alm.

Along the way there are a number of memorials to walkers who have been killed by lightning – a grim reminder of the dangers of walking along exposed mountain ridges in stormy weather.

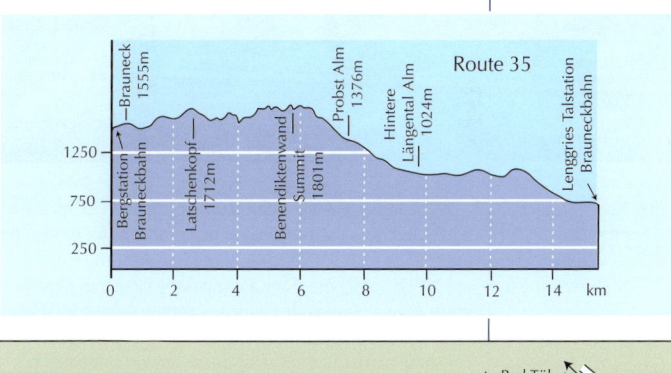

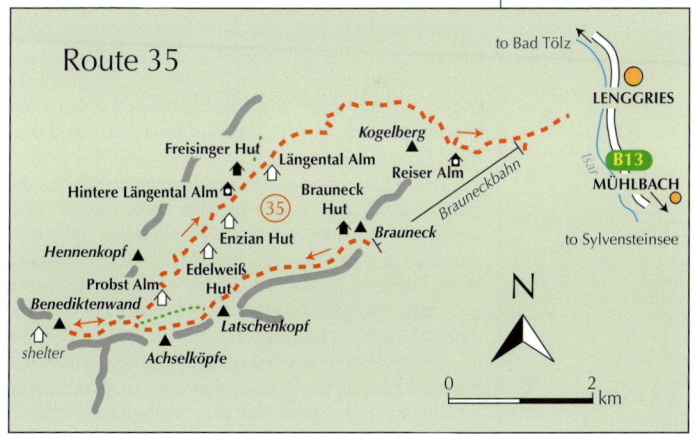

Ibex have established themselves in the vicinity of the Benediktenwand

The route over the **Achselköpfe** is somewhat exposed in places but does not present any real problems for those with experience in the mountains. There is a good chance of seeing ibex around here. They are relatively tame and photographers have a reasonable chance of getting some good close-up shots. The fork to Probst Alm is located in a dip or saddle. For some reason it is not signposted directly at the fork but a little further on. The trail downhill is easy to find, however, and is marked on the map as path 466. Those who wish could first climb up the steep slope to the west and visit the **Benediktenwand** summit (1801m). This detour would take about 1hr one way.

Probst Alm hut is already visible from the saddle, and the trail which zigzags down to it is not too hard on the knees. Turn left at the hut in the direction (signposted) of Längental and Lenggries. At a point below the hut it is necessary to cross a stream at the point where it drops over a cliff – depending on the weather and time of the year this short stretch could be very slippery, so take care! The trail now weaves through a very pretty stretch of open woodland. It is worth pausing along this section of the route for a backward glance as the sheer cliffs of the Probstenwand form a very impressive backdrop. After passing a blockhouse belonging to the Touristenbund Edelweiß the path widens into a dirt road, leaves the woods and enters the meadows of **Längental Alm** (*refreshments available in summer at the pretty Hintere Längental Alm hut*). The nearby Freisinger Hut is not serviced.

A short distance further down the road turn right, near a house standing alone in the fields, and follow path 469 towards Lenggries. You first cross a boggy area (wooden planks help you across the muddiest patches) where there are lots of wild orchids in spring. For much of the rest of the way the trail goes through forest but shortly after passing the turn-off to **Reiser Alm** (*closed Mon*) it passes through pastureland to arrive at the car park next to the Brauneckbahn.

ROUTE 36
The Seekarkreuz (1601m)

Start	Lenggries
Parking	Car park near Hohenburger Forellen (trout hatchery)
Transport	Local buses
Distance	12.2km/7.5 miles
Height gain	884m (2900ft)
Height loss	884m (2900ft)
Time	4hrs
Grade	1
Refreshments	Lenggrieser Hut
Accommodation	Lenggrieser Hut
Map	Kompass-Wanderkarte No 8: Tegernsee – Schliersee – Wendelstein

This walk on the east side of the Isar Valley offers, when compared to walks around the Brauneck and Benediktenwand, relative peace and quiet. This in itself would be adequate compensation for the lack of any chairlifts, but the modest

Walking in the Bavarian Alps

summit of the Seekarkreuz can also impress with a magnificent panorama. In spring the descent along the Grasleite track is especially pretty; when myriad liverworts add a splash of blue colour to the tawny-brown slopes.

By driving to the car park near the trout hatchery you save ½hr walking. Starting point for those who would rather walk is the tourist information office (*Verkehrsamt*) – those who start from the railway station can get to the *Verkehrsamt* along Bahnhofstrasse. Follow Karwendelstrasse to the southern end of town, turn left into Hohenburgstrasse and continue to the trout hatchery.

If you are driving turn right at the Hohenburger Forellen trout hatchery, drive over a small bridge and park on the left-hand side of the road next to the bridge. Walk back to the hatchery and follow the sign 'Hirschbachtal – Lenggrieser Hütte – Seekar' along what is at first a paved road. It runs through a pretty landscape of meadows backed by forest-cloaked hills with nothing but the tinkling of cowbells to disturb the rural tranquillity of the scene. Soon after passing a small farmhouse bearing the name **Geisreuth** what is now a gravel road enters the woods. Keeping close to the banks of a pretty mountain stream you come to a fork near a concrete bridge. Our route is signposted here as path 612 and turns right.

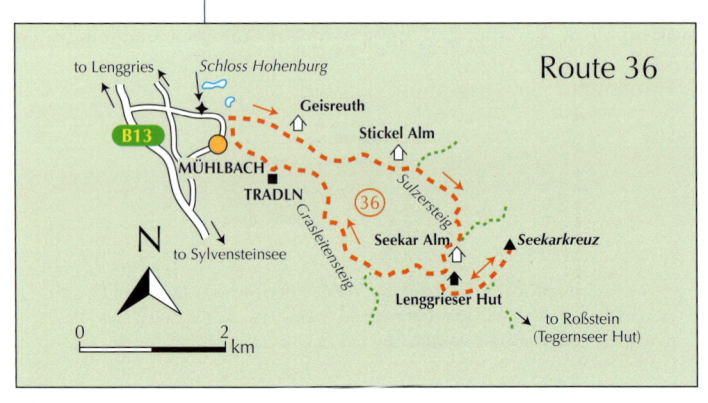

ROUTE 36 – THE SEEKARKREUZ

Seekar Alm, near Lenggrieser Hut

This section is known as the Sulzersteig and is described as being *Feucht* or wet – by no means an exaggeration in spring. The track climbs uphill alongside a stream, crossing a couple of wooden footbridges on the way. After about 1hr climbing through attractive deciduous forest it arrives in an area of meadows, which tells you that you are in the vicinity of **Seekar Alm** (1334m). Keep to the path here as the pastures are subject to erosion. From the alm huts it is only a short walk to **Lenggrieser Hut** (1338m) (*self-service refreshments*). The grassy summit of the **Seekarkreuz** is reached in about 45mins from the hut along a clearly waymarked trail. Excellent views!

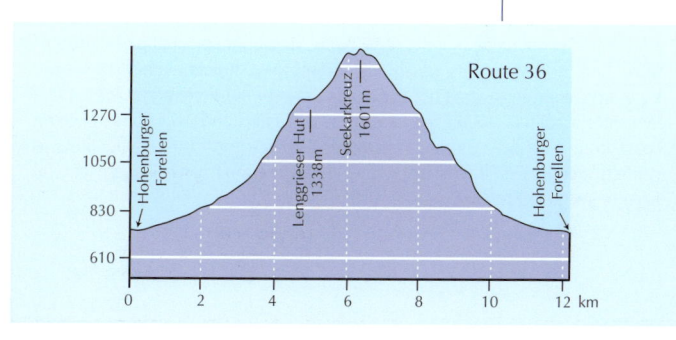

Return to Lenggrieser Hut and then turn left (west) along path 621. This route descends along the forested slopes of the Grasleitenkopf on a track known as the Grasleitensteig. Just after it leaves the woods and enters meadows you are suddenly confronted by a splendid view over the Isar Valley. In the distance is the Benediktenwand, whereas the foreground is dominated by the River Isar, winding its way past scattered copses of trees and rural villages in what appears, in the soft light of the late afternoon, to be an almost enchanted landscape. Accompanied once again by the tinkling of cowbells you soon reach the tiny hamlet of **Tradln**. Here the asphalted road starts and brings you through the small farming village of **Mühlbach** back to the car park.

Extension

Starting from Lenggrieser Hut, an interesting possibility for a hut-to-hut tour would be to follow path 621 southeast via Mariaeck and Roßsteinalm to Tegernseer Hut (2hrs; see Route 41). A slightly longer alternative goes over the Seekarkreuz, then descends to Rauhalm and Schwarzenentenalm before climbing up to Tegernseer Hut via Buchstein Hut.

TEGERNSEE

*Tourist office: Kurverwaltung Tegernsee, Haus des Gastes, Hauptstrasse 2, D-83684 Tegernsee. Tel: (08022) 180 140, fax: (08022) 3758; website: **www.tegernsee.de**, e-mail: info@tegernsee.de*

Like many towns fringing the Alps, Tegernsee enjoys the status of *Kurort* (health resort or spa) and has a wide range of recreational facilities with which to pamper its guests. But what really attracts visitors here is its location on the eastern shore of the beautiful lake of the same name, its well-manicured parks and gardens, and (for some) its plush restaurants and hotels with lake views. Accommodation in town is not particularly cheap, but there are at least a few campsites scattered around the lake (at Sankt Quirin and near Rottach-Egern). Apart from a railway station, Tegernsee also has good bus connections to Munich, Schliersee, Bayrischzell and to destinations in the Tegernseer Tal (Kreuth, Wildbad Kreuth).

ROUTE 37
Above Tegernsee

Start	Tegernsee railway station
Parking	Car park at railway station
Transport	Local buses
Distance	11km/7 miles
Height gain	692m (2270ft)
Height loss	723m (2372ft)
Time	4½hrs
Grade	1
Refreshments	Berggasthaus Riederstein (Galaun)
Accommodation	Berggasthaus Riederstein (Galaun)
Map	Kompass-Wanderkarte No 8: Tegernsee – Schliersee – Wendelstein

Wonderful views over Tegernsee, a lake cruise and a meal in a rustic Bavarian pub are the salient features of this route. If the weather is right you can also go for a swim in the lake before catching the boat back to the starting point.

From the railway station follow Bahnhofstrasse to Steinmetzplatz and then go left along Lärchenwaldstrasse and Kleinbergstrasse. The latter goes steeply uphill alongside a stream and offers some nice views back down to the lake. At the top of Kleinbergstrasse turn left and follow path T3 (signposted). Turn right onto the Auerweg, then a short distance later (after a sharp bend) turn right again along a track leading uphill and into the woods – this turn-off is not signposted, so keep your eyes peeled. Eventually the track comes to a sign pointing the way to the Riederstein (path T4). It now climbs more steeply for a while but then levels out, dips, and arrives at a gravel road. Follow this road for a short distance, then turn into the woods along a track marked with red dots. It is easy walking along here and it is not long before you arrive at **Berggasthaus Riederstein**

WALKING IN THE BAVARIAN ALPS

(marked on some maps as Galaun Haus, 1070m), which lies directly below the rock pinnacle of the Riederstein itself.

The tiny chapel perched dramatically on top of the Riederstein can be reached via the steeply climbing steps of a pilgrimage trail (Kreuzweg; turn left after the *Gasthaus*). The view from the chapel over Tegernsee and the mountains to the south is quite impressive. However, those who continue further east (path N3) will find the view from the top of the **Baumgartenschneid** (1449m; 1hr) even more breathtaking!

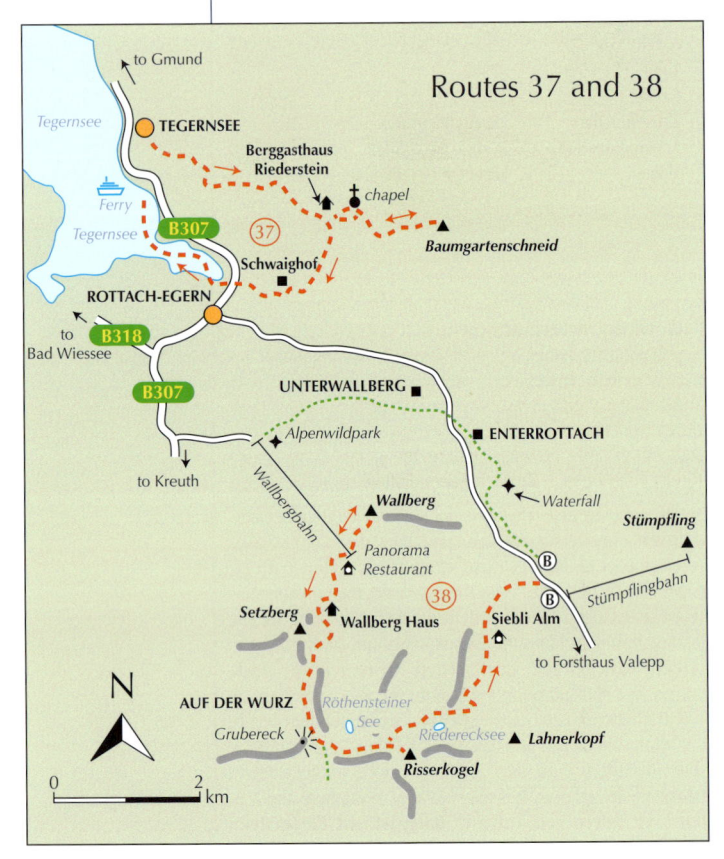

ROUTE 37 – ABOVE TEGERNSEE

In spring its grassy summit is dotted with dark blue gentians and other wildflowers. This is a good place for a picnic if you have resisted the temptation to eat earlier on.

Return the same way as far as the Berggasthaus. From here follow a gravel road downhill in the direction of Tegernsee and Rottach (path RS). Somewhat over halfway down the Höhenweg to Tegernsee branches right, but our route continues down to where the gravel road meets Riedersteinstrasse in **Rottach-Egern**. Follow this street down

A relaxing cruise across Tegernsee to Bräustüberl pier provides a comfortable end to this varied route

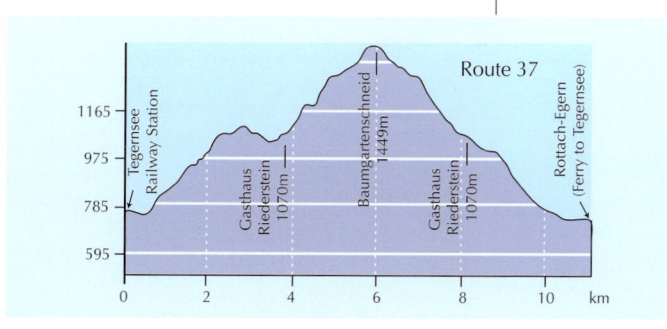

to the lake. Cross the main road, go past a car park and follow a path left along the lake shore. This takes you around the Kur-Kongress-Saal and past a bathing area (Strandbad) near where the passenger launch docks. The boat will bring you to the Schloss/Bräustüberl pier in Tegernsee from where it is less than 1km back to the railway station.

The ferry to Tegernsee runs roughly every 30mins 11.00–19.00 in summer (timetables at the tourist office) and docks at the Schloss/Bräustüberl pier. A smaller version of the famous Hofbräuhaus in Munich, the Bräustüberl is a noisy, cheerful place serving food and frothing mugs of beer or potent schnapps. It is open 09.00–23.00.

ROUTE 38
Wallberg (1722m) and Risserkogel (1826m)

Start	Rottach-Egern
Parking	Car park next to the Wallbergbahn
Transport	Buses 9550 and 9556 from Tegernsee to Wallberg; bus 9560 from bus stop on toll road back to Rottach-Egern/Tegernsee Bahnhof
Distance	9.3km/5.5 miles
Height gain	326m (1069ft)
Height loss	867m (2844ft)
Time	6½hrs (4½hrs if bus is used)
Grade	2
Refreshments	Wallberg Panorama Restaurant, Wallberg Haus, Siebli Alm (summer)
Accommodation	Wallberg Haus
Map	Kompass-Wanderkarte No 8: Tegernsee – Schliersee – Wendelstein

ROUTE 38 – WALLBERG AND RISSERKOGEL

The Wallberg summit is popular with both hang-gliding pilots and hikers, all of whom take advantage of the easy access provided by the Wallbergbahn from Rottach-Egern. It can get quite busy on a fine summer's day but the splendid panorama makes the ascent worth it. Once the summit is left behind the trail becomes quieter and promises still more fine views on its way to the Risserkogel. After descending to the valley those who are tired can catch a bus back to the starting point – remember to check timetables beforehand.

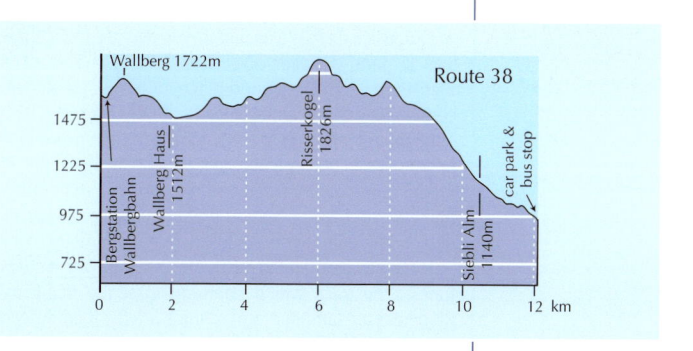

Take the cable railway up to the Wallberg Panorama Restaurant – the walk up from the valley requires about 2hrs. The summit of the **Wallberg** (1722m) can be reached from the restaurant in 20mins. To the north there is a wonderful view over Tegernsee, and to the south it is possible to make out the peaks of the Ötztal and Zillertal Alps in Austria.

After visiting the summit return to the restaurant. From here a wide path descends in a southerly direction past a picturesque chapel to **Wallberg Haus** (1512m; 15mins). Those who want an easy day can turn right before reaching Wallberg Haus and follow the clearly marked path back to the bottom of the cable railway.

As the trail up to the summit of the Setzberg (1712m) does not promise any better views than those from the Wallberg it is just as well to take the level path around its eastern flanks and then to continue along a ridge to the Grubereck (1671m). This route goes through a forested area marked on the map as **Auf der Wurz**.

In the early 19th century the original forest was cleared in order to supply the saltworks in Rosenheim with wood. As was so often the case the earlier mixed forest was replaced with a spruce monoculture. These conifers grow more quickly than broadleaf trees and promised quick returns for the timber industry. Unfortunately, such 'plantation' forests are also more vulnerable to insect pests and diseases and reforestation efforts in recent years have introduced a healthier, more natural mixture of spruce, fir and various broadleaf species.

At Grubereck there is a beautiful view over the Rothensteiner See (a tarn) towards the bare rock pinnacle of the Blankenstein. This is a good place for a brief pause before continuing east along the ridge to the **Risserkogel** (1826m; 1hr). Though the path to the summit is a little exposed and rather steep in places it does not present any real difficulties for the sure-footed. From the summit return a short distance the way you have come and then turn right onto a steeply descending path that leads to the foot of the Blankenstein.

The onward route to Siebli Alm is signposted at the bottom of the track which continues past the tree-fringed Riedereckseee (another tarn), climbs briefly, then descends past Riedereck Alm to **Siebli Alm** (*refreshments in summer*). From the alm buildings turn left along a paved road that leads to an intersection near Siebli Hunting Lodge. Turn right here and follow the road down through forest to a bus stop on the toll road to Enterrottach. Hikers now have the choice of either marching onwards via **Enterrottach** to **Rottach-Egern** or, if the limbs are complaining, catching the bus.

The trail to the Risserkogel

ROUTE 39 – WILDBAD KREUTH TO THE SCHILDENSTEIN

Those who decide to (or have to) walk can make a worthwhile detour to the pretty Rottachfall (waterfall), just over halfway to Enterrottach. From the village follow path E1 to the left (not to the right via Unterwallberg) and walk along the foot of the **Wallberg**, past a wildlife park (Alpenwildpark), back to the Wallbergbahn cable railway.

ROUTE 39
Wildbad Kreuth to the Schildenstein (1613m)

Start	Wildbad Kreuth, south of Tegernsee
Parking	At Siebenhütten bus stop on B307 (German Alpine Road)
Transport	Bus 9550 from Tegernsee and Kreuth to Haltestelle Siebenhütten
Distance	13km/8 miles
Height gain	813m (2667ft)
Height loss	813m (2667ft)
Time	5hrs
Grade	2
Refreshments	Königs Alm
Map	Kompass-Wanderkarte No 8: Tegernsee – Schliersee – Wendelstein

Those who wish could make this interesting but relatively easy walk a bit more challenging by using the route via the Wolfsschlucht, which is also mentioned as an alternative for climbing the Blauberge (Route 40). After climbing the Schildenstein use the ascent route described below for the descent. About the same amount of time is required for this variation.

There is a car park shaded by trees, next to the bridge over the Weißach, on the opposite side of the road from the bus stop. The bus stop is located around 1km west of the former spa resort of Wildbad Kreuth on the B307.

WALKING IN THE BAVARIAN ALPS

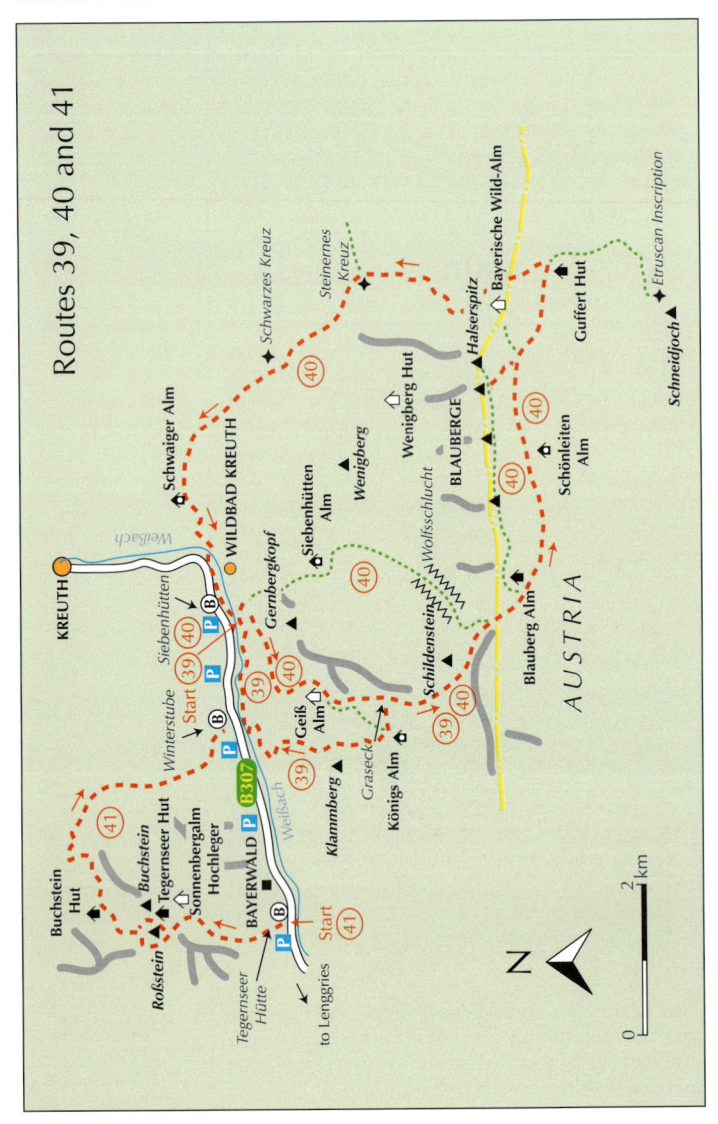

ROUTE 39 – WILDBAD KREUTH TO THE SCHILDENSTEIN

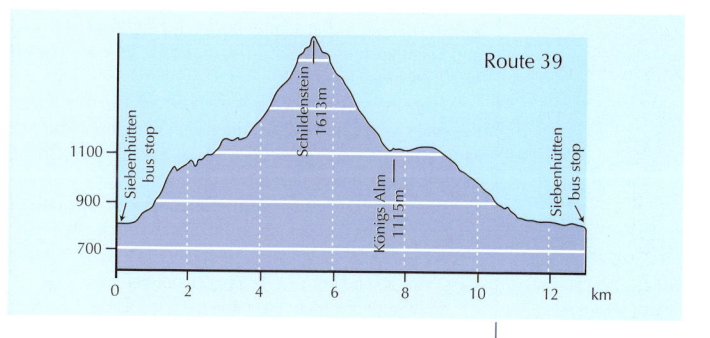

Cross the bridge over the River Weißach and, after walking a short distance in the direction of Siebenhütten Alm, turn right towards Geiß Alm. For the most part the path climbs steeply through forest before it levels off at the point where it swings south to **Geiß Alm** (1100m; *drinking water only*). There are good views from here over the Weißach Valley towards the twin peaks of the Roßstein and Buchstein (see Route 41).

Above the alm the path divides: the right fork goes down to Königs Alm (20mins) but this route follows the left fork uphill, along the edge of the woods, to **Graseck** (1179m). Still shaded by trees continue up one last steep

A splendid panorama over the Alps unfolds from the Schildenstein summit

191

stretch of track to the saddle between Platteneck (1618m) and **Schildenstein** (1613m). The meadows here are a good spot for a break.

From the saddle go a few steps downhill and then follow the steep path up to the Schildenstein's summit (15mins). Most will agree that the panorama at the top is worth the modest effort involved. To the north the summits of the Roßstein, Wallberg and (northwest) Brauneck (all goals of routes in this section) are clearly visible. To the south are the jagged peaks of Austria's Karwendel mountains. Similar views can be had from the Platteneck (further west).

For the return route the same track is followed as far as **Graseck**. Turn left here to **Königs Alm** (1115m), then follow the track going due north, on the left side of the Klammbach gorge. ◄ Down in the valley turn right and walk along the right bank of the River Weißach back to the starting point.

> In winter part of this route along the gorge (near where the road starts) is used as a toboggan run (Naturrodelbahn on map).

ROUTE 40
The Blauberge (Blue Mountains)

Start	Wildbad Kreuth
Parking	Car park at Siebenhütten bus stop (Haltestelle)
Transport	Bus 9550 from Tegernsee and Kreuth to Haltestelle Siebenhütten
Distance	22km/13.5 miles
Height gain	760m (2493ft)
Height loss	760m (2493ft)
Time	8–9hrs (2 days, overnight at Guffert Hut)
Grade	2–3
Refreshments	Blauberg Alm, Schönleiten Alm, Guffert Hut, Schwaiger Alm, (Siebenhütten Alm)
Accommodation	Blauberg Alm, Guffert Hut
Map	Kompass-Wanderkarte No 8: Tegernsee – Schliersee – Wendelstein

ROUTE 40 – THE BLAUBERGE (BLUE MOUNTAINS)

The Blauberge massif's steep, rocky northern flanks are in direct contrast to the gentle alm pastureland that characterises its southern slopes. The first route described below takes advantage of the massif's gentler side whereas its variant takes the walker directly along the sometimes exposed ridge to its highest point, the Halserspitz. Both the 'easy' and 'hard' variations of this route are quite long, but it is possible to spend the night at Guffert Hut (formerly Ludwig-Aschenbrenner Hut) if you wish to break it up.

Follow Route 39 as far as the saddle between the **Schildenstein** and Platteneck. From here continue southeast, past the track down into the Wolfsschlucht, to a fork in the trail on the German–Austrian border. The left fork leads in the direction of the Halserspitz (highly recommended for those with the necessary head for heights, see alternative route) but this route takes the right fork further southeast to **Blauberg Alm** (1540m). Those with an appetite should make a point of trying some of the tasty cheeses that are made here – it is also possible to climb up to the ridge from the alm, so there is no need to pass on a snack if you choose the ridge walk. Without any significant ups or downs the path further east continues below the Blauberge ridge to **Schönleiten Alm** (1478m). Though the views from the alm are nice enough those who want more can continue east for about 1200m to where a path climbs up to the Karspitz (1800m; 25mins), on the Blauberge ridge. Return the same way.

A short distance further on from where the side track up to the Karspitz begins the main track divides. This route

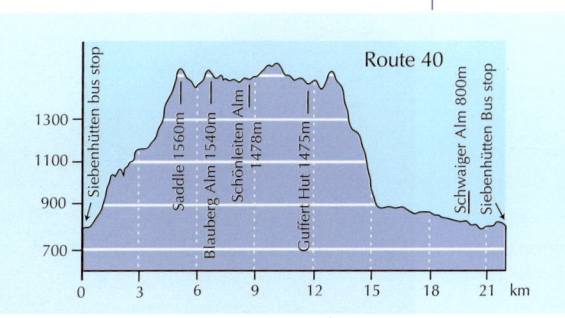

Carved into rock near Guffert Hut is a 2000-plus-year-old Etruscan-Raetian inscription, located south of the hut (1hr) at the site of a spring below the Schneidjoch.

follows the right fork to the beautifully situated **Guffert Hut** (1475m). The left fork brings you directly to the **Bayerische Wild-Alm** on the other side of the border. ◄

From Guffert Hut the gently undulating track heads north over the border, passes Bayerische Wild-Alm, and continues around the northeast flank of the **Halserspitz**. The trail now descends to the area of the Bayrbach Alm and from here (in some places steeply) to the small **Steinernes Kreuz** (Stone Cross; 882m) in the Langenau Valley. Now it is easy walking along a forestry road (a popular stretch for mountain-bikers) in a northwesterly direction to **Schwaiger Alm** (800m) and to a road junction. Turn left in the direction of **Wildbad Kreuth**, then a short distance further on go right over a bridge. Now continue left along the B307 road back to the starting point (30mins).

Alternative route

Grade 3: From the **Siebenhütten** bus stop cross the River Weißach and continue south to **Siebenhütten Alm** (837m). Now follow the path via **Königs Hut** in the direction of the **Wolfsschlucht** (Wolf's Gorge). Red waymarks guide you along the gravel river bed of the Felsweißach to where the valley ends in a nearly vertical wall of rock. A narrow, and in some places rather exposed, track snakes its way up the rock face to the saddle between **Schildenstein** and the Blauberg ridge.

The walk east along the ridge of the Blauberge massif offers spectacular views but it requires both sure-footedness

The trail to Halserspitz on the Blauberge ridge

ROUTE 41 – THE ROSSTEIN

and a head for heights. Peaks along the way are the Blaubergschneid (1786m), Blaubergkopf (1786m), Karspitz (1800m) and the **Halserspitz** (1861m). From the summit of the Halserspitz return to the Karspitz and follow a track downhill (southeast) which links up with the trail coming from **Schönleiten Alm**. The rest of the route is identical to that described above.

> **Note** Those inexperienced in the mountains are warned against attempting the route (not shown on the sketch map) down from the Halserspitz to Wenigberg Hut. It involves one difficult passage which can be extremely dangerous if the track is wet or there is still snow lying. Fatalities have occurred along here.

ROUTE 41
The Roßstein (1697m)

Start	Bus stop Tegernseer Hütte, west of Bayerwald on B307 (between Lenggries and Kreuth)
Parking	Car park at bus stop Tegernseer Hütte
Transport	Bus No 9550 from Tegernsee and Kreuth to Haltestelle Tegernseer Hütte
Distance	11km/7 miles
Height gain	828m (2716ft)
Height loss	868m (2848ft)
Time	5hrs
Grade	2
Refreshments	Tegernseer Hut, Buchstein Hut
Accommodation	Tegernseer Hut, Buchstein Hut
Map	Kompass-Wanderkarte No 8: Tegernsee – Schliersee – Wendelstein

Walking in the Bavarian Alps

That fish once swam around the Roßstein and its neighbour the Buchstein is a fact which is perhaps only obvious to the geologist: the two limestone peaks were once part of a coral reef that was formed over 200 million years ago. Those with a trained eye might even be able to find fossilised coral and other marine organisms preserved in the rock. Of more immediate interest to the thirsty wanderer is the magnificently situated Tegernseer Hut with its tiny *Biergarten*. Perched above the abyss like an eagle's nest it is as much a goal as the peaks themselves.

The clearly marked track winds its way steeply uphill through the woods, first passing Sonnbergalm-Niederleger (1144m) before arriving at the huts of **Sonnbergalm-Hochleger** (1500m). From here it continues through meadows; ahead the bare rock peaks of the Roßstein and Buchstein become ever more apparent, contrasting as they do with the green surroundings. En route a short detour to the left (unmarked) can be made to the grassy summit of the Sonnberg (1572m). It offers some good views and relative peace and quiet – Tegernseer Hut further on up the track is a popular destination and is often crowded on weekends.

Back on the main track, near the rock pinnacle known as the Roßsteinnadel, experienced hikers can follow the direct route to Tegernseer Hut along the Bayerwaldsteig. This easy scramble is aided by wire ropes, though a head for heights is necessary.

For those who decide that discretion is the better part of valour then the so-called Altweibersteig (Old Woman's Track) remains as an alternative. Do not be put off by the

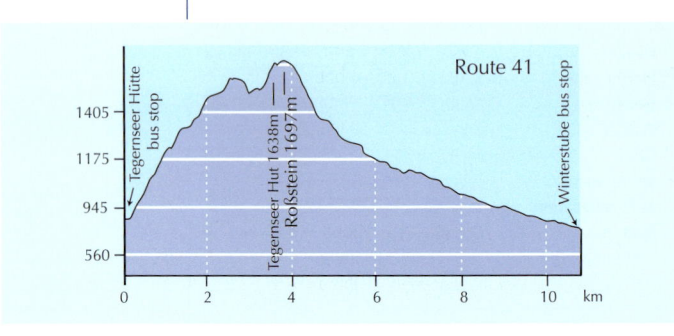

ROUTE 41 – THE ROßSTEIN

Bayerwaldsteig to Tegernseer Hut

name! This track, which continues on from the Nadel, is a very pleasant walk and brings you in about 20mins to the near vicinity of Roßstein Alm. Instead of going down to the alm, however, this route turns right to enter the large basin just northwest of the **Roßstein** and **Buchstein**. The track passes through an area of dwarf pines and scree, passes the track coming up from **Buchstein Hut** and climbs up to **Tegernseer Hut** (1638m), on the saddle between the two peaks. The easy climb from the hut to the Roßstein's summit takes no more than 10mins. The views at the top belong to the best in this part of the Bavarian Alps!

> The Buchstein can also be climbed in about 10–15mins from the hut, but the ascent is much more difficult and requires some rock-climbing experience. Combined with the Bayerwaldsteig it would make this a Grade 3 rather than 2 walk.

For the descent return to the point where the track forks right in the direction of **Buchstein Hut** and follow it down to the Schwarzenbach stream. Here the track turns right to enter a small gorge and eventually brings you to the Königsalm-Winterstube bus stop. Those who parked their cars at Tegernseer Hut (and missed the bus) can, instead of walking 3km along the busy road, cross it and follow the path on the other side.

BAYRISCHZELL

*Tourist office: Tourist-Info Bayrischzell, Kirchplatz 2, D-83735 Bayrischzell. Tel: (08023) 648, fax: (08023) 103; website: **www.bayrischzell.de**, e-mail: tourist-info@bayrischzell.de*

Nestled at the foot of the Wendelstein, the small town of Bayrischzell has managed to preserve much of its typical Bavarian character despite the encroachments of modern tourism. For the mountain walker the town makes an ideal base, not only for the ascent of the Wendelstein but also for routes in the vicinity of the Rotwand. A very scenic stretch of the B307 winds its way from Bayrischzell to Hotel Tatzelwurm, where a number of trails lead through alm pastures and forest to such peaks as the Brünnstein and Grosser Traithen. Also worth visiting is the Spitzingsee, a pretty lake to the southwest. Bayrischzell can be reached by train from Munich and by bus and train from Miesbach and Schliersee. There is a youth hostel on the road to Tatzelwurm and campsites near Aurach and Fischbachau (both northwest).

VALLEY WALKS
Map: Kompass-Wanderkarte No 8.

vii AROUND THE SPITZINGSEE (1hr) Starting at the southern end of the lake follow the road in the direction of the Stümpflingbahn (chairlift) but before reaching it turn right. A very picturesque trail now runs north along the lake's western shore. From the north end of the lake path K25 hugs the eastern shoreline on its way back to the starting point.

viii TO KRONBERGER ALM (2½hrs) This walk begins at the bridge over the Arzbach stream (car park). To get there drive east from Bayrischzell in the direction of Tatzelwurm (B307). From the bridge follow a small farm road north past Untere Arzmoos Alm to the picturesquely situated Obere Arzmoos Alm. At Kronberger Alm turn sharp left and continue south. You soon come to a swampy stretch of track that runs through an area of upland moor. After passing through a patch of woods cross a field (path is a bit unclear here) and then continue on a good path along a partly wooded slope to Jackelberger Alm. Continue to Schweinsteiger Alm, then follow an asphalt road south to the B307. This leads you back to the bridge.

ROUTE 42
The Wendelstein (1838m)

Start	Brannenburg am Inn
Parking	Next to Wendelstein-Zahnradbahn (rack railway)
Transport	Wendelstein-Ringlinie bus from Bayrischzell railway station to Brannenburg and Zahnradbahn station
Distance	10.5km/6.5 miles
Height gain	98m (321ft)
Height loss	1322m (4337ft)
Time	4½hrs
Grade	2
Refreshments	Wendelstein Haus, Breitenberg Hut
Accommodation	Breitenberg Hut
Map	Kompass-Wanderkarte No 8: Tegernsee – Schliersee – Wendelstein

Crammed on the summit of the Wendelstein is an observatory, a meteorological station, a television transmitting tower, a restaurant (of course) and a church. It can be reached by cable railway from Osterhofen (southwest) and rack railway from Brannenburg am Inn (northeast). Not exactly a lonely summit? Be that as it may, the alpine panorama that can be enjoyed at the top is justly famous (assuming of course that the weather is on your side). The route described below takes advantage of the rack railway, a more leisurely alternative to the cable railway.

WALKING IN THE BAVARIAN ALPS

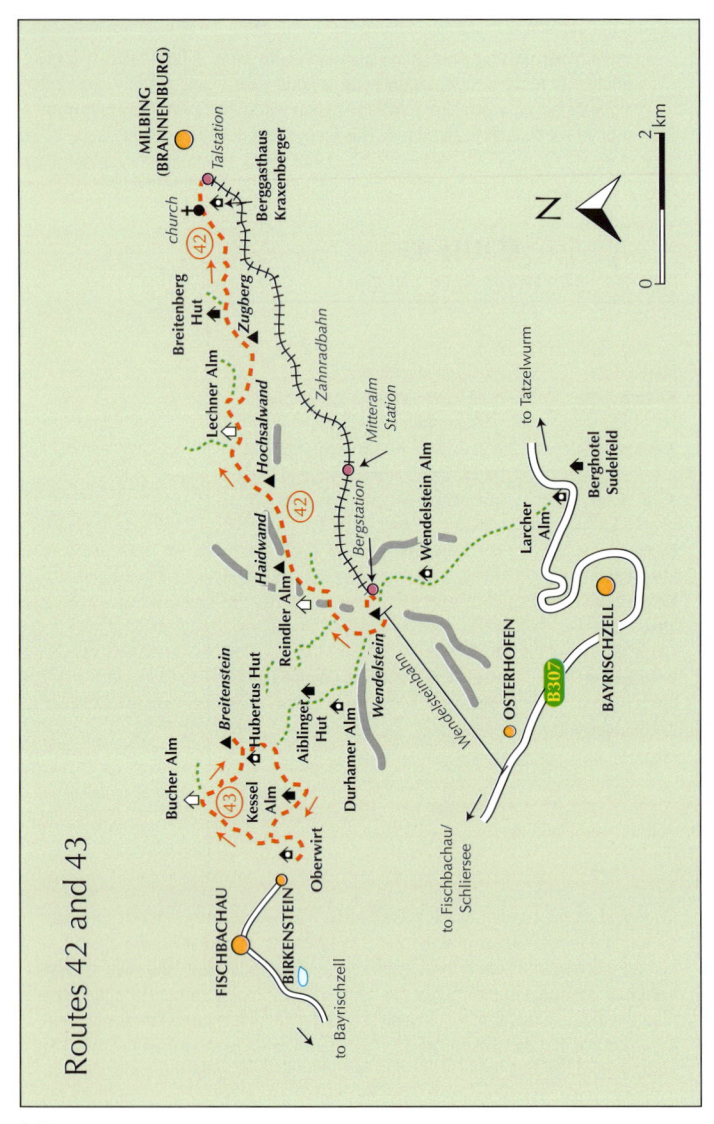

ROUTE 42 – THE WENDELSTEIN

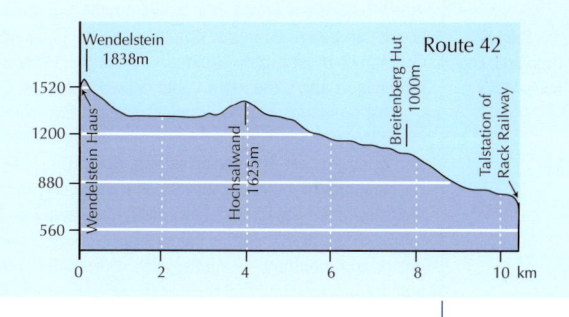

Wendelstein-Zahnradbahn (rack railway)
The historic Wendelstein rack railway started operation in 1912 as Germany's first mountain railway. To reach a point just below the summit the old locomotive had to overcome a difference in altitude of 1217m and a gradient of up to 24 percent over a distance of 7½km. It achieved this in just under 1hr. In comparison the cable railway only requires 6mins to overcome 932m in altitude. The new rack railway (the historic train still runs on special occasions) which came into operation in 1991 requires 25mins for the trip. Many visitors take the one up, the other down and return to the starting point by bus. Special tickets can be bought for this circular trip, which is worth considering if you only want to do the circular Panoramaweg.

The buses of the Wendelstein-Ringlinie run once a day from Bayrischzell to the valley station (Talstation) of the rack railway. From the rack railway station buses run twice daily back to Bayrischzell. For more information and up-to-date timetables visit the website: www.wendelstein-ringlinie.de or tel: (08066) 906333.

From the upper station of the rack railway the **Wendelstein** summit is reached along a well-made but steep track known as the Panoramaweg – the actual ascent begins on the west side of the summit from the upper station (*Bergstation*) of the cable railway (20mins). The views at the top can be impressive at any time of the year but in autumn, when the air is especially clear, they are quite breathtaking. Below the summit, on the mountain's south face at an altitude of 1740m, is the Wendelstein cave (Wendelsteinhöhle). It was formed millions of years ago by movements in the earth's crust and gradually enlarged to its present size by water erosion, but many will find the ice cave near Marktschellenberg more interesting

The entire Gipfel-Panoramaweg takes 50mins.

(Route 63). As it is only a short walk from the rack railway station it can be visited before commencing the Panoramaweg. Germany's most highly situated church, the Wendelstein-Kirchlein, is also close to the cable railway station. ◀

For the return walk to Brannenburg start from the terrace of the Wendelstein Haus restaurant (part of cable railway station complex). At first zigzag steeply downhill close to the cable railway (not the rack railway on the eastern side!) in the direction of Fischbachau (signposted), then swing right and follow the path that circles the mountain's west flank (signposted Brannenburg – Reindler Alm). Eventually come to a junction with the trail that runs south and to the right, back to the Wendelstein. Turn left here, then after only a short distance, left again along the signposted trail to **Reindler Alm**. A short walk through fields brings you to the alm huts and what, from now on, is a much less 'busy' section of track.

It is easy going over meadows (red dots mark the route) to the **Hochsalwand** (1625m), which can be climbed along its west ridge. There are good views from here back to the Wendelstein, and the route of the rack railway is clearly visible. From the summit return to the main track, descend steeply along a path secured with wire cables, pass below the Lechnerkopf and then follow the grassy ridge in the direction of the Rampoldplatte (1422m). Shortly before reaching the summit with its cross, which is already visible ahead, turn right and zigzag steeply down grass slopes to

The views from the Wendelstein are second to none

Lechner Alm. Now follow the alm road a short distance northeast before turning right, along a trail through woods and meadows, towards the **Zugberg** and **Breitenberg Hut**.

From the hut follow the track down to St Margarethen. Turn right at the church and pass **Berggasthaus Kraxenberger** from where it is only a short walk to the lower station of the rack railway.

Ascent from Bayrischzell

For all those who would prefer to get to the top of the Wendelstein under their own steam the best place to start is near Berghotel Sudelfeld, east of town on the road to Tatzelwurm. The route follows path B1a via **Larcher Alm** to **Wendelstein Alm** and then path B1 via the Zeller Scharte to the summit (2½hrs). Either return the same way or take one of several tracks back to Bayrischzell.

ROUTE 43
The Breitenstein (1622m)

Start	Birkenstein, near Fischbachau
Parking	Car park in Birkenstein
Transport	From Bayrischzell: train to Fischbachau and then bus 9552 to Birkenstein or bus 1088 to Fischbachau Kirche, then bus 9552 to Birkenstein, or Wendelstein-Ringline A (bus)
Distance	8km/5 miles
Height gain	771m (2529ft)
Height loss	771m (2529ft)
Time	3½hrs
Grade	1
Refreshments	Hubertus Hut, Kessel Alm
Accommodation	Kessel Alm
Map	Kompass-Wanderkarte No 8: Tegernsee – Schliersee – Wendelstein

Near the start of this pleasant half-day route is a very interesting pilgrimage chapel (*Wallfahrtskirche*) that is well worth a look. The interior is quite striking: the walls are covered from top to bottom with colourful votive pictures, and a large rococo altar almost seems to fill the entire room. Walkers should note, however, that a reasonable standard of dress is required of those who enter the chapel – normal walking attire is acceptable, but those who are skimpily clad are advised to change first.

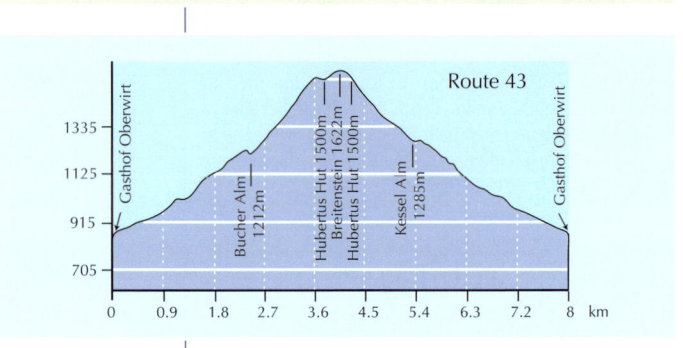

[Elevation profile: Route 43 – Gasthof Oberwirt, Bucher Alm 1212m, Hubertus Hut 1500m, Breitenstein 1622m, Hubertus Hut 1500m, Kessel Alm 1285m, Gasthof Oberwirt; distance 0 to 8 km; elevation 705 to 1335m]

The signpost pointing the way to Kessel Alm is near Gasthof Oberwirt (closed at time of writing). The route follows a gravel road uphill for a while in the direction of Kessel Alm but then branches left at a signposted junction to **Bucher Alm** (path B4). This road is only followed for a relatively short distance before another sign directs you uphill along a simple forest trail (path 4a, Bucheralm–Breitenstein). From the alm hut you can enjoy some nice views over the Leitzach Valley and towards Elbach (north).

The trail turns southeast (path B4) from the alm and climbs steeply up the Breitenstein's northern flanks. Shortly before reaching **Hubertus Hut** (1500m) it levels out and the going becomes much easier. The small hut is nicely situated with a beautiful view towards the Wendelstein, which seems no more than a stone's throw away. If it is wet, and there are a lot of people walking, it can get rather cramped inside but there is a nice atmosphere about the place. The walk up to the **Breitenstein**'s main summit (1622m) requires no more than ¼hr from here. Though the views from the top are not as grandiose as those from the Wendelstein you probably won't have to share them with quite so many people.

The track descends quite steeply from the hut until it comes to a couple of storage huts next to a fork. ▶ Our route continues right to **Kessel Alm** (1285m), already visible a short distance further downhill. A tiny chapel behind the alm restaurant is worth visiting as there is a nice view from here over the Leitzach Valley. Otherwise it is an easy walk down the Kessel Alm road back to **Birkenstein** and Gasthof Oberwirt.

The trail to the left leads past Aiblinger Hut (*accommodation*) and Durhamer Alm to the Wendelstein (2½hrs).

Those who would like to end the day's walking with a swim can follow a gravel path southwest through woods and fields to a small lake known as the Wolfsee (30mins from the Oberwirt). The refreshing dip can be followed by a relaxing meal in the nearby *Gasthof*'s beer garden. Return to Birkenstein along the same route or go via Bichl (path W6).

ROUTE 44
Taubensteinbahn – Soinsee – Taubenstein Haus

Start	Spitzingsee
Parking	Car park at Taubensteinbahn
Transport	Train (Bayerische Oberlandbahn) from Bayrischzell to Fischhausen-Neuhaus, then Bus 9562 from Neuhaus Bahnhof to Taubensteinbahn
Distance	9.1km/5.5 miles
Height gain	600m (1968ft)
Height loss	600m (1968ft)
Time	5½hrs
Grade	2
Refreshments	Bergstation Taubensteinbahn, Taubenstein Haus, Rotwand Haus
Accommodation	Taubenstein Haus, Rotwand Haus
Maps	Kompass-Wanderkarte No 8: Tegernsee – Schliersee – Wendelstein

WALKING IN THE BAVARIAN ALPS

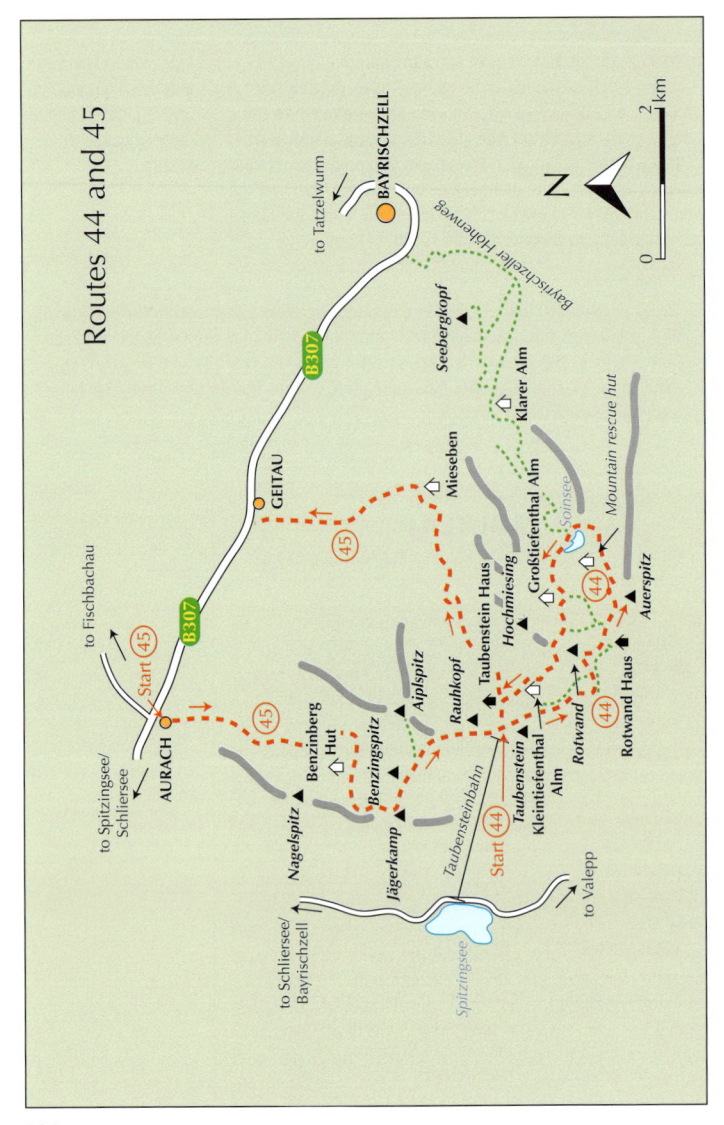

Route 44 – Taubensteinbahn – Soinsee – Taubenstein Haus

This lovely walk offers views galore as well as an idyllic mountain lake where you can cool off on a hot day – so don't forget your togs. The Taubensteinbahn saves you a long uphill walk from Spitzingsee (2hrs) so there should be plenty of time to savour the magnificent scenery. Nevertheless, remember to check the timetables before starting! The last cable car down to the valley usually goes at 16.30.

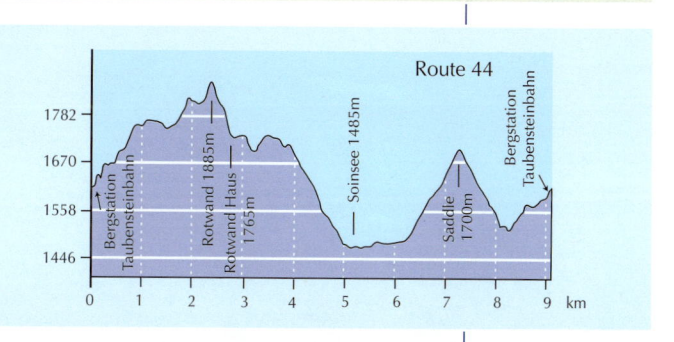

At the upper station of the Taubensteinbahn follow the trail that climbs southeast past the **Taubenstein** (1693m). Those with a head for heights can enjoy an easy scramble to the summit cross for a fine panorama. Otherwise, continue up to a saddle, ignore a trail to the left that runs down to Kleintiefenthal Alm, and continue instead straight ahead along the west slopes of the Lempersberg. Great views! The track is quite level until it reaches the saddle between Lempersberg, Klammstein and Rotwand. Rotwand Haus is already visible from here but instead of walking directly to the hut climb a narrower path along the base of the **Rotwand** (it rises above you to the left) and then curve left to the summit (1885m). The panorama at the top is magnificent, surpassing that of the Taubenstein earlier on. A great swathe of the northern Limestone Alps opens up to the eye, from the Berchtesgaden Alps in the east to the Allgäu Alps in the west. Looking further south it is also possible to make out such peaks as the Großvenediger and Großglockner in Austria's Hohe Tauern. From the summit it is no longer far to the hut.

Rotwand

A dip in the lake's clear, cold waters is guaranteed to refresh any hot and tired walker.

After leaving **Rotwand Haus** (1765m; the first hut in the Alps to have all its power supplied by a combination of wind and solar energy) continue on to the Kümpflscharte. The trail (marked on map as B4A) now descends between the Ruchenköpfe and **Auerspitz**, passing a Bergwachthütte (mountain rescue hut) on its way to the prettily situated Soinsee (1485m). ◄

The route continues from the lake along a level forestry road to **Großtiefenthal Alm**. From here a path climbs steeply up to the saddle between the **Hochmiesing** and **Rotwand** before descending in about 15mins to **Kleintiefenthal Alm**. Around 20m on from the last of the alm buildings a small track branches left from the alm access road. This track takes you through an area of upland moor directly to **Taubenstein Haus**. After a rest and a cold drink it is no longer far back up to the cable railway.

ROUTE 45
Jägerkamp (1746m), (Aiplspitz), Taubenstein (1693m) and Taubenstein Haus

Start	Aurach
Parking	In Aurach
Transport	Bus 1088 from Bayrischzell to Aurach, Wendelstein-Ringlinie A (bus) or train to Fischbachau and then a short walk to Aurach
Distance	15.2km/9.5 miles
Height gain	972m (3189ft)
Height loss	969m (3179ft)
Time	6hrs
Grade	2
Refreshments	Bergstation Taubensteinbahn, Taubenstein Haus
Accommodation	Taubenstein Haus, Rotwand Haus
Maps	Kompass-Wanderkarte No 8: Tegernsee – Schliersee – Wendelstein

The route up to the Jägerkamp and Taubenstein described here is a less popular alternative to the ride up with the Taubensteinbahn from the Spitzingsee. Those who want to avoid the long uphill climb from Aurach (and who do not mind the expense of the cable railway) could start at the lake. This might be a good alternative if you just want to base yourself at one of the huts and walk from there.

Aurach is situated on the German Alpine Road (B307) between Bayrischzell and Fischhausen. From near Gasthof Mairhofer in **Aurach** (*restaurant*) follow Benzing Strasse south into the Aurach Valley (Aurachtal). After walking through the woods for about 45mins leave the road and follow a steep zigzag track uphill towards **Benzingberg Hut** (1180m). Unfortunately, the turn-off is not signposted but you go left, across a gravel river bed. The track is well defined once you actually find it. Continue past the hut then

WALKING IN THE BAVARIAN ALPS

> Those who feel like it can make a ½hr detour (not waymarked) from the saddle to the top of the Nagelspitz (1551m) from where there is a fantastic view over the Schliersee.

at a fork turn right (west) along what is now an almost level track to Benzing Alm (1346m). From here it is another steep climb through pastures to the saddle between the Jägerkamp and Nagelspitz. ◄

Still climbing steeply carry on from the saddle south along a ridge to the summit of the **Jägerkamp** (1746m). Good views over the mountains to the south, while to the north and northeast Schliersee and the Wendelstein (transmitting tower on summit) are clearly visible. For the descent go southeast to a fork just above Schnittlauchmoos Alm. The trail on your left goes up to the summit of the **Aiplspitz** (1758m). However, as this track is a bit exposed in places it is only suitable for those with a head for heights. Otherwise continue down past the alm hut to a saddle from where the track climbs up a grassy slope to the **Rauhkopf** (1691m) and then down again to the upper station of the Taubensteinbahn. From here it is only a 20min detour to the summit of the **Taubenstein** (1693m). **Taubenstein Haus** (1567m) can be seen from the cable railway station and is quickly reached along a path that branches right from the route that was followed down from the Rauhkopf.

Compared to the rather faceless modern restaurant at the top of the Taubensteinbahn the old-fashioned *Gaststube* (dining-room) at Taubenstein Haus has plenty of character. The hut is old and comparatively small. Those who stay here will have to do without showers, but there is hot water in the basins. As the hut can only sleep 60 the larger Rotwand Haus (at the foot of the Rotwand) offers an alternative if it is full in summer.

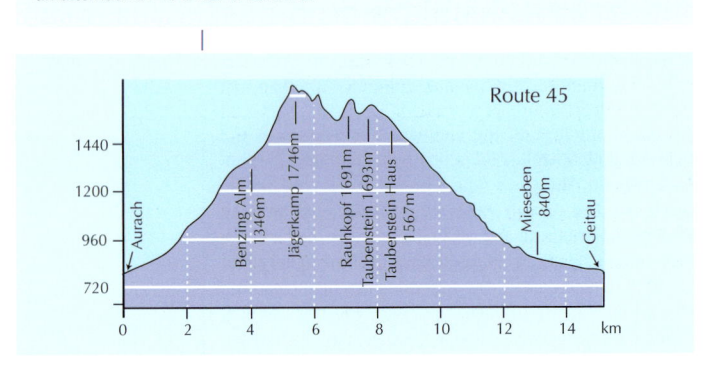

ROUTE 45 – JÄGERKAMP, (AIPLSPITZ), TAUBENSTEIN AND TAUBENSTEIN HAUS

Taubenstein summit

The descent route from Taubenstein Haus follows an alm access road via **Mieseben** to **Geitau** (marked as routes B6 and K4 on map). There is a bus stop and train station (on other side of B307) at Geitau, roughly 3½km southeast of Aurach as the crow flies.

Two-day tour
Spend the night at Taubenstein Haus – or at Rotwand Haus further along the trail. Next day return to the upper station of the Taubensteinbahn (from Taubenstein Haus) and follow the trail as described in Route 42 as far as Soinsee. Instead of taking the route to Großtiefenthal Alm take the road that leads northeast from this tarn down to Schellenberg Alm (1350m). A bit further on from the alm leave the road and follow a track (path B4) towards Niederhofer Alm (1050m). Shortly before the alm turn left (north) to Klarer Alm. The trail now follows the Bayrischzeller Höhenweg (High Level Walk) to Bayrischzell. This route allows an excursion to the Seebergkopf (1538m), the highest point on the Seeberg.

ROUTE 46
Tatzelwurm – Brünnstein – Tatzelwurm

Start	Gasthaus Tatzelwurm
Parking	Car park across road from Gasthaus Tatzelwurm
Transport	From Bayrischzell to Gasthaus Tatzelwurm with Wendelstein Ringlinie bus
Distance	14.5km/9 miles
Height gain	854m (2802ft)
Height loss	854m (2802ft)
Time	5hrs
Grade	1–2
Refreshments	Gasthaus Tatzelwurm, Brünnstein Haus
Accommodation	Gasthaus Tatzelwurm, Brünnstein Haus
Maps	Kompass-Wanderkarte No 8: Tegernsee – Schliersee – Wendelstein

Except for a bit of easy scambling on the way to the hut and the steep ascent to the Brünnstein summit, this walk should present no problems. Even without climbing to the summit there are some wonderful views, and for the most part the route follows comfortable alm roads. The second half of the walk is especially easy going, as it is mostly downhill at a modest gradient.

The pretty gorge and the waterfall near Gasthaus Tatzelwurm are associated with the saga of the dreaded *Tatzelwurm*, a fire-breathing dragon that once struck fear into the hearts of the locals. The nicely situated *Gasthaus* offers meals and accommodation; www.tatzelwurm.de; tel: (08034) 30 080.

From **Gasthaus Tatzelwurm** (764m) a short walk uphill through the woods (follow the blue dots) and past the impressive waterfall brings you up to a large car park. Now

ROUTE 46 – TATZELWURM – BRÜNNSTEIN – TATZELWURM

follow the trail uphill on the left (waymarked as path 657). This leads southeast through woods and meadows to where it meets with an alm road. Still moving southeast and waymarked as path 657 the road is followed past **Schoißer Alm** (900m) to the point where it curves back to the northwest. Here path 657 leaves the alm road and climbs through the woods along a narrow track. The track traverses the gully of the Kaserbach stream, and just before it links up with the road to Groß Alm there is a bit of easy scrambling with the help of a wire cable.

Cross the road and pass through alm meadows to the lightly wooded northeastern slopes of the Brünnstein. Eventually the track curves around to the southwest, and shortly before reaching **Brünnstein Haus** (1342m) it levels

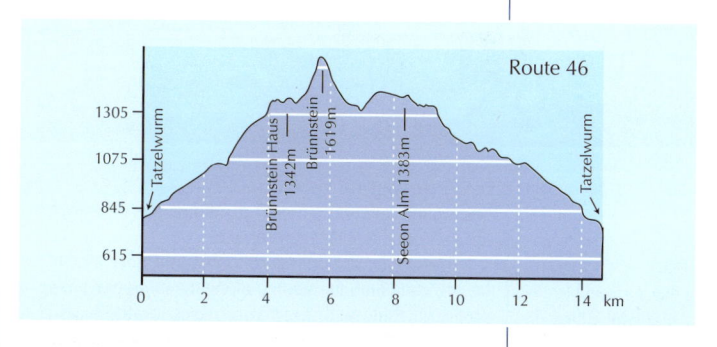

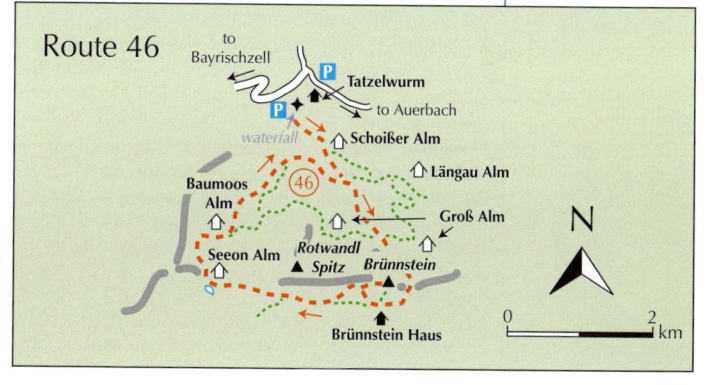

Seeon Alm

Reliable sources have it that you can identify at least 200 peaks from near the tiny chapel at the top.

out. There are great views across to the Kaisergebirge along this section, and the splendid panorama can be enjoyed at leisure from the hut's sunny terrace.

Those who are both sure-footed and have a head for heights can climb the summit along the Julius-Mayr-Steig, a protected route with fixed wire ropes to aid the ascent. Otherwise, choose the easier path which reaches the summit along the **Brünnstein**'s west ridge. ◄

Instead of returning the same way you can continue west via Himmelmoos Alm (1326m) towards **Seeon Alm** (1383m) on path 651. Shortly after Seeon Alm path 651 descends a short distance, then it is fairly level walking along steep slopes until the point where the trail descends again on what is now path 655 to **Baumoos Alm** (1197m). After the alm it is easy walking along an access road through meadows to where path 655 intersects with the ascent route from Tatzelwurm (path 657). Passing **Schoißer Alm** on the way, the trail arrives back at the starting point in around 30mins.

View back down the Unzental (Route 55)

PART V
THE CHIEMGAU ALPS

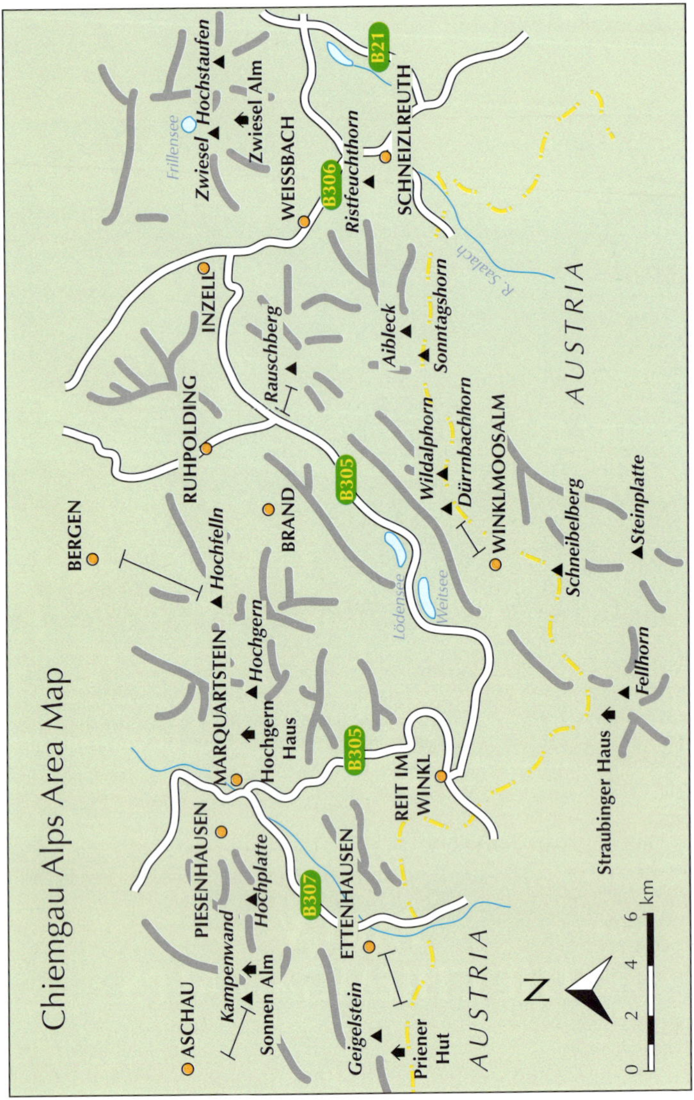
Chiemgau Alps Area Map
ASCHAU
Kampenwand
Sonnen Alm
PIESENHAUSEN
Hochplatte
B307
ETTENHAUSEN
Geigelstein
Priener Hut
AUSTRIA
MARQUARTSTEIN
Hochgern
Hochgern Haus
B305
REIT IM WINKL
BERGEN
Hochfelln
BRAND
RUHPOLDING
Lödensee
Weitsee
WINKLMOOSALM
Schneibelberg
Steinplatte
Fellhorn
Straubinger Haus
Wildalphorn
Dürrnbachhorn
Rauschberg
INZELL
Aibleck
Sonntagshorn
AUSTRIA
R. Saalach
Frillensee
Zwiesel
Hochstaufen
Zwiesel Alm
WEISSBACH
B306
Ristfeuchthorn
SCHNEIZLREUTH
B21
N
0
2
4
6
km

PART V
THE CHIEMGAU ALPS

The Chiemgau Alps

The Chiemgauer Alpen – or Chiemgauer Berge as they are known in German – are situated between the rivers Inn and Saalach. The highest peak in the region is the Sonntagshorn (1960m), which is situated directly on the German–Austrian border. However, the southern boundaries of the group do not end at the border but extend to the Austrian towns of Erl and Niederndorf in the west and Unken in the east. The Fellhorn and Steinplatte mark the southernmost limits of the group's 'intrusion' into Austria.

That the Chiemgau Alps have not escaped the effects of large-scale commercial development can be clearly seen at such places as Winklmoos Alm and the Steinplatte, where ski lifts have 'scarred' the landscape. Fortunately a large area (between Reit im Winkl and Weißbach) has been set aside as a nature reserve (Naturschutzgebiet Chiemgauer Alpen). Here there are no ski slopes, and cable cars only reach those peaks on the fringe. One of the most scenically interesting stretches of the German Alpine Road (between Reit im Winkl and Ruhpolding) goes through this reserve, winding past a string of pretty lakes. The Weitsee is the largest, and is a popular place to swim in summer.

WALKING IN THE BAVARIAN ALPS

MARQUARTSTEIN
*Tourist office: Tourist Information, Rathausplatz 1, D-83250 Marquartstein. Tel: (08641) 699 558, fax: (08641) 699 559; website: **www.marquartstein.de**, e-mail: info@marquartstein.de*

That section of Marquartstein to the west of the River Tiroler Ache makes a rather nondescript impression on most visitors: the same tidy, well-swept streets lined by equally tidy little shops that one can expect to find just about anywhere in the Alps (or elsewhere in Germany). However, this impression changes somewhat when one crosses to the east bank of the river. Here lies Alt-Marquartstein with its narrow alleys and a few old houses still decorated with frescoes in the traditional style. Nothing overwhelming, it is true, but what remains is quite picturesque and conveys something of what the village must originally have looked like. The *Burg* (castle), which is also located here, was once the residence of Graf Marquart II, a medieval Casanova who came to a sticky end at the hands of a jealous ex-lover. As a footnote it is worth mentioning that the composer Richard Strauss was a regular summer guest in Marquartstein. While 'relaxing' amidst the mountain scenery he composed such works as *Elektra* and *Salome*.

Marquartstein has no railway station, but there are direct connections to Prien on Chiemsee from Frankfurt and a number of other German cities. From Prien you can catch a bus. Those travelling by car can use the motorway Munich–Salzburg (A8) and take either the Bernau exit or the exits Übersee-Feldwies and Grabenstätt. There is a campsite to the southwest near Mettenham, and some nice bed and breakfasts in Piesenhausen on the road to the Hochplatte chairlift.

VALLEY WALKS
Map: Kompass-Wanderkarte No 10.

ix **THE SMUGGLER'S TRAIL (Schmugglerweg) (2½hrs)** The so-called Smuggler's Trail begins at Ettenhausen (southwest of Marquartstein on the road to Kössen in Austria) and crosses the border to Austria. After passing a small lake and a waterfall the trail continues through meadows and woods to the Entenlochklamm (a gorge) where the border is crossed. Shortly after the gorge turn left, cross a bridge over the Tiroler Ache stream, and walk up to the idyllically situated Gasthof Klobenstein (*refreshments*). Just above the *Gasthof* is a very interesting pilgrimage church. Return the same way. **Note** Remember to take a passport!

ROUTE 47
From the Kampenwand (1669m) to the Geigelstein (1801m)

Start	Marquartstein-Niedernfels
Parking	Next to Hochplattenbahn (chair-lift)
Transport	Bus 9509 runs between Ettenhausen and Marquartstein
Distance	21km/13 miles
Height gain	1819m (5968ft)
Height loss	1740m (5708ft)
Time	3 days
Grade	2–3
Refreshments	Platten Alm, Steinling Alm, Berggasthof Kampenwand, Sonnen Alm, Priener Hut, Wuhrstein Alm
Accommodation	Sonnen Alm, Priener Hut
Map	Kompass-Wanderkarte No 10: Chiemsee – Simssee

Many people rate the ridge walk to the Kampenwand as the finest in the entire Chiemgau Alps. Splendid views the whole way! Apart from a bit of healthy uphill sweating at the start, the only really difficult part on Day 1 is the crossing of the Kampenwand. The section up to the Hochplatte is quite easy (if steep) and can be done by anybody who is reasonably fit. Day 2 involves covering quite a lot of ground, and there is one very steep section, but the magnificent views from the Geigelstein and a comfortable mountain hut at the end of the walk make up for this. On Day 3 the only bit of 'hard work' is the ascent of the Breitenstein, otherwise it is downhill all the way.

Day 1 (3½–4½hrs)
The Hochplatte chairlift takes you in 10mins to an altitude of 1050m, thus saving 1hr walking. At the top follow waymark 4 southwest. It is a long, steady climb along a gravel road to

WALKING IN THE BAVARIAN ALPS

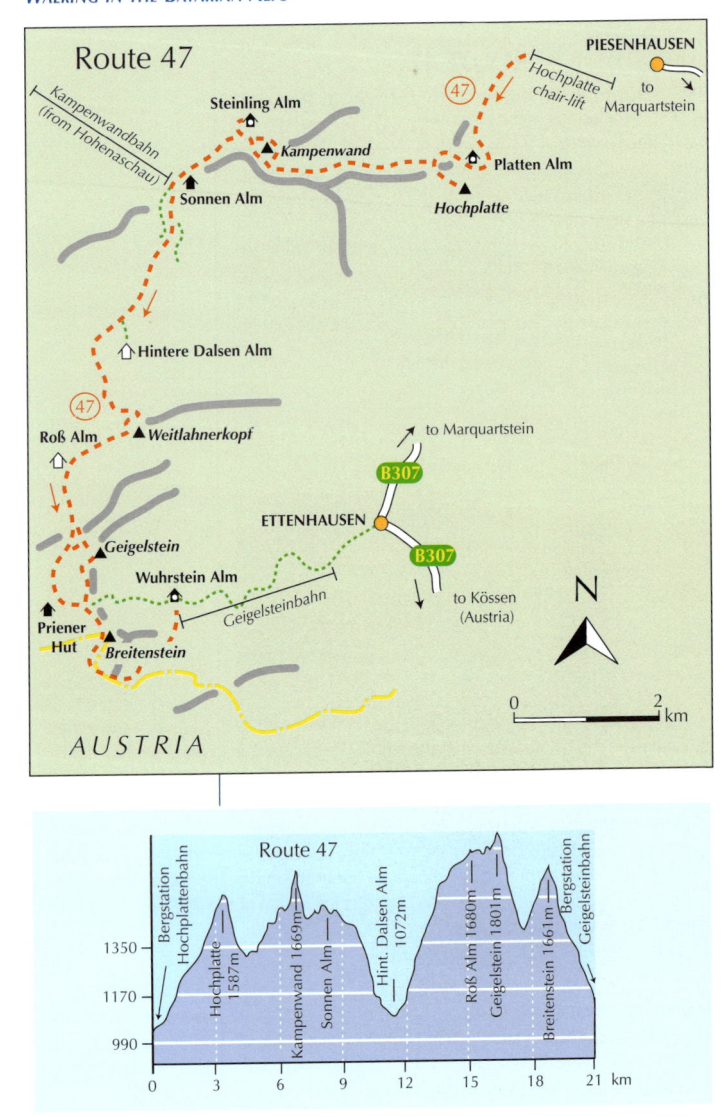

Route 47

Kampenwandbahn (from Hohenaschau)
Steinling Alm
Kampenwand
Sonnen Alm
Hochplatte chair-lift
Platten Alm
Hochplatte
PIESENHAUSEN
to Marquartstein

Hintere Dalsen Alm
Roß Alm
Weitlahnerkopf
Geigelstein
Wuhrstein Alm
Priener Hut
Breitenstein
Geigelsteinbahn
ETTENHAUSEN
B307
to Marquartstein
B307
to Kössen (Austria)

N

0   2 km

AUSTRIA

Route 47

Bergstation Hochplattenbahn
Hochplatte 1587m
Kampenwand 1669m
Sonnen Alm
Hint. Dalsen Alm 1072m
Roß Alm 1680m
Geigelstein 1801m
Breitenstein 1661m
Bergstation Geigelsteinbahn

1350
1170
990

0   3   6   9   12   15   18   21 km

ROUTE 47 – FROM THE KAMPENWAND TO THE GEIGELSTEIN

the **Platten Alm** but you have some great views on the way. At the alm the road climbs more steeply to a saddle between the Friedenrath and Hochplatte. A track branches left and up to the **Hochplatte** summit (½hr). After enjoying the panorama return to the main track and turn left towards the Kampenwand. It is already visible ahead as a humped ridge of bare grey-white rock that bears some resemblance to the back of a stegosaurus.

The crossing to the Kampenwand (part of the European long-distance walk E4) is one of the most rewarding ridge walks in the Chiemgau Alps. It takes roughly 1hr to get to a point just below the **Kampenwand** summit, and those with

The Kampenwand from the track to Dalsen Alm

sufficient confidence can climb directly up and over it (½hr to top). ◄ Alternatively go round it to the right and cross the Kampenwand at a lower point: the track goes first downhill a short way then climbs up a rocky section which is secured by wire ropes. It is an easy descent to **Steinling Alm** which you can already see below. The alm hut offers the opportunity for a rest and a snack, otherwise continue another 20mins along a comfortable trail to the upper station of the Kampenwandbahn. Shortly before reaching the cable car station you will come to **Sonnen Alm**, where you can spend the night.

Before you get to the top there is one tricky bit over a tilted slab of rock where you will need the help of the wire ropes.

Day 2 (4–4½hrs)

The onward route to the Geigelstein and Priener Haus is clearly signposted from the Kampenwandbahn. The trail first descends, then it is fairly level walking for a while. Good views back to the Kampenwand. Eventually you start a long descent through the woods to Dalsen Alm (path 66). When the track reaches a gravel road turn right, walk a few metres, then turn left (signposted 'Weitlahner – Geigelstein'). The track continues briefly through the woods then enters the pastures above **Hintere Dalsen Alm**. Soon after the track commences its steep climb up to the Weitlahnerkopf. If you look back yesterday's route between the Hochplatte and Kampenwand is clearly visible. Roughly two-thirds of the way up the track enters the woods again before coming out at a grassy clearing just below the **Weitlahnerkopf**. Great views and a good place for a rest after the strenuous climb.

Before reaching the summit you have to traverse what can be a very muddy stretch of track and then clamber up a rocky slope – wire ropes help where it is steepest. At the top a track goes left to the summit cross. After admiring the views continue southwest to **Roß Alm**. It is easy going along what is now a fairly level track. In autumn the pastures are dotted with hundreds of carline thistles which are, like most alpine plants these days, protected. From the alm huts the track climbs once more then levels out again. Fantastic views to the south. Before long you come to a fork from where you can begin your ascent of the **Geigelstein**. You could also continue directly down to Priener Hut, but it is a long hot climb back up if you decide to do the summit later. From the fork it is only a matter of 15mins to the top. At

Route 47 – From the Kampenwand to the Geigelstein

1801m this is the highest peak in the western Chiemgau Alps, and the view is accordingly impressive.

A steep descent down a grass slope brings you to **Priener Hut** and the end of today's walk. As Alpine Club huts go it is surprisingly luxurious; they even have double rooms! Other comforts include hot showers and a proper little restaurant on the ground floor. The evening might be spent on the terrace watching the sun set behind the saw-tooth ridge of the Kaisergebirge.

Day 3 (1½hrs to chairlift)

Before descending to Ettenhausen it is worth climbing the **Breitenstein**. Though lower than the Geigelstein the views are still very good. The track starts climbing immediately from the hut but levels out a little just before it arrives at a fork. Those in a hurry can walk directly down to **Wuhrstein Alm** from here, otherwise turn right to the summit. After enjoying the views descend southwest along a steep track to another fork. Here the trail (signposted 'Seilbahn – Wuhrsteinalm') continues downhill to the pastures of the now-abandoned Karl Alm and then along lightly wooded slopes to the Geigelsteinbahn (chairlift). En route there are beautiful views over the valley towards Unterwössen and Marquartstein. As the last lift does not go down until 16.30 you should reach it in plenty of time. At the bottom it is ½km to the bus stop in **Ettenhausen**.

> Due to the uncertain financial situation of the Geigelsteinbahn in recent years it may not always be running. Enquire at the tourist office in Schleching beforehand; tel: (08649) 220. If the chairlift is not operating it will take 1–1½ hrs to reach Ettenhausen from Wuhrsteinalm.

Last bus from Ettenhausen to Marquartstein at 18.10 (check!). The bus drops you off near the centre of **Marquartstein** (Rathaus) from where it takes about 30mins to get to the car park by the Hochplattenbahn. There is also a bus to the chairlift but it does not run regularly.

WALKING IN THE BAVARIAN ALPS

ROUTE 48
Marquartstein to the Hochgern

Start	Marquartstein
Parking	Car park above castle (Burg)
Transport	Local buses
Distance	15.3km/9.5 miles
Height gain	1133m (3717ft)
Height loss	1133m (3717ft)
Time	5½hrs
Grade	2
Refreshments	Staudacher Alm, Hochgern Haus, Enzian Hut, Agergschwendt Alm
Accommodation	Hochgern Haus
Map	Kompass-Wanderkarte No 10: Chiemsee – Simssee

Though the first section of this walk is a longish uphill slog it does, in the end, promise some of the best views in the area and is relatively free of the crowds that one might expect if the summit were accessible by cable car.

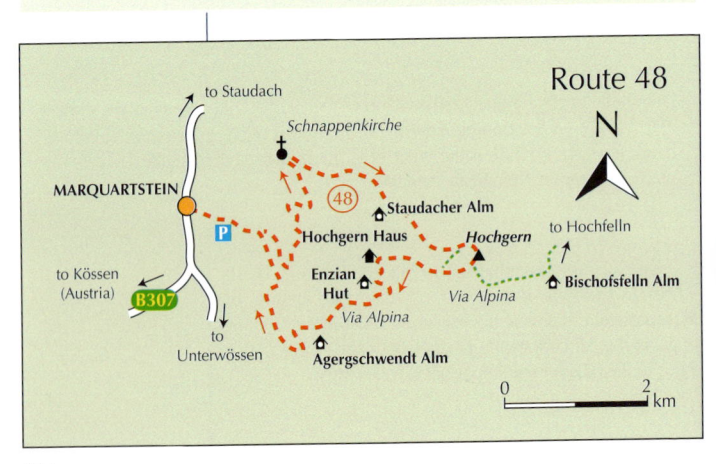

ROUTE 48 – MARQUARTSTEIN TO THE HOCHGERN

Starting point is the car park in the woods above the local castle (*Burg*). From the upper end of the car park take the right-hand path and continue through the woods until you come to a fork. From here follow the sign 'Schnappenberg' (path 53) to the left. The steadily climbing trail is quite clearly waymarked from now on and you should have no trouble finding your way. After about 1½hrs' walking through the woods the **Schnappenkirche**, a small church, is reached. Excellent views over Chiemsee to the north. The church is usually open, but apart from a few faded frescoes on the walls it is quite simply furnished. The gravel road that you have been following so far is left after the church and is exchanged for a proper track (path 3) that leads uphill into the woods towards Staudacher Alm. After climbing over a stile and passing through a small grassy clearing the track levels out, descending only slightly before it climbs gently up to the alm meadows and huts. Prettily situated **Staudacher Alm** is a good spot for a break.

Alpine salamanders are commonly seen along the track when it's wet

Those who have the (mis)fortune to walk this route when it is wet or misty have a good chance of seeing salamanders. Particularly common are the jet-black alpine salamander (*Salamandra atra*), but the strikingly coloured spotted salamander (*Salamandra salamandra*) can also be seen. The latter is the larger of the two (up to 20cm long), and the poison secreted through its skin is deadly for small creatures – not for humans, but it is better not to touch them.

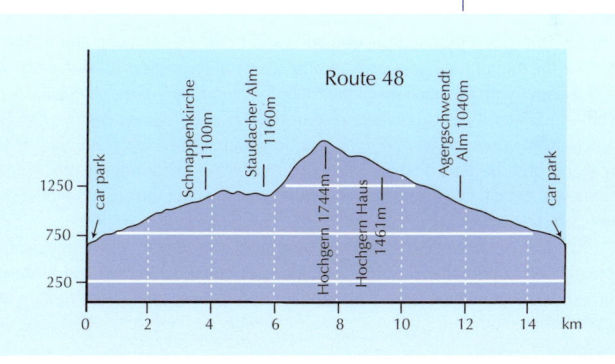

From the alm path 5 (signposted) continues through the meadows, then enters the woods where it starts climbing quite steeply to the **Hochgern** summit. Some care is necessary if it is wet as the track gets very slippery. After enjoying the panorama at the top go a short distance back along the ascent route, then continue west along a broad, well-defined trail towards **Hochgern Haus**. From here a windy access road leads down past **Enzian Hut** to **Agergschwendt Alm** (1hr). Continue along the road until you reach an intersection, then turn right towards **Marquartstein**.

Alternative route

This route can be linked with Route 52, thus connecting two peaks in the Chiemgau famed for their views. From the summit of the **Hochgern** head south, down a very steep track, then go in a northeasterly direction towards **Bischofsfelln Alm** (*refreshments*). After the alm go north to Hinter-Alm, then east to where the track joins a road near Eschlmoos Dienst Hut. From the hut continue first a short distance north, then go east along path 56 to the Thoraukopf and from there up to the Hochfelln summit (3½hrs from Hochgern). Either continue down to Bergen with the cable car or on foot, or walk to Ruhpolding.

REIT IM WINKL

*Tourist office: Tourist-Info, Dorfstrasse 38, D-83242 Reit im Winkl. Tel: (08640) 80 020, fax: (08640) 80 029; website: **www.reitimwinkl.de**, e-mail: info@reit-im-winkl.de*

In winter the skiers descend on Reit im Winkl in their thousands, and in summer it is the turn of mountain walkers and other holidaymakers to feed the local cash registers with the contents of their rapidly dwindling wallets. And what for? Well – in winter there is nowhere else in the Bavarian Alps where you can be so certain of good snow conditions, and in summer the town is an ideal base for walks both in the Chiemgau Alps and the Tyrol – the border is only a few kilometres distant. The town is quite picturesque, but over the years has become very commercialised.

Reit im Winkl can be reached by bus from Marquartstein, and there are also connections to Winklmoos Alm, Ruhpolding, Prien am Chiemsee and Munich. There is a campsite quite near town and another at Seegatterl, near the turn-off to Winklmoos Alm.

ROUTE 49
To Hindenburg Hut, Straubinger Haus and the Fellhorn

Start	Reit im Winkl-Blindau
Parking	At Steinbachbrücke
Transport	Private minibus runs to Hindenburg Hut; check times at the tourist office in Reit im Winkl
Distance	17km/10.5 miles
Height gain	1044m (3425ft)
Height loss	1044m (3425ft)
Time	5hrs
Grade	1
Refreshments	Hindenburg Hut, Straubinger Haus
Accommodation	Straubinger Haus
Map	Kompass-Wanderkarte No 14: Berchtesgadener Land – Chiemgauer Alpen

This beautiful route is probably at its most attractive in late spring or early summer when the wildflowers are at their decorative best. However, in autumn the weather is often more stable and then it is the larch that adds a vivid splash of golden colour to the landscape. **Note** Remember your passport as there is a border crossing.

Starting point is the Steinbachbrücke (a bridge) at the southern end of town. You will have to park your car here as the road to Hindenburg Hut is closed to private vehicles. A minibus runs between **Blindau** and the hut and stops at the bridge. If you do walk along the road, which is rather steep, it will take roughly 1hr to get to the hut.

WALKING IN THE BAVARIAN ALPS

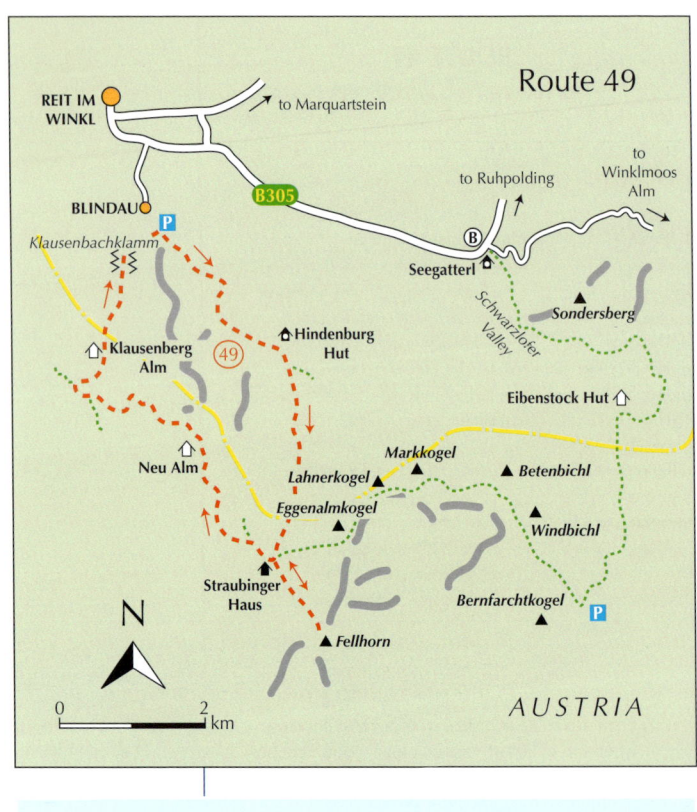

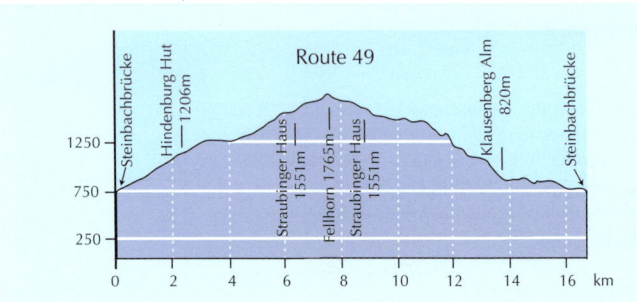

Route 49

Route 49 – To Hindenburg Hut, Straubinger Haus and the Fellhorn

The minibus between Blindau and Hindenburg Hut runs roughly every ½hr from around 09.00 during the season (check times). It also runs on demand (tel: 08640 8425 or tel: 0171 543 7923). There is a phone booth about 200m further back along the road from the bridge.

From **Hindenburg Hut** follow an asphalted road in the direction of Obere Hemmersuppenalm. This first short stretch is especially idyllic in spring and early summer when the surrounding meadows are covered by a golden carpet of wildflowers. Once you reach the signpost to **Straubinger Haus** (path 152) you leave the road, pass a few farm buildings and then continue on a track through an area of open woodland. This is where the so-called Filzenweg begins, a trail which passes through an attractive upland moor – again lots of wildflowers. After leaving the moor and crossing into Austria the trail starts climbing more steeply and it is not long before **Straubinger Haus** comes into view.

Though the views are already very good from the hut they are even better from the **Fellhorn**'s summit (1765m). The route is clearly signposted and it requires a good ½hr's

Fellhorn summit

Just before town it is worth visiting a small but impressive gorge known as the **Klausenbachklamm** (signposted). After leaving the *Klamm* turn right at the first group of houses and walk along the edge of the woods to the car park by the bridge.

walking to reach the summit cross. Fantastic panorama! The view extends over the snow-capped peaks of the Austrian Alps, and looking back towards Germany you can make out the blue expanse of Chiemsee. The impressive wall of bare rock that dominates the foreground to the south belongs to the Wilder Kaiser massif.

For the descent from **Straubinger Haus** follow the signpost 'Kössen/Reit im Winkl', and then a short distance further down the trail (10mins) turn left at the sign 'Neualm – Klausenbergalm – Blindau'. The fork to the right returns to Reit im Winkl via Hindenburg Hut. After a good ½hr the track (path 27) brings you through a very attractive area of forest to **Neu Alm**. From here follow a steep path down to the huts and meadows of Weißenstein Alm, and then (walking at first towards Kössen) continue on to **Klausenberg Alm**. The German border lies just beyond the alm, and after crossing it a gravel road is followed back towards Blindau. ◄

Variation

This route can be turned into a very attractive two-day trip by continuing from Straubinger Haus to Seegatterl: spend the night at Straubinger Haus then go via Eggenalmkogel (1685m), Lahnerkogel (1595m) and Windbichl (also spelled Windbühel) to the car park below the Bernfarchtkogel (3hrs; a good sense of direction is necessary – do not walk the route when it is misty). Continue in a northerly direction and descend to Seegatterl via the Schwarzlofer Valley (c.3hrs). From here catch the bus back to Reit im Winkl (check timetables beforehand).

ROUTE 50
Winklmoos Alm and Dürrnbachhorn

Start	Winklmoos Alm
Parking	Large car park at Winklmoos Alm
Transport	Bus 9507 from Reit im Winkl
Distance	11km/7 miles
Height gain	589m (1932ft)
Height loss	625m (2050ft)
Time	4½hrs
Grade	1
Refreshments	Restaurants at Winklmoos Alm, Bergstation of chairlift, Wild Alm
Accommodation	Traunsteiner Ski Hut, Alpengasthof Winklmoosalm
Map	Kompass-Wanderkarte No 14: Berchtesgadener Land – Chiemgauer Alpen

The Dürrnbachhorn's precipitous north face stands in marked contrast to the gentler southern slopes which are cloaked by forest and meadows. In early summer the slopes above Dürrnbach Alm are especially pretty, sprinkled with bright yellow globeflowers and white anemones; reason enough to pack your camera and to forgo the expense of the chairlift.

To get to Winklmoos Alm drive east of Reit im Winkl to Seegatterl. From here take the signposted toll road to Winklmoos Alm. There is also a bus from Reit im Winkl to the alm. **Note** As this walk enters Austria you should carry a passport.

Winklmoos Alm is situated 10km east of Reit im Winkl. In winter the alm's high plateau is popular for winter sport, but numerous walking trails make it an equally popular destination in summer. There is a good range of accommodation, from the simple walking hut facilities of Traunsteiner Hut to more luxurious *Gasthöfe*. For more information enquire at the tourist office in Reit im Winkl, or visit the German language website: www.winklmoosalm.de.

WALKING IN THE BAVARIAN ALPS

Routes 50 and 51

[Map showing Routes 50 and 51 in the Bavarian Alps, featuring locations including Dürrnbachhorn, Wildalphorn, Rieger Kaser Alm, Bergstation, Finsterbach Alm, Hochgimpling, Wild Alm, Winklmoos Alm, Seegatterl, Sondesberg, Martinsbichl, Eibenstock Hut, Scheibelberg, Möser Alm, Straubinger Haus, Bernfarchtkogel, Stallen Alm, Kammerköhr, Steinplatte (Kammerköhr), and Panoramaweg. Roads indicated include B305 to Ruhpolding, toll road, and routes to Reit im Winkl. Start point marked for Routes 50 and 51 near Zigeuner-Marterl. Scale: 0–2km.]

The walk up to the Dürrnbachhorn begins at the foot of the chairlift. Those who wish can cut out some 400m of climbing by taking the lift to the Dürrnbacheck (1590m). Otherwise follow the trail through the woods to Dürrnbach Alm. From here cross under the chairlift and continue on through the woods to the chairlift's upper station (45mins). Another 30mins' climbing brings you to the summit of the

ROUTE 50 – WINKLMOOS ALM AND DÜRRNBACHHORN

Chapel in the meadows at Winklmoos Alm

Dürrnbachhorn (1776m) from where you can enjoy a panorama that stretches from the Berchtesgaden Alps to the Wettersteingebirge. Wonderful bird's-eye view of the lakes (Weitsee, Mittersee and Lödensee) in the Chiemgau Alps nature reserve. ▶

The main route continues first east and then south (descending steeply) to where the trail forks: the right fork

If time allows a detour can be made along a somewhat exposed ridge (head for heights!) with fine views to the **Wildalphorn** (1690m).

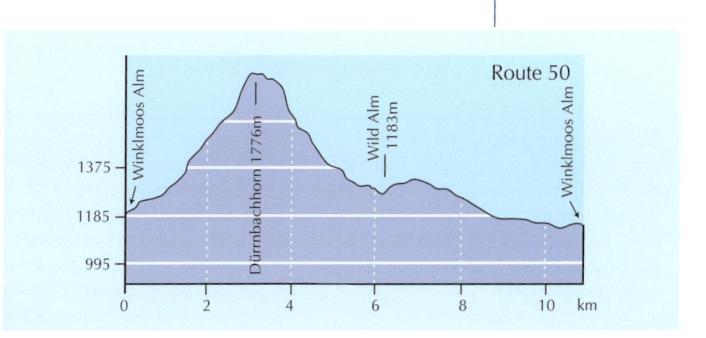

goes via Finsterbach Alm directly back to the starting point but this route follows the left fork, crossing alm meadows to **Rieger Kaser Alm** and then down to **Wild Alm**. From here you follow path 15 and then the pretty Landweg back to **Winklmoos Alm**.

ROUTE 51
Winklmoos Alm to the Steinplatte (Kammerköhr) (1869m)

Start	Winklmoos Alm
Parking	Car park at Winklmoos Alm
Transport	Bus 9507 Reit im Winkl – Winklmoos Alm. Toll road up to alm
Distance	17.5km/11 miles
Height gain	724m (2375ft)
Height loss	724m (2375ft)
Time	5½hrs
Grade	1
Refreshments	Restaurants at Winklmoos Alm, Möser Alm, Kammerköhr, Stallen Alm
Accommodation	Traunsteiner Ski Hut, Alpengasthof Winklmoosalm
Map	Kompass-Wanderkarte No 14: Berchtesgadener Land – Chiemgauer Alpen

Not everyone is going to like the fact that this route goes through one of the most popular ski fields in the region. There are prettier sights than chairlift pylons and ski huts, but the relatively easy walking and wonderful views from the top of the Steinplatte make this a nice (if rather long) outing for families with younger children. The second half of the route is quite different in character, as it leaves the ski slopes behind and passes through some very pretty stretches of forest. **Note** Do not forget your passport as the trail crosses the border to Austria.

ROUTE 51 – WINKLMOOS ALM TO THE STEINPLATTE (KAMMERKÖHR)

From the large car park at **Winklmoos Alm** walk past Alpengasthof Winklmoosalm and the Winklalm-Stüberl and then follow path 11 in the direction of the Scheibelberg (signposted). The route follows a gravel road for a short distance, but then turns onto a gently climbing track that runs along the German–Austrian border. ▶ At a point just below the **Scheibelberg**'s modest summit (1465m) the track divides. Those who wish can climb it by turning to the right, otherwise continue left over the border into Austria. Before long the ski slopes and lifts surrounding **Möser Alm** come into view. The *Gasthof* here is a huge place that was obviously built for the hordes that descend upon it during the ski season.

Continue south in the direction of Gasthaus Kammerköhr along a narrow road that winds uphill through the ski fields. On the way you pass a tiny wooden chapel dedicated to St Hubertus, the patron saint of hunters. From the *Gasthaus* (again a rather cavernous place) a steep path climbs up to the summit of the **Kammerköhr** (1869m), or Steinplatte, as the Tyroleans prefer to call it (45mins). The magnificent view at the top (looking south) encompasses the jagged peaks of the Loferer Steinberge with the Hohen Tauern and Zillertal Alps in the background.

Return the same way, past the *Gasthaus*, to the signposted turn-off to **Stallen Alm** (path 7), where there is yet another large restaurant that seems to be pining for the return of snow and the fat wallets of *après*-skiers. Follow the sign here down to Parkplatz Steinplatte. Walk through the large car park, go past a chairlift station and descend into the valley.

> In spring this first stretch can be very wet and muddy, though wooden planks save your boots from the worst.

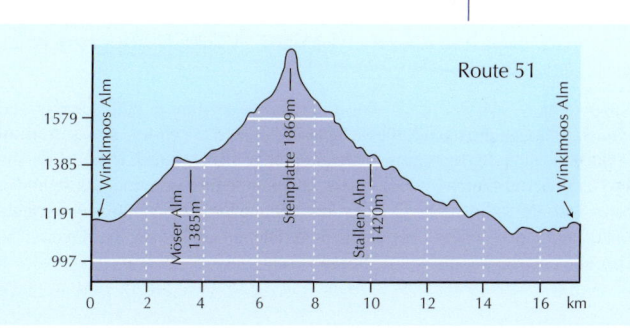

Alpine chough

Some distance further on from the chairlift you come to a fork. The right fork goes back to Möser Alm but our route continues straight ahead towards Winklmoos Alm – you follow a stream. At **Eibenstock Hut** (a log cabin set in beautiful deciduous forest back on the German side of the border) turn right along path 18. This trail brings you through the woods and back to **Winklmoos Alm**.

RUHPOLDING AND INZELL

*Tourist office: Tourist-Information, Hauptstrasse 60, D-83324 Ruhpolding. Tel: (08663) 88 060, fax: (08663) 880 620; website: **www.ruhpolding.de**, e-mail: tourismus@ruhpolding.de*

*Inzeller Touristik GmbH, Rathausplatz 5, D-83334 Inzell (also office at bus station). Tel: (08665) 98 850, fax: (08665) 988 530; website: **www.inzell.de**, e-mail: info@inzell.de*

Ruhpolding is, like Reit im Winkl, a popular destination in both summer and winter. Although the town has by no means escaped the effects of mass tourism it is still possible to discover picturesque little corners here and there where the eye can rest on a pretty house fresco. There are a few very good museums in town with interesting collections of folk and religious art, and a magnificently decorated parish church (Pfarrkirche St Georg), a must if you are interested in baroque and rococo art.

ROUTE 51 – WINKLMOOS ALM TO THE STEINPLATTE (KAMMERKÖHR)

Another 9km further east visitors will find the holiday resort of Inzell less commercialised than Ruhpolding but the village itself is also less interesting. However, for a walking holiday this is not so important as the surrounding landscape is quite beautiful, and some 150km of well-maintained walking trails make it easy to explore.

Ruhpolding has a railway station (regular connections to all larger German cities) and can be reached by bus from Reit im Winkl. There are also bus connections to Inzell, Bad Reichenhall and Berchtesgaden. Ruhpolding's campsite is to the south of town at the foot of the Rauschberg (not far from the cable railway). Inzell's youth hostel is a few kilometres north of town at Panholz, whereas the campsite is to the south near Gasthof Zwing (on the B305).

VALLEY WALKS
Map: Kompass-Wanderkarte No 14.

x **AROUND THE FALKENSTEIN (2hrs)** This circular walk begins next to the *Eisstadion* (ice-skating rink) in Inzell. Walking in a clockwise direction (path no 11) head first to Burgstall (castle ruin) and then walk via the Falkensee and Gasthof Zwing back to the starting point. Shortly after Burgstall a detour can be made to the right to the Krottensee, a very pretty lake surrounded by forest. Bathing is possible in the Zwingsee, not far from the *Eisstadion*.

xi **AROUND FRILLENSEE (1½hrs)** The Frillensee is reputedly one of Central Europe's coldest lakes; it is covered by ice from November right through to April. The lake lies a few kilometres east of Inzell at the foot of the Hochstaufen (1771m). To get to it follow path no 14 from Gasthof Adlgaß. A pleasant trail circles the lake.

WALKING IN THE BAVARIAN ALPS

ROUTE 52
The Hochfelln (1671m)

Start	Staudigl Hut, near Glockenschmiede (historic bell foundry), a few kilometres south-west of Ruhpolding
Parking	At Staudigl Hut (also bus stop)
Transport	Local buses
Distance	13km/8 miles
Height gain	951m (3120ft)
Height loss	951m (3120ft)
Time	5hrs
Grade	1–2
Refreshments	Hochfelln Haus, Thorau Alm
Map	Kompass-Wanderkarte No 14: Berchtesgadener Land – Chiemgauer Alpen

The view from the Hochfelln is one of the best in the Chiemgau Alps, and in ideal conditions it is meant to encompass some 400 peaks. Unfortunately, easy access from Bergen with Germany's second-longest cable railway means that the summit is a very popular destination, so be prepared for crowds in summer. Of interest near the start of this route is a bell foundry museum.

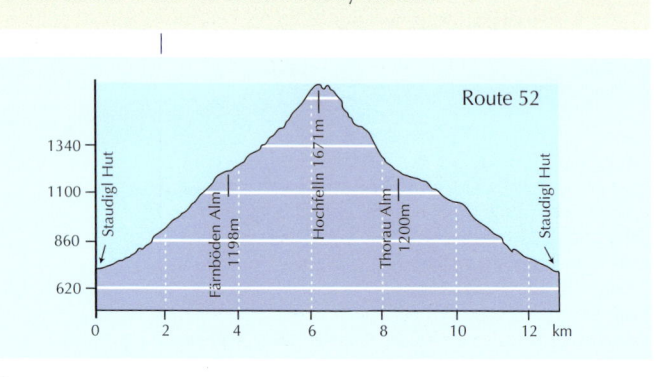

ROUTE 52 – THE HOCHFELLN

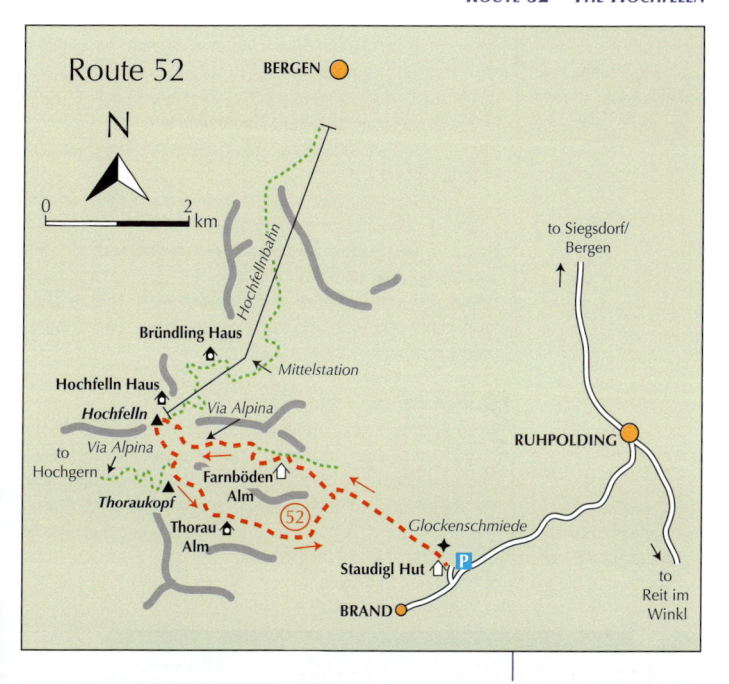

The Glockenschmiede Bell Foundry – established over 300 years ago – is one of the last of its kind in Bavaria. Apart from cowbells the foundry also produced tools such as scythes and axes. Now preserved as a museum, it ceased operation in 1955. Open: mid-May–1 July, Mon–Fri 10.00–12.00 and 14.00–16.00; 1 July–15 Sept, daily 10.00–16.00; 15 Sept–10 Oct, Mon–Fri 10.00–12.00 and 14.00–16.00.

From the car park by **Staudigl Hut** follow the asphalted road right and after roughly 400m cross a small bridge before turning left to the bell foundry. From here follow the forestry road, which runs alongside a stream, in the direction of Thorau-Hochfelln. After 1hr or so's steep uphill walking the road swings southwest. About 200m further on there is a sharp turn to the right which takes you along an access road

See also the note under Route 48 for a route linking the Hochfelln to the Hochgern.

(path 65) to **Farnböden Alm**. In another 20mins the junction with the path that climbs up from Hinterreit is reached. Continue through forest and across the pastures of Felln Alm and then climb steeply up to **Hochfelln Haus**. The imposing 7m high cross on the summit was erected in 1886 in honour of King Ludwig I. ◄

The descent route (path 66) begins by the summit chapel (Hochfellnkapelle). Go first along the Thorauschneid ridge to the hollow between the Weißgrabenkopf and Thoraukopf. The path swings southeast (right) here and soon brings you to the sprinkling of huts that mark **Thorau Alm**. From there you simply follow the alm access road through pine forest back to the starting point.

Shorter alternative route (3hrs)

From **Bergen**, a small town to the northwest of Ruhpolding, take the two-stage cable railway to the top of the Hochfelln. The route begins with a zigzag descent to **Brundling Alm** (*refreshments*) and offers plenty of fine views along the way. From the hut it is just a matter of following the clearly marked trail (No 8, Hochfellnweg) along the Schwarze Ache stream back to **Bergen**.

Brundling Alm is a good place for a snack on the route down to Bergen

ROUTE 53
The Rauschberg

Start	Ruhpolding
Parking	At Rauschbergbahn, southeast of Ruhpolding
Transport	Bus 9506 to Rauschbergbahn Talstation
Distance	9.8km/6 miles
Height gain	26m (85ft)
Height loss	982m (3222ft)
Time	3½hrs
Grade	1
Refreshments	Rauschberg Haus, Restaurant Taubensee
Map	Kompass-Wanderkarte No 14: Berchtesgadener Land – Chiemgauer Alpen

On this route the best views are at the beginning, but the walk down is not without interest, and it ends by a picturesque little lake which would be a nice picnic spot if one wishes to avoid the expense of a nearby restaurant. Apart from walkers the Rauschberg summit is also a popular starting point for hang-glider pilots (there is a hang-gliding school here), and their take-offs seem to attract as much attention as the alpine panorama. Also of interest on the summit is 'Adam's Hand', a steel sculpture over 6m high that points to Rome.

Because it is a long climb up to the top of the Rauschberg most people will probably take advantage of the cable railway. After admiring the impressive view from the summit of the Vorderer Rauschberg (1645m; 5mins stroll to summit cross) follow the alpine nature trail (Alpenlehrpfad) along the ridge to the summit of the **Hinterer Rauschberg** (Roßgassenkopf; 1671m) where, once again, there is a magnificent view. Return the same way, then turn left near a sign to the 'Jagdhütte'. This brings you down to the main walking trail. A number of paths run together here, so though our

WALKING IN THE BAVARIAN ALPS

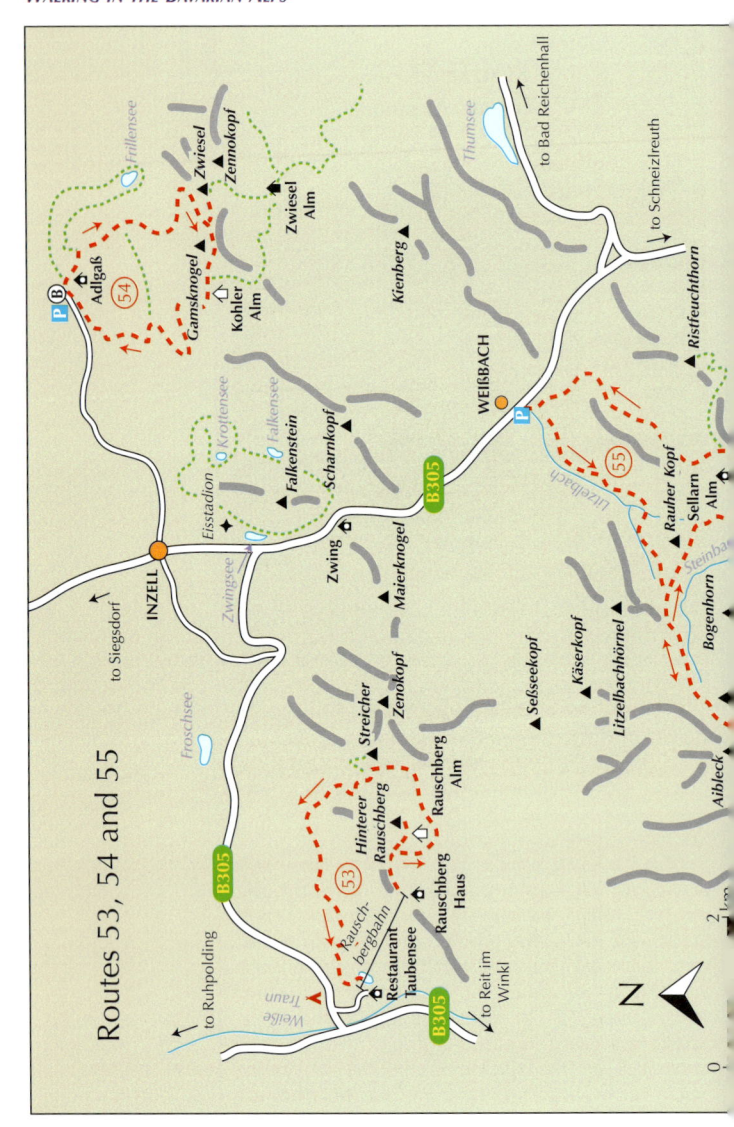

ROUTE 53 – THE RAUSCHBERG

Taubensee at the foot of the Rauschberg

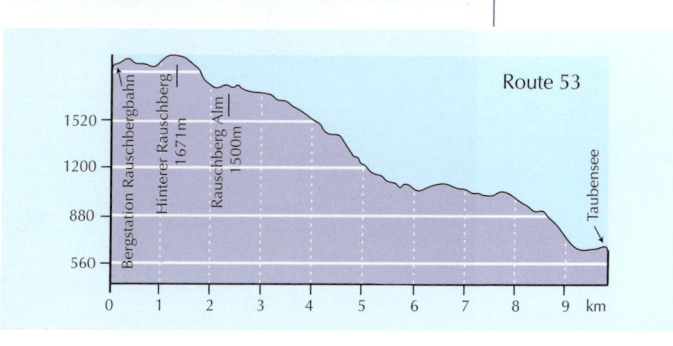

route actually follows path 2 we also follow paths 19 and 20 for a while.

From now on it is downhill all the way. The gravel road is followed in a southerly direction past the huts of **Rauschberg Alm**, after which it turns northeast. At the turn-off to the **Streicher** (signposted 'Inzeller Skihütte/Kaitelalm') it starts descending more steeply. Good views to Chiemsee on this stretch. Eventually you come to a signpost that points you left to the Rauschbergbahn and Ruhpolding. The road is fairly level here but is rather dull up to the point where it ceases and a track begins. The track descends through an attractive area of mixed forest and is a pleasant change from the hot and dusty gravel road. It brings you down to the B305 (German Alpine Road), but then forks left up to the Taubensee on path 21. From the pretty lake which lies directly at the foot of the Rauschberg it is only a short walk back to the lower station of the Rauschbergbahn.

The Zwiesel

ROUTE 54
From Inzell-Adlgaß to the Zwiesel (1782m)

Start	Adlgaß, northeast of Inzell
Parking	Next to Gasthof Adlgaß
Transport	Local buses (*Dorflinie*); for details contact tourist office in Inzell
Distance	11km/7 miles
Height gain	981m (3218ft)
Height loss	981m (3218ft)
Time	6–7hrs
Grade	3
Refreshments	Gasthof (Forsthaus) Adlgaß, Zwiesel Alm
Accommodation	Zwiesel Alm
Map	Kompass-Wanderkarte No 14: Berchtesgadener Land – Chiemgauer Alpen

Breathtaking views over the Inzell Valley, Chiemsee, Berchtesgaden Alps, Chiemgau Alps and Kaisergebirge are the reward for this strenuous ascent of the Zwiesel. **Note** The crossing between the Zwiesel and Gamsknogel is not for the inexperienced.

From **Gasthof Adlgaß** follow waymark 24 southeast, climbing all the while, to a forest road. Cross it, continue a short distance further south and, after crossing another road, start climbing more steeply along a forested ridge. Eventually the track curves to the east, allowing a view down on to the Frillensee, before swinging right to the saddle between the Gamsknogel and Zwiesel. A rocky path climbs up to the **Zwiesel**'s summit which is reached in around 15mins. ▶ Those who wish to avoid the crossing between Gamsknogel and Kohler Alm can continue southeast to the **Zennokopf** (1756m) and then follow the track down to **Zwiesel Alm** (Kaiser-Wilhelm-Haus; 1386m). From there follow path 23 around the western flanks of the Hinterstaufen and up to **Kohler Alm** (1450m).

At 1782m it is the highest point on the Hochstaufen massif.

WALKING IN THE BAVARIAN ALPS

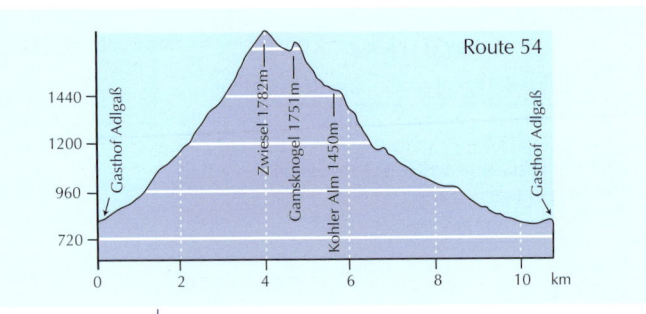

Walkers who feel they can manage a bit of easy scrambling and who have a head for heights can retrace their steps to the saddle and reach **Kohler Alm** via the **Gamsknogel** (1751m).

From the alm follow path 23 downhill through forest and, just before arriving at Einsiedl, turn right along path 31 to **Adlgaß**.

ROUTE 55
The Aibleck (1756m)

Start	Weißbach, south of Inzell on B305
Parking	Car park off the Sägmühlweg
Transport	Bus 9526 from Inzell to Weißbach
Distance	18.2km/11 miles
Height gain	1149m (3769ft)
Height loss	1149m (3769ft)
Time	6½hrs
Grade	2–3
Refreshments	Restaurants in Weißbach, Sellarn Alm
Map	Kompass-Wanderkarte No 14: Berchtesgadener Land – Chiemgauer Alpen

ROUTE 55 – THE AIBLECK

> No huts offering accommodation, no cable cars, no crowds! It can get a bit lonely on this long but interesting route to the Aibleck, a peak which lies in the shadow of its higher neighbour the Sonntagshorn. Most people who want to climb the latter do it from the Austrian side, as the ascent route from the Heutal is quite easy and takes no more than 3hrs. This route, on the other hand, requires rather more stamina and a degree of pathfinding ability as the way is a little unclear at one point. **Note** A good map is essential.

Coming from the direction of Inzell drive past Gasthof Stabach in **Weißbach** and then turn off to the right along Sägmühlweg. A short distance further down the road turn right again, over a bridge, and you will come to a small parking area.

From the car park go left over another small bridge, walk a short distance along a gravel road, then turn right along a trail that leads up into the woods (signposted 'Sonntagshorn'). The path gradually becomes narrower and after roughly 1hr it crosses the Litzelbach stream. From here it gets steeper and the scenery wilder. Some parts of the track, which edges its way along what is an occasionally precipitous slope, are very narrow indeed and require extra care. After a while you arrive at a dead-end gravel road. This is where the track forks right and uphill to the Aibleck and Sonntagshorn (signposted 'Sonntagshorn').

From now on the route gradually takes on more of an alpine character as it penetrates deeper into the Unzental (Unzen Valley). After climbing steadily through the woods

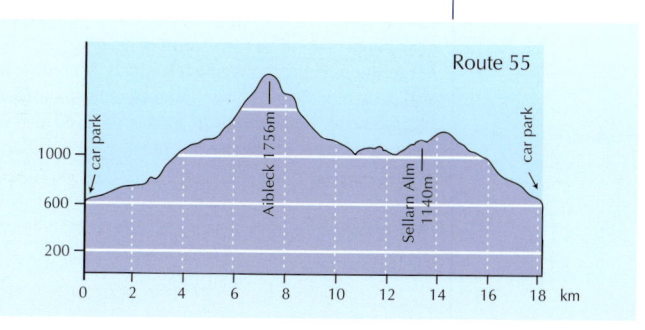

Care is needed here if the bridge is very wet and certainly if it is icy.

for a while you come to a simple wooden footbridge over a small waterfall. ◄ A short distance further on wire ropes secure a particularly exposed section of track – this does not present any real problems. After negotiating a few more slightly tricky stretches (where the path may be washed away) a large grassy clearing is reached near the valley's end. This is quite an idyllic, if isolated, spot and a good place to rest before completing the final stretch to the Aibleck which, together with the Ochsenhorn, dominates the view to the southwest.

From the clearing the track climbs back into the woods and then crosses rocky slopes covered by dwarf pines. It is now a very steep climb along a narrow, rocky path to the saddle between the Aibleck and Ochsenkopf. Once it is reached the views are great. Especially impressive is the vast, bare rock pyramid of the Sonntagshorn (1961m) to the southwest (another 2hrs, only for the experienced). The summit of the **Aibleck** is reached by turning right and climbing up through a corridor of dwarf pines. Return the same way to turn off at the gravel road.

Though the route to **Sellarn Alm** is not signposted or waymarked here it is simply a matter of following the road (nice views into the valley) to where it bends sharply downhill. The road to the alm branches left and uphill, just before the bend. You should see a red rectangle with a white bar above and below as a waymark along here. At the alm it is possible to buy fresh milk (*frische Milch*) and simple snacks in summer.

The track continues steeply uphill through pastures, but levels out once it enters the woods. After a short while the turn-off to the Ristfeuchthorn is reached, and the very energetic could climb it in 1½hrs. Most of us, however, will turn left in the direction of **Weißbach** which, according to the sign, is no more than 1hr away. The rest of the route is downhill, following for the most part another unpaved road which leads directly back to the starting point.

A narrow section of track on the Aibleck route

WALKING IN THE BAVARIAN ALPS

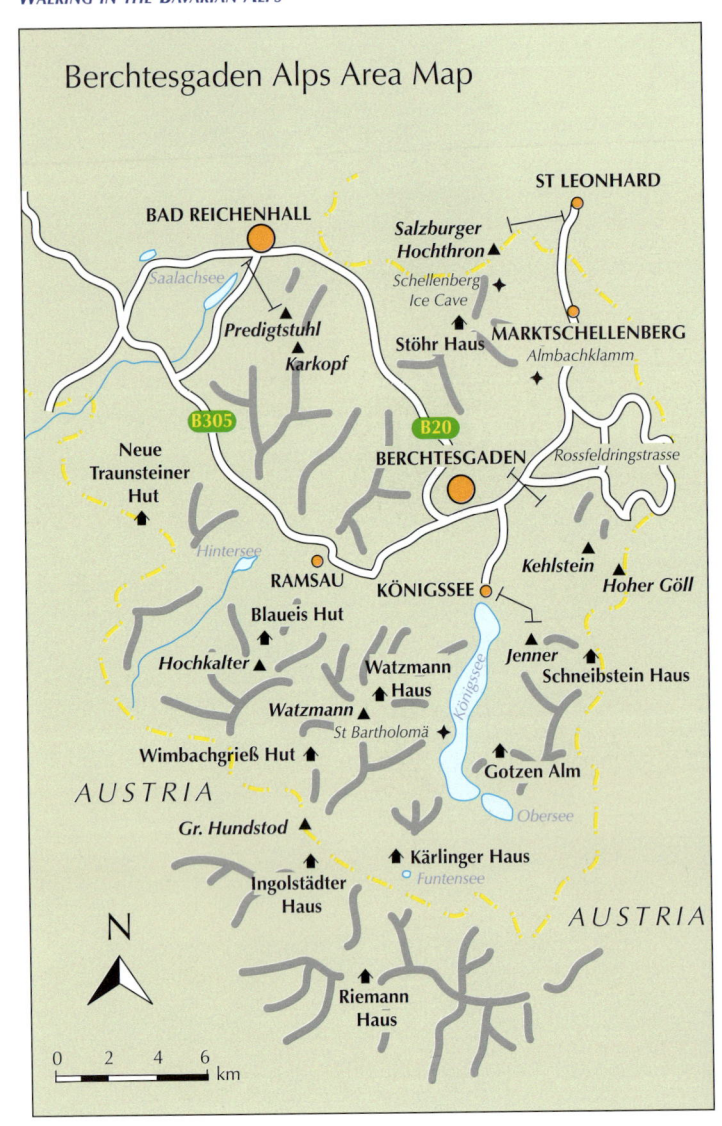

Berchtesgaden Alps Area Map

The Wimbach Valley (Route 60)

PART VI
THE BERCHTESGADEN ALPS

PART VI
THE BERCHTESGADEN ALPS

The Berchtesgadener Alpen are situated between the rivers Saalach and Salzach and are part of a very popular tourist region known as Berchtesgadener Land. Looking at a map this small, triangular corner of Bavaria seems to thrust its way into Austria like an outstretched tongue, greedy for more of the alpine grandeur it has already tasted. Among the highest peaks are the Watzmann, Hochkalter, Hoher Göll and Hocheisspitze, all of which are well over 2000m. But above all it is the Watzmann – at 2713m the second-highest mountain in Germany – that captures the imagination of most visitors. Its characteristic, pleasingly symmetrical form dominates the landscape with a kind of Wagnerian grandeur that has certainly helped to make the Berchtesgaden region the most visited in the Bavarian Alps. Days out in this picture-postcard landscape will be counted among the highlights of any walking tour to Germany.

Picture-postcard view of Ramsau church, with the Reiteralpe in the background

That so much beauty needs protection is almost a truism in this age of mass tourism and the exploitation of nature. Several of the routes described in this section take place within Berchtesgaden National Park, formed in 1978 to replace an earlier nature reserve around Königssee. Here nature is left to itself (very rare in the Alps, where the commercial interests of ski-lift operators and hotel proprietors usually come first). Within the park plants and animals are strictly protected, and visitors are asked not to leave the walking trails or drop litter. For more information visit the Nationalpark-Haus Berchtesgaden at Franziskanerplatz 7 in Berchtesgaden (tel: 08652 64343). It is open daily 09.00–17.00.

PART VI – THE BERCHTESGADEN ALPS

BAD REICHENHALL
Tourist office: Tourist-Info Bad Reichenhall, Wittelsbacherstr. 15, D-83435 Bad Reichenhall.
Tel: (08651) 606 151,
fax: (08651) 606 133, website:
***www.bad-reichenhall.de**,*
e-mail: info@bad-reichenhall.de

A prosperous spa town in the Saalach Valley, Bad Reichenhall was already important in Roman times because of its rich salt deposits. Though the salt trade brought the town great wealth in the Middle Ages there is not much to be seen from this period as many of the older buildings were destroyed by devastating fires that have ravaged the town so often in the past. Worth visiting are some fine old churches such as St Aegidien and St Nikolaus, as well as the Münster St Zeno (the largest Romanesque church in Bavaria) with its interesting cloister. In view of the importance of salt in the town's history the Alte Saline (old saltworks) also justifies a visit. Just across the border the Austrian city of Salzburg offers all the museums and historical sights that one could wish for, and a visit is an excellent way to while away a rainy day.

The Saltworks Museum in Bad Reichenhall is worth a visit on rest days

Bad Reichenhall is quickly reached on the A8 motorway from Munich, or the B305 (German Alpine Road) from Ruhpolding and Inzell. The town has a railway station and campsite.

VALLEY WALKS
Map: Kompass-Wanderkarte No 14.

xii **AROUND THE THUMSEE (2½hrs)** From the centre of Bad Reichenhall make your way to the Kretabrücke (Kreta Bridge) which takes you across the River Saalach to the suburb of Karlstein (pick up a free map from the tourist office). Now follow Schmalschlägerstrasse to the St-Pankratius-Kirche (a baroque church) and the ruins of Karlstein Castle (Ruine Karlstein). The climb up to the castle ruins is worth it as there are good views at the top. After visiting the castle continue southwest along Schmalschlägerstrasse, then turn right through a patch of woods to reach the path that descends to Gasthof Madlbauer on the shores of the Thumsee. Follow the path around the lake to the car park near the pretty *Seerosenteich* (water-lily pond). Cross the road, pass the pond, then go via Seebichl along the Soleleitungsweg (Old Saltwater Pipeline Trail) to Amalienruh. A path leads from here back to town.

ROUTE 56
The Lattengebirge (Predigtstuhl)

Start	Bad Reichenhall
Parking	Next to cable railway (Predigtstuhlbahn)
Transport	Bus 841 from bus stop 'Sellboden' to Bad Reichenhall
Distance	7.8km/5 miles
Height gain	131m (430ft)
Height loss	1060m (3477ft)
Time	4hrs
Grade	2
Refreshments	Predigtstuhl Hotel, Gasthof Schlegelmulde
Accommodation	Predigtstuhl Hotel
Map	Kompass-Wanderkarte No 14: Berchtesgadener Land – Chiemgauer Alpen

The ride up in the cable car is quite dramatic – especially the last section where it scales the jagged cliffs just below the upper station. However, it is with a feeling of relief that many of the passengers leave the tiny cabin in which (usually crammed like sardines) they have been hanging over the abyss, all faith pinned on what seems to be an impossibly thin steel cable and German engineering skill. With both feet on terra firma the scenery glimpsed on the way up can be appreciated at greater leisure, but as the views get even better further on it is just as well to continue along an easy trail in the direction of the Hochschlegel.

The trail leads quickly to **Gasthof Schlegelmulde** which, on warm sunny days, seems to be a favourite spot for sunbathers. From here the path winds its way up to the cross at the top of the **Hochschlegel** where there is usually a crowd of walkers enjoying the panorama. More often than not one is also joined by several Alpine choughs, inquisitive black crow-like birds with bright yellow bills that have long since

ROUTE 56 – THE LATTENGEBIRGE (PREDIGTSTUHL)

learned that scavenging titbits from alpine tourists is much easier than hunting for their own food.

Continuing southeast the summit of the **Karkopf** is reached along a path that branches off the main route and climbs fairly steeply up slopes covered by dwarf pines. At the

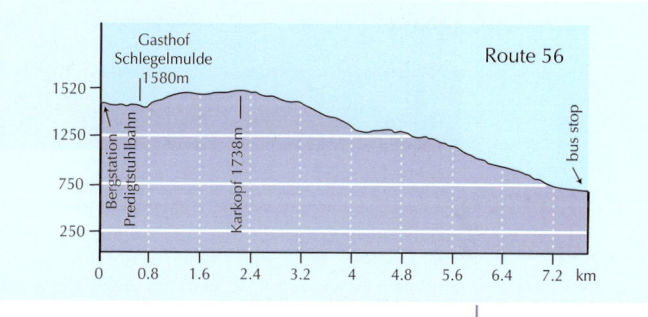

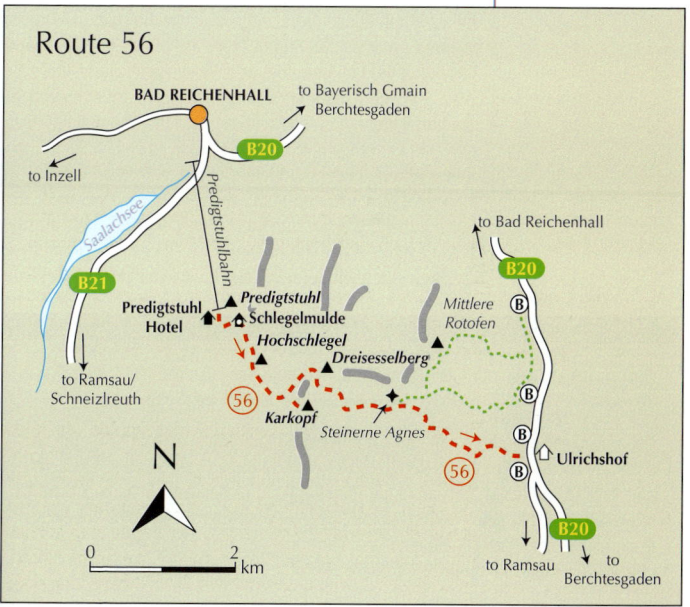

The Hochstaufen from the Lattengebirge

top there are views across to the Berchtesgadener Hochthron, the Reiteralpe, Watzmann and Hochkalter. Return to where you turned off, then go right in the direction of the **Dreisesselberg**. The detour to the top of this peak takes 5–10mins. Otherwise the path descends steeply into a rocky, scree-filled basin directly below the precipitous east face of the Karkopf. For the rest of the descent the path (477) goes through open woodland but there are plenty of clear views towards the Hagengebirge and Watzmann along the way. After passing a bizarre-looking rock formation known as **Steinerne Agnes** you soon arrive at a fork. The quickest way down to the valley is to continue along path 477. At the bottom a paved access road leads to the main road where you turn right (at **Ulrichshof**) and after walking only a short distance arrive at the bus stop for Bad Reichenhall – on the same side of the road as the railway line. There is a phone box nearby if you want to catch a taxi back to town (another 9km).

RAMSAU

*Tourist office: Haus des Gastes, Im Tal 2, D-83486 Ramsau. Tel: (08657) 9889-20, fax: (08657) 772; website: **www.ramsau.de**, e-mail: info@ramsau.de*

The photograph of the small church in Ramsau, preferably in autumn, with the dramatic rock wall of the Reiteralpe rising behind it, has graced more calendars and tourist brochures than anybody might care to remember. A visual cliché it might be, but that takes nothing away from the pleasure of regarding the scene *in situ*. It is the scenic beauty of the surroundings that recommends Ramsau above all else, and autumn is certainly one of the nicest times to be here.

ROUTE 56 – THE LATTENGEBIRGE (PREDIGTSTUHL)

There is plenty of accommodation in the village and also around the Hintersee, an idyllic lake a few kilometres further west. The closest campsite is northwest, off the B305, at Vordersimon. Ramsau can be reached by bus from Berchtesgaden.

VALLEY WALKS

Map: Kompass-Wanderkarte No 14.

xiii **THE ZAUBERWALD (Enchanted Wood)** This pleasant stroll through the Zauberwald takes about 1hr. Park at the large car park near the eastern shore of the Hintersee. From the souvenir kiosk on the lake shore walk (northeast) through the woods fringing the lake until you come to a sign pointing right in the direction of Wirtshaus Zauberwald. Eventually you will come to a small bridge about 200m before the Wirtshaus. Follow the sign 'Zauberwald' right and continue uphill into the woods. The track gets prettier and prettier the further you walk. Once the stretch of track that runs next to the Ramsauer Ache stream is reached you are walking through a picturesque landscape strewn with moss-covered boulders and shaded by beautiful deciduous forest. There are plenty of opportunities to sit and enjoy the scenery along the way. The well-maintained path soon brings you back to the kiosk. Those who want to extend this walk could also consider circling the lake, which would take another 1hr. **Note** The Zauberwald has been recently declared one the 100 loveliest geotopes (a place of geological significance) in Bavaria.

xiv **THE MALERWEG (Artist's Trail; 1½–3hrs)** Commemorated here are the many 19th-century artists who were inspired by the fabulous mountain scenery around Ramsau. They included such well-known German landscape artists as Ferdinand Waldmüller, Carl Rottman and Hubert von Herkomer. A fascinating feature of the walk is that at the various stations you can compare a copy of one of their paintings to the scene as it is today. The circular walk begins at the Neuhausenbrücke (bridge) in Ramsau, then continues west to the lovely lake of Hintersee from where it returns to the starting point. The entire route requires about 3hrs, though there are a number of possibilities for shortening it. A detailed map of the route is available from Ramsau's tourist information.

xv **THE SALZHANDELSWEG (Salt Trade Path; 1½–2½hrs)** In long bygone days this trail was on an important trade route from Berchtesgaden via the Hirschbichl Pass to the Pinzgau in Austria. It starts from the Berchtesgaden National Park information office at the southwestern end of Hintersee.

Walk a short distance along the Hirschbichl road into the valley, then turn left onto the Adlerweg (Eagle's Trail, path 481). This trail is followed until it joins the road again near Bind Alm. At the alm there are refreshments, and you can now either return the same way or (recommended) continue over the Hirschbichlpass to Weißbach in the Pinzgau. This allows you to follow the Route der Klammen (Gorge Route) via Gasthof Lohfeyer into the beautiful Seisenbergklamm (gorge). Instead of walking you can return to Hintersee with the Wanderbus Hirschbichl. It runs daily mid-May–mid-Oct 08.00–16.30. Check times beforehand!

ROUTE 57
To the Alm Meadows above Ramsau

Start	Ramsau
Parking	In Ramsau
Transport	Local buses
Distance	12.2km/7.5 miles
Height gain	841m (2759ft)
Height loss	629m (2063ft)
Time	5–6hrs
Grade	2
Refreshments	Wirtshaus Wachterl
Map	Kompass-Wanderkarte No 14: Berchtesgadener Land – Chiemgauer Alpen

Much of the Bavarian Alps would have a very different aspect were it not for the farmers who make a modest living grazing their cattle on the high meadows of the surrounding mountains. Along with the periodic mowing of the grass for hay, only the grazing of dairy cows prevents the natural reversion of the delightful wildflower-covered grassy slopes to forest. The absence of the cows would mean the loss of something that is considered typical of this part of the Alps. They are the subject of innumerable postcards, and the tinkling of cowbells is a familiar sound to anyone who spends time here.

ROUTE 57 – TO THE ALM MEADOWS ABOVE RAMSAU

The following route takes you through the alm pastures above Ramsau and into scenery that is, in many ways, typical not only for Berchtesgaden but also for many other areas mentioned in this guidebook. Those who read German will be able to learn more about mountain farming from the information boards along the trail; for others the beautiful landscapes are reward enough.

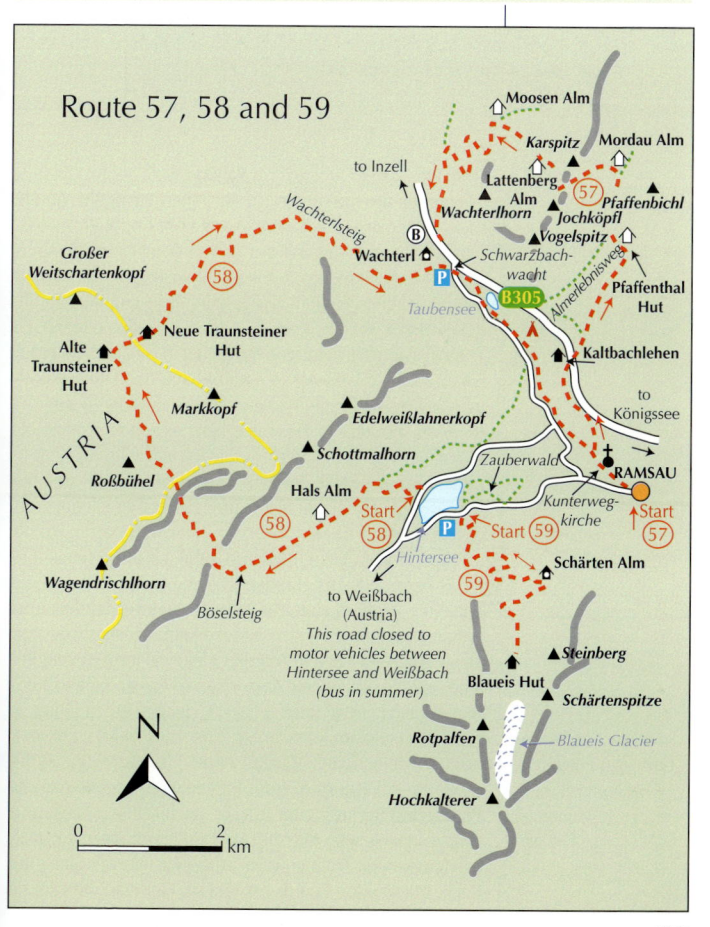

WALKING IN THE BAVARIAN ALPS

Route 57

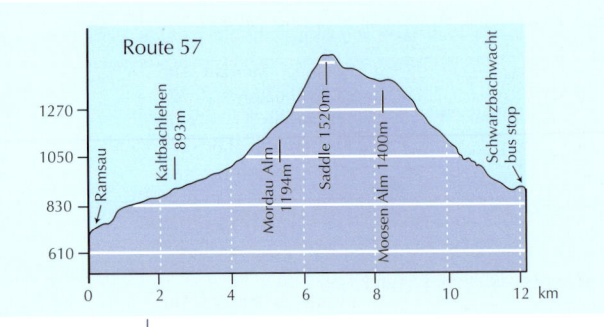

Elevation profile showing: Ramsau, Kaltbachlehen 893m, Mordau Alm 1194m, Saddle 1520m, Moosen Alm 1400m, Schwarzbachwacht bus stop — over approximately 12 km.

From the Gasthof Oberwirt in **Ramsau** walk a short distance west along the main road 'Im Tal', then turn right, off the road, and follow a track that leads uphill through woods. This pilgrimage trail, known as the Kunterweg, passes a small chapel on its way to the Kunterwegkirche. Pause for a look at the church's attractive interior, then continue uphill, past a track which branches left along the Lattenbach stream. The trail soon widens into a paved access road, which leaves the woods to pass through fields strewn with wildflowers in spring. An imposing panorama of the surrounding mountains is revealed here and confirms that this region belongs to the loveliest that the Bavarian Alps has to offer. A short while later the small alm road (still the Kunterweg) connects with the Deutsche Alpenstraße (German Alpine Road).

The route now turns left and follows the Alpenstrasse as far as **Pension Kaltbachlehen** (*lodgings*). At this point you leave the Alpenstrasse and follow an alm road that runs uphill opposite the pension and the Kaltbachlehen bus stop. This signposted route to Mordau Alm runs through pastureland dotted with grazing dairy cows in the spring and summer months. In a short while a signposted junction is reached (1hr from Ramsau). ◄ This route bears right, in a northerly direction to Mordau Alm (1¼hrs according to the sign). Near a group of buildings marked on the map as **Pfaffenthal** the trail climbs right, up into the woods, and soon connects with the 'official' Alm-Erlebnisweg en route to Mordau Alm. From now on, at regular intervals along the track, information boards explain (in German) the various

> The left branch heads northwest to Schwarzbachwacht via Taubensee (45mins).

ROUTE 57 – TO THE ALM MEADOWS ABOVE RAMSAU

aspects of dairy farming in alpine regions and also give details on the alpine environment.

Continuing uphill the meadows of **Mordau Alm** (1194m) are soon reached. Near the first buildings a small track branches left, off the alm road in the direction of Lattenberg Alm and Moosen Alm. It climbs first above and roughly parallel to the alm (slightly northwest) but then swings sharp left (southwest) to climb steeply up to the saddle between the Jochköpfl and Karspitz. Most of the climb goes through forest, and once at the top it is an easy downhill walk to **Lattenberg Alm** (1460m). From here a short stretch through forest brings you down to **Moosen Alm** (1400m). ▸

> In the pastures around here you will notice circular, funnel-shaped depressions (dolines) where the underlying limestone rock has dissolved and subsided.

Moosen Alm is one of the few remaining examples of the so-called Rundumkaser, the oldest form of *Kaser* (as the alm huts in the Berchtesgaden region are known). In this type of hut the windowless living area is surrounded by the stall. Those living in the hut profited from the warmth provided by the animals, but only an opening in the roof provided a minimum of light for the gloomy interior.

The onward route is signposted 'Wachterl' (path 470, T9 on map), and the wide gravel road in the vicinity of the alm soon narrows to a rocky mountain trail. This stretch of

Wayside altar and meadows at the top of the Kunterweg from Ramsau

the route is particularly scenic, with magnificent views down into the valley below and across to the Reiteralpe massif on the opposite side. At the signposted turn-off to Anthaupten-Alm the trail widens again to a comfortable gravel road. Do not go right to Anthaupten-Alm but continue left and downhill to Schwarzbachwacht (not signposted). It's now plain sailing all the way down to the German Alpine Road near **Wirtshaus Wachterl**. Here it is possible to catch the bus back to **Ramsau** (check timetables beforehand). Otherwise, continue past Taubensee and the camping ground and then follow the Alte Reichenhaller Strasse, a minor road, towards Hintersee and Ramsau. A short distance after crossing the Triebenbachstrasse (telephone booth at the intersection) leave the Reichenhaller Strasse along a track on the left. This trail runs along a pretty stretch of the Lattenbach stream, past the Kunterwegkirche and back to the starting point in town.

ROUTE 58

The Reiteralpe Massif: Hintersee to Neue Traunsteiner Hut

Start	Hintersee
Parking	Car park near Gasthof Alpenhof
Transport	Bus 845 from Ramsau to Hintersee
Distance	15.5km/9.5 miles
Height gain	1241m (4071ft)
Height loss	1153m (3783ft)
Time	8½–10hrs (2 days)
Grade	2–3
Refreshments	Neue Traunsteiner Hut
Accommodation	Neue Traunsteiner Hut
Map	Kompass-Wanderkarte No 14: Berchtesgadener Land – Chiemgauer Alpen

ROUTE 58 – THE REITERALPE MASSIF: HINTERSEE TO NEUE TRAUNSTEINER HUT

The Reiteralpe massif consists of an expansive karst plateau fringed by steep and, especially to the south, often precipitous slopes. Whereas the formidable rock faces and peaks – Großes Mühlsturzhorn (2234m), the Grundübelhörner (2096m) – to the south are the domain of skilled rock climbers the northern regions are a paradise for both mountain walkers and the botanically minded. Especially worth mentioning are the rare cembra pines (*Pinus cembra*), ancient trees that can live to be over 1000 years old. They grow at altitudes of up to 2500m and their seeds, like those of some other pines, are edible. The soft wood is prized for furniture and carving, but these days anything made from cembra would probably cost a small fortune.

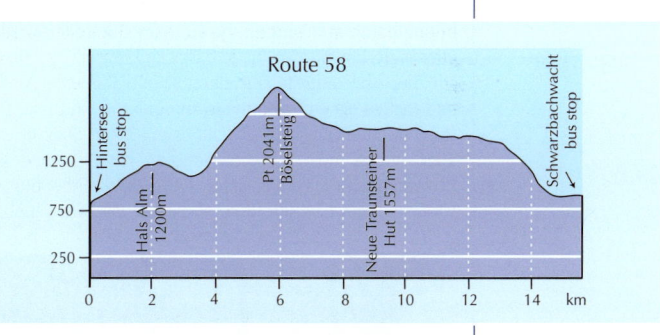

This ascent of the Reiteralpe massif begins at the bus stop near the CVJM hostel (German equivalent of YMCA; tel: [08657] 98 870) in Hintersee. A narrow path (signposted Hals Alm) leads uphill from the road and takes you northwest to the edge of the woods and a good trail that climbs easily through mixed forest. Gradually the trail gets steeper and after about 1hr reaches a meadow from where you have an unimpeded view over Ramsau and its surroundings. The next goal of the tour, the picturesquely situated **Hals Alm**, is clearly visible on a grassy saddle below the Halskopf (1285m). From Hals Alm (1200m) the trail continues without climbing for a short while, but then loses about 100m in altitude as it descends into the Halsgrube.

This is where the first really strenuous climb begins as the path winds steeply upwards through scree and rock. The fixed wire ropes of the Böselsteig then guide you quickly over two exposed rock faces. This is the most difficult stretch of the route, but it can be mastered in not much more than 10mins. Leaving the Böselsteig behind the trail now crosses a small depression, starts climbing again and then after one more steep ascent reaches the high plateau of the Reiteralpe.

The direct route to the hut is through the Steinberggasse: at first descend in a northwesterly direction through rocky terrain into a sparsely vegetated valley. Follow the gently undulating trail to the meadows of Reiter Alm (1500m) and continue on what is now a level path to first the old and then the new **Traunsteiner Huts**. Both offer accommodation (only for groups in Alte Traunsteiner Hut) but only the 'new' hut on the German side of the border offers refreshments.

The best route for the descent into the valley is the trail (path 470) going northeast through the Saugasse. The steep descent down the Wachterlsteig is not difficult and after, at the most, 3hrs you should have reached the Schwarzbachwacht bus stop. Either catch the bus to Hintersee or follow the route of the old saltwater pipeline

Passage through snow near Neue Traunsteiner Hut

(Soleleitung) for another 1½hrs until, shortly before **Ramsau**, you join the König-Max-Weg which takes you back to the lake and your departure point.

Excursions from Neue Traunsteiner Hut
Those who are prepared to stay a few nights will find that the Neue Traunsteiner Hut makes a good base for exploring the Reiteralpe. Among the peaks worth climbing from here are the Großer Weitschartenkopf (1980m), Wagendrischlhorn (2253m) and Edelweißlahnerkopf (1953m).

ROUTE 59
The Hochkalter Massif: Ramsau to Blaueis Hut

Start	Hintersee
Parking	Seeklause car park (just before the Hintersee)
Transport	Bus 846 to Hintersee from Berchtesgaden and Ramsau
Distance	5km/3 miles (one way)
Height gain	891m (2923ft)
Height loss	891m (2923ft)
Time	4hrs
Grade	2
Refreshments	Schärten Alm, Blaueis Hut
Accommodation	Blaueis Hut
Map	Kompass-Wanderkarte No 14: Berchtesgadener Land – Chiemgauer Alpen

Apart from beautiful mountain scenery another attraction of this route is the Blaueis glacier. Though it is only about 1km long and 300m wide it can claim the distinction of being the northernmost glacier in the Alps. If you study the ice carefully you should be able to make out some reddish patches. These are caused by a species of algae which thrives nearly all over the world in the seemingly hostile environment of glacial ice.

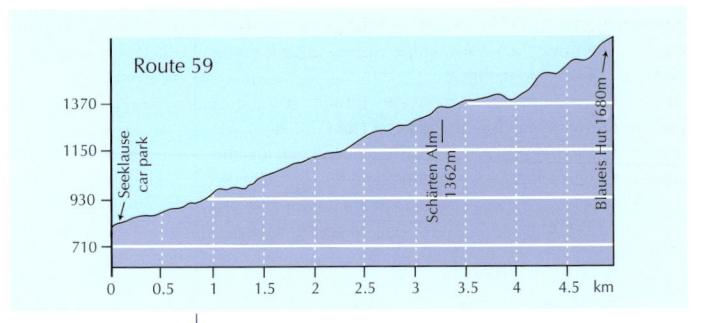

WALKING IN THE BAVARIAN ALPS

Route 59

Elevation profile: Seeklause car park to Blaueis Hut 1680m, via Schärten Alm 1362m. Distances 0 to 4.5km; elevations 710, 930, 1150, 1370m.

From the large car park situated at the edge of the woods start walking uphill along path 482. This forest path soon gives way to a gravel and dirt road which continues up to Schärten Alm. At one point on the way up there is a magnificent view over the Hintersee with the Reiteralpe in the background. At **Schärten Alm** (1362m) there is a rustic old wooden hut where you can stop for refreshments and enjoy the wonderful views. It is a lovely spot with a great deal of the charm that is sometimes missing at the larger mountain huts.

Continue along the trail which remains level for a short distance before descending somewhat to a point where it curves sharply to the left. The view around the corner is breathtaking. You are suddenly confronted with the craggy

Blaueis Hut

alpine majesty of the Hochkalter and the glistening white tongue of snow and ice below it: the Blaueis (Blue Ice) glacier. The trail starts climbing again and eventually you reach steps which climb even more steeply through a stand of larch to the beautifully situated **Blaueis Hut** (1680m). From the hut it is about 40mins up to the edge of the glacier. ▶ Return the same way.

Do not venture onto the glacier (crevasses!) unless you are properly equipped and have the necessary experience on snow and ice.

ROUTE 60
Wimbachklamm, Wimbachtal and Wimbachgrieß Hut

Start	Wimbach Bridge (Wimbachbrücke; on main road between Berchtesgaden and Ramsau)
Parking	At Wimbach Bridge
Transport	Bus 846 to bridge from Ramsau or Berchtesgaden
Distance	8.5km/5 miles (one way)
Height gain	700m (2296ft)
Height loss	700m (2296ft)
Time	4hrs
Grade	1
Refreshments	Wimbachschloss, Wimbachgrieß Hut
Accommodation	Wimbachgrieß Hut
Map	Kompass-Wanderkarte No 14: Berchtesgadener Land – Chiemgauer Alpen

This deservedly popular route allows anybody who is modestly fit to experience the beauty of the Berchtesgaden Alps at close quarters. There are plenty of benches on which to relax along the way, as well as lots of nice picnic spots. Start early in the morning, especially in summer, to avoid the afternoon heat and the largest crowds.

> There is also a path to the right which bypasses the *Klamm*.

From the car park near the **Wimbach Bridge** walk up a paved road past meadows and a few houses to the *Klamm* entrance. ◄

The entrance fee is quite modest, and although it does not take much more than 15mins to walk the *Klamm* it is worth it. From high above numerous waterfalls splash their way down the gorge's mossy green walls, while from the safety of the boardwalk you can look down onto the roaring torrent of water as it squeezes its way through a corset of stone. The overall effect is as picturesque as it is impressive. Keep your tickets because if you come back the same way you may need to show them.

Once you leave the *Klamm* continue along the river on a very gently climbing path. The valley has a quite idyllic aspect, and in the distance you can already see the jagged alpine peaks which mark the end of the Wimbachtal and this route. Not long after what is marked on the map as

The Wimbach roars and splashes its way through the Wimbachklamm

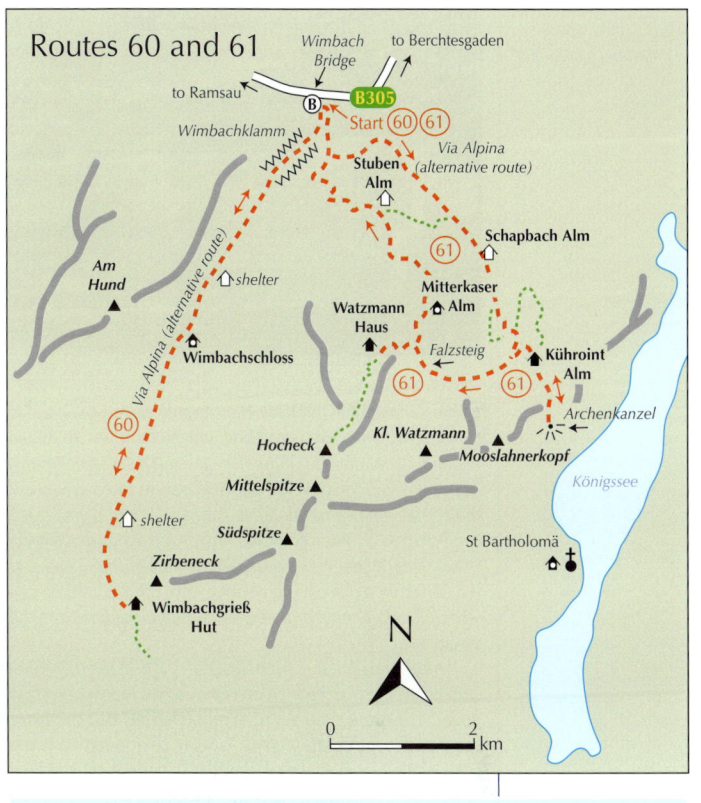

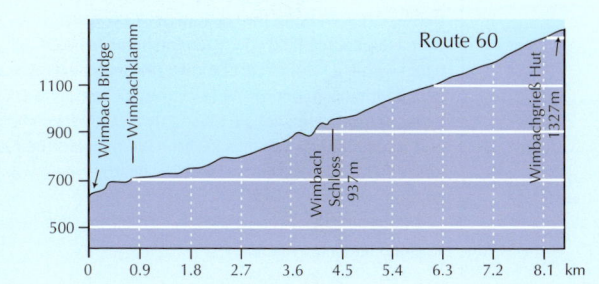

ROUTE 60 – WIMBACHKLAMM, WIMBACHTAL AND WIMBACHGRIEß HUT

Wimbachgrieß Hut

Unterstandshütte (shelter) the stream disappears to be replaced by a vast dry gravel bed which continues up to and beyond the **Wimbachschloss**. The going is a bit steeper now, but as the trail remains for the most part in open woodland there is at least some shade. Before you know it you reach the Schloss, a rather grandiose name for what is a simple restaurant (once a hunting lodge). However, many will find it a convenient place to pause for a cool drink. Children can work off excess energy in the small playground next to the restaurant.

After the Wimbachschloss the path starts climbing somewhat more steeply again but it is still reasonably easy going. The closer you get to **Wimbachgrieß Hut** the more spectacular the scenery gets. Especially impressive is the view of the Hochkalter to your right; in spring you can hear and see the avalanches roaring down its bare, precipitous flanks. After walking through an area of dwarf pines and over a large scree field you reach the hut. It is beautifully situated within a semi-circle of mountains with the Hochkalter massif forming an impressive backdrop to the northwest. The tables in front of the hut are invariably crowded with hungry and thirsty hikers. For those who have brought their own lunch there is a large grassy meadow nearby where you can picnic.

Returning the same way it takes about 1½–2hrs (without stops) to reach the *Klamm*.

ROUTE 61
Kühroint Alm (Watzmann Haus and Hocheck)

Start	Wimbach Bridge (Wimbachbrücke) on the road from Berchtesgaden to Ramsau
Parking	At Wimbach Bridge
Transport	Bus 846 to bridge from Ramsau or Berchtesgaden
Distance	15.7km/9.5 miles
Height gain	1303m (4275ft)
Height loss	1303m (4275ft)
Time	4½hrs
Grade	1
Refreshments	Kühroint Alm, (Watzmann Haus)
Accommodation	Kühroint Alm, (Watzmann Haus)
Map	Kompass-Wanderkarte No 14: Berchtesgadener Land – Chiemgauer Alpen

The most characteristic and imposing mountain formation in the Berchtesgaden Alps is the mighty Watzmann massif, and during this route to Kühroint Alm there are plenty of opportunities to admire it at close quarters. An additional highlight is the picture-postcard view over Königssee from the Archenkanzel viewpoint – absolutely magnificent!

From the car park near the **Wimbach Bridge** (Wimbachbrücke; 624m) cross the Wimbach stream, then follow the signpost 'Kührointalm' which points you uphill along a path through the woods. You soon reach a gravel road (closed to private vehicles) which is now followed to the alm. Although the road is fringed by forest it would be a hot walk in summer, so it is advisable to get an early start. The first few kilometres are not all that exciting and you climb steadily, but not too steeply, all the way. Your first decent view of the Watzmann is by the Diensthütte (service

WALKING IN THE BAVARIAN ALPS

hut; 988m), where a couple of benches are provided. It is better to save your first refreshment stop for **Schapbach Alm** (1040m) about 600m further on, as the view of the Watzmann massif from here is even more impressive. At the alm it is sometimes possible to buy fresh milk.

The next stretch of the route up to **Kühroint Alm** (1420m; waymark 442) is rather steep, so it pays to make sure that there is something to drink in your backpack. The reward for the sweaty climb is another impressive view of the Watzmann and perhaps a snack at the hut – there is also an information office for Berchtesgaden National Park. ◄

An excursion to the viewpoint **Archenkanzel** (1346m) is worthwhile; 15–20mins walk from the alm, with a fabulous view over the Königssee.

To get back to the Wimbach Bridge either return the same way (quickest) or turn left (west) at the Diensthütte and follow path 444 via **Stuben Alm** (1203m). **Note** The latter adds 1km to the route and involves climbing again.

To Watzmann Haus (6–7hrs)

For those who would like to turn the above into a longer and more challenging route (Grade 3) it is worth considering the climb up to Watzmann Haus from **Kühroint Alm**. The route (path 442) is quite easy going at first. Walk along a mountain slope through woods (lots of larches, very picturesque in autumn) until you come to some cliffs below and within view of Watzmann Haus, which is perched high above. This is where the only really difficult bit of the walk begins. To get up to the hut you must first ascend the cliffs along the so-called Falzsteig. The Steig (a steep mountain track) is very narrow, but the ascent is made fairly safe by wire ropes which are fastened into the rock. Although it is quite short

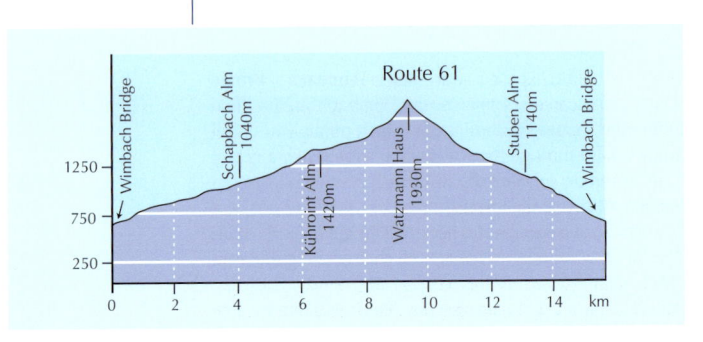

ROUTE 61 – KÜHROINT ALM (WATZMANN HAUS AND HOCHECK)

The Watzmann massif from Schönau (near Königssee)

and not unduly exposed, it does require some care and a reasonable degree of agility in steep rocky terrain. The inexperienced should think twice about attempting it when the track has been made slippery by rain or ice. Once this section has been successfully navigated it is a steep zigzag climb up to **Watzmann Haus**.

The track up to the **Hocheck** (2651m), the lowest of the Watzmann's three summits, is clearly marked from Watzmann Haus (adds 2hrs). Though it presents no particular difficulties appropriate care should be taken. Once at the top you are greeted by a magnificent alpine panorama that stretches as far as the Central Alps and deep into Berchtesgadener Land. **Note** The way further south over the Mittelspitze (2713m) and Südspitze (2712m) is *definitely* not for the inexperienced, so most walkers will probably return the same way to Watzmann Haus.

For the descent to Wimbach Bridge follow path 441 through the woods, passing **Mitterkaser Alm** and **Stuben Alm** on the way.

BERCHTESGADEN

Tourist office: Tourist-Information, Maximilianstr. 9, D-83471 Berchtesgaden. Tel: (08652) 944 5300, fax: (08652) 967 381;
*website: **www.berchtesgaden.de**, e-mail: info.kurhaus@berchtesgaden.de*

Berchtesgaden is a pleasant mountain resort with an attractive marketplace fringed by historic buildings. Though the mountains will be the major draw for people using this guidebook, there are a few attractions in town such as the Schloss Museum and Salzbergwerk (Salt Mine Museum) that deserve a visit if the weather is less than perfect. There is also the Obersalzberg (1000m) to the east where Adolf Hitler created a holiday retreat for himself and the Nazi élite. The ruins of the complex can be visited, as is the case with Kehlstein Haus (also known as Hitler's teahouse, see Route 65) further south, on the Kehlstein (1837m). Great views! Also well worth an excursion is the panoramic Rossfeldringstrasse. This toll road is the highest in Germany, and reaches an altitude of 1600m.

Berchtesgaden can be reached from Bad Reichenhall by train. Those travelling by road will find the B20 the quickest route from Bad Reichenhall, whereas those coming from Ruhpolding or Inzell will most likely take the B305 via Ramsau. There are a couple of camping grounds south of town on the road to Königssee, but the first one you come to is best avoided as it is close to the road and rather noisy. The youth hostel is at Strub, just west of town.

ROUTE 62
The Untersberg Massif

Start	St Leonhard (Austria)
Parking	At cable railway
Transport	Bus 840 from Berchtesgaden to Untersbergseilbahn (St Leonhard)
Distance	15.2km/9.5 miles
Height gain	167m (548ft)
Height loss	1386m (4547ft)
Time	6–7hrs
Grade	2
Refreshments	Upper terminus cable car, Stöhr Haus, Rost Alm
Accommodation	Stöhr Haus
Map	Kompass-Wanderkarte No 14: Berchtesgadener Land – Chiemgauer Alpen

This is one of the easiest and scenically most rewarding of the 'high-level' walks in Berchtesgadener Land. It is best saved for a very fine day (no haze) in order to ensure that you can enjoy the magnificent views to the fullest.

Catch the bus from Berchtesgaden to St Leonhard. From St Leonhard take the Untersbergseilbahn (cable railway) up to the summit of the **Geiereck** (1805m). The alpine panorama at the top is quite spectacular and sets the tone for the greater part of this route: to the south the Steinernes Meer (see Route 68), Hochkönig and Watzmann; to the west the Chiemgau Alps, Kaiser Mountains and Zugspitze; to the east the mountains of the Salzkammergut, Hoher Dachstein and Schladminger Tauern. A more fitting introduction to a mountain walk is hard to imagine!

The first goal, the **Salzburger Hochthron** (1853m), lies only 20mins away along path 417. It is not uncommon to see chamois along this section of track in spite of the fact that the Untersbergbahn station is so close. Apart from a few ups and

WALKING IN THE BAVARIAN ALPS

The Stöhrweg down from Stöhr Haus

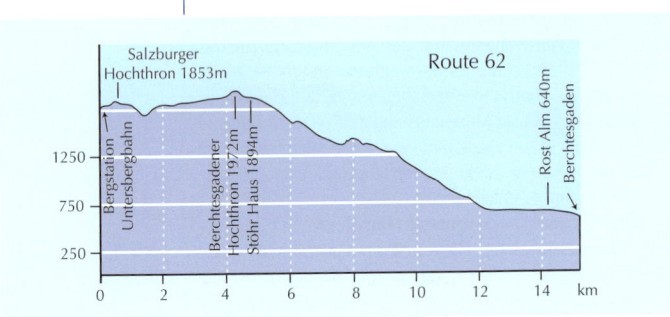

ROUTE 62 – THE UNTERSBERG MASSIF

downs the track along the ridge is fairly level until it dips down very steeply into a saddle (marked as the Mittagsscharte on the Kompass map) from where the track to Toni-Lenz Hut and the Schellenberg Ice Cave (Thomas-Eder-Steig; see Route 63) branches left – roughly 1hr from the cable railway.

It is a steep climb up the other side of the saddle. Once at the top it is easy going along a gently undulating path the

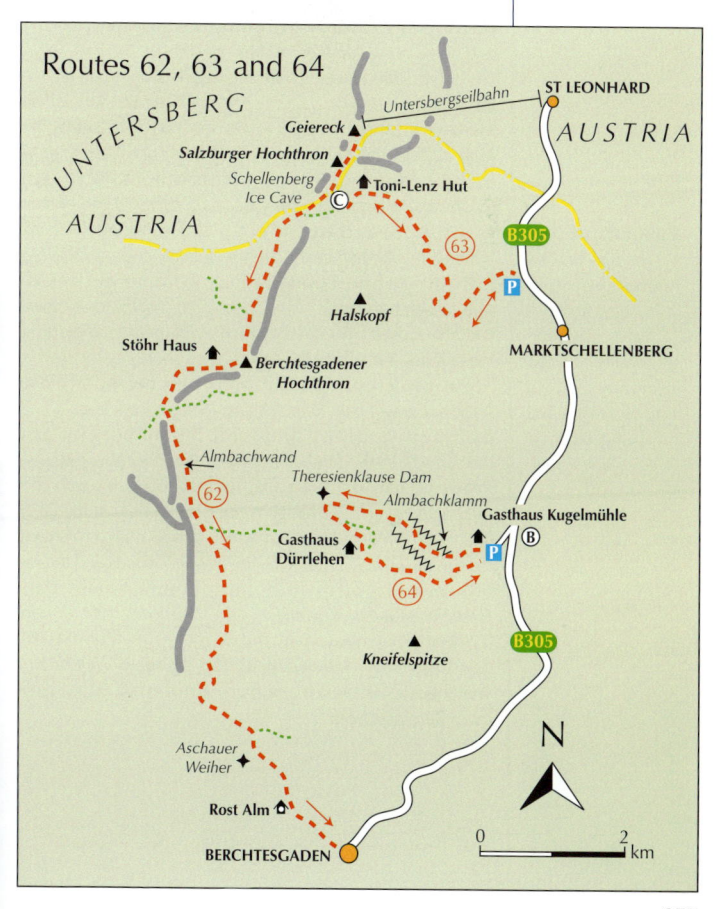

> As there is very little or no shade it is wise to wear a hat and to take plenty to drink.

rest of the way to Stöhr Haus. If visibility is good the views in all directions are tremendous. For the most part the track winds its way through thickets of shrub-like dwarf pines on the edge of the Untersberg plateau – a fascinating landscape. ◄ After some 3hrs' walking the **Berchtesgadener Hochthron** (1972m) is reached. The views are great, and if you have brought something to eat with you and want to enjoy it in relative peace and quiet this is the place. **Stöhr Haus** is only a 15min walk away but it is generally crowded and noisy in the summer months.

From Stöhr Haus the descent begins along path 417 in the direction of Maria Gern. After passing the turn-off to Marktschellenberg the track levels out and passes below the high cliffs of the **Almbachwand**. Though normally a good track the going is made somewhat harder if it is still covered by snow – this can be the case even towards the end of May. ◄ At the southern end of the Almbachwand the track widens (it is known as the Stöhrweg here) and you reach a fork. Go right here, leaving the route to Maria Gern for path 468 to Berchtesgaden – it is signposted 'Aschauer-Weiher/Bischofswiesen'. The track, which eventually changes to a forest road, remains in the woods until shortly before town. At the next fork go right, but shortly after turning off along what is a gravel path keep a sharp lookout for a track going downhill to the left (not signposted). This will bring you past the turn-off to the Rauher Kopf and down to Maximilians-Reitweg (a long-distance path). Turn left along this path and then right towards **Aschauer-Weiher** (swimming in the lake) and the Berchtesgadener *Trimmweg* (fitness trail), crossing a road in the process. After walking through woods and meadows leave the fitness trail along Rostwaldstrasse. Pass Gaststätte-Café Rostalm and follow the sign 'Lockstein/Berchtesgaden' and then the sign 'Zum Markt' past Gästehaus Mitterweinfeld. The Weinfeld-Weg brings you down to the church and *Rathaus* (town hall) at the centre of **Berchtesgaden**.

> If the drifts are deep you may have to traverse very steep snow banks in places where the mountainside drops almost vertically; a head for heights and sure-footedness is essential.

ROUTE 63
Schellenberg Ice Cave

Start	Marktschellenberg
Parking	Eishöhle car park on B305
Transport	From Berchtesgaden railway station take bus no 2940 to the Haltestelle (bus stop) Eishöhle, near Marktschellenberg
Distance	5.4km/3.5 miles (one way)
Height gain	1098m (3602ft)
Height loss	1098m (3602ft)
Time	4hrs
Grade	2
Refreshments	Toni-Lenz Hut
Accommodation	Toni-Lenz Hut
Map	Kompass-Wanderkarte No 14: Berchtesgadener Land – Chiemgauer Alpen

The Schellenberg Ice Cave (Schellenberger Eishöhle; 1570m) is the largest ice cave in Germany open to the general public – the Kolowrat Cave on the north side of the Geiereck (in Austria) is even larger, but is only accessible for well-equipped speleologists. As the temperature inside is around 0°C warm (and waterproof!) clothing is essential. It is open mid-May–end Oct. There are hourly guided tours from 10.00–16.00 which last about 40mins (www.eishoehle.net).

The trail (path 463) is clearly signposted as 'Toni-Lenz-Hütte' and 'Eishöhle' and should present no navigational problems. The actual track begins about 1km outside **Marktschellenberg** on the road to Salzburg (B305). At the start of the track there is a car park as well as a bus stop for buses running between Berchtesgaden and Salzburg.

On the other side of the road from the car park the track begins its long climb through the woods. After rain there is a good chance of seeing spotted salamanders along the path.

WALKING IN THE BAVARIAN ALPS

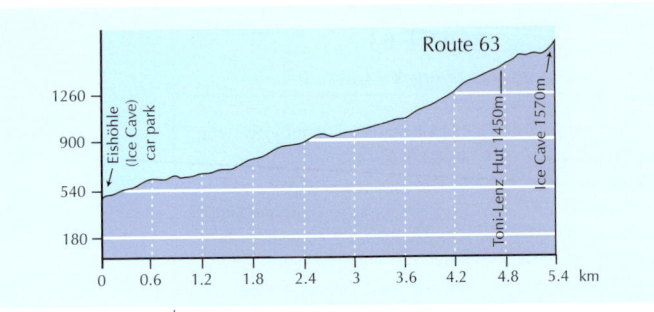

Route 63 elevation profile: from Eishöhle (Ice Cave) car park at 0 km to Toni-Lenz Hut 1450m and Ice Cave 1570m at approximately 5.4 km.

View down to the valley of the Berchtesgadener Ache (river) from Toni-Lenz Hut

ROUTE 64 – THE ALMBACHKLAMM

Before arriving at **Toni-Lenz Hut** (1450m) the woods are left behind and the track enters an area of low bushes, dwarf pines and alpenrose (very pretty when in flower). Some 2½hrs after commencing the (in places very steep) climb from the car park the hut is reached. Wonderful views from the terrace and a cosy atmosphere inside. From here it is another 20mins or so to the cave entrance (entry fee).

Inside the cave visitors are provided with carbide lamps. The journey into the icy depths proceeds along a wooden walkway, past walls of glittering ice to the cave's deepest point, the Fuggerhalle, 55m below the surface. On the way back to the entrance you pass through the Mörkdom (Mörk Cathedral). Currents of air have carved the ice here into curious shapes and, with a little imagination, you can recognise such objects as a pulpit, an altar and a confessional.

Either return the same way or continue up to the Untersberg along the exciting Thomas-Eder-Steig (see also Route 62).

The Thomas-Eder-Steig from the Eishöhle up to the Mittagsscharte was constructed in 1937. It takes mountain walkers across a vertical rock face via a series of four tunnels with wire cables, where necessary, to aid the ascent. The ice cave can also be reached via the *Steig* from the Untersberg cable-car station (1½–2hrs). A head for heights is necessary.

ROUTE 64
The Almbachklamm

Start	Gasthaus Kugelmühle (roughly halfway between Berchtesgaden and Marktschellenberg on the B305)
Parking	At Gasthaus Kugelmühle
Transport	Bus 840 from Berchtesgaden
Distance	7km/4.5 miles
Height gain	339m (1112ft)
Height loss	339m (1112ft)

Time	2½hrs
Grade	1
Refreshments	Gasthaus Kugelmühle, Gasthaus Dürrlehen
Accommodation	Gasthaus Kugelmühle
Map	Kompass-Wanderkarte No 14: Berchtesgadener Land – Chiemgauer Alpen

This route along the very beautiful Almbachklamm makes a nice and easy half-day outing. Up until 1963 logs were floated down the Almbach stream to a spot near the present *Gasthaus*. Here they were gathered and transported to the timber mills. To facilitate this work a dam was built in the early 19th century on the upper reaches of the *Klamm* (gorge). Named in honour of the Bavarian Queen Therese, the Theresienklause dam is 14m high, 6m wide and 17m long. The reservoir behind the dam had a capacity of up to 15,000 cubic metres, which swept the logs below downstream when the floodgates were opened. The *Klamm* is normally open from 1 May–31 Oct, and there is an entry fee.

At the entrance to the *Klamm*, and next to the *Gasthaus* (tel: [08650] 461, www.gasthaus-kugelmuehle.de), is Germany's last *Kugelmühle* (marble-grinding mill). In this simple device roughly cut stone blocks are placed in grooved discs where they are rolled into a spherical shape by the action of water. There were once over 100 such mills in the Berchtesgaden region. They were run by the poor local mountain farmers and provided an extra source of income. Though marble balls were once in demand for early firearms their heyday came in the 18th century when they were exported all over the world for the popular children's game of marbles. The later mass production of marbles from clay and glass brought about the demise of the marble-grinding mills. Now popular as souvenirs the finished marble ball has a diameter of 3–10cm.

The *Klamm* is made accessible by steps and paths carved from the rock, a tunnel and 29 bridges. The roar of gushing water, waterfalls and the wild beauty of the (at some points very narrow) gorge make the walk uphill to the **Theresianklause Dam** quite impressive. Those who carefully examine the banks of the swift flowing Almbach stream

Route 64 – The Almbachklamm

The water-driven marble mill next to the Gasthaus

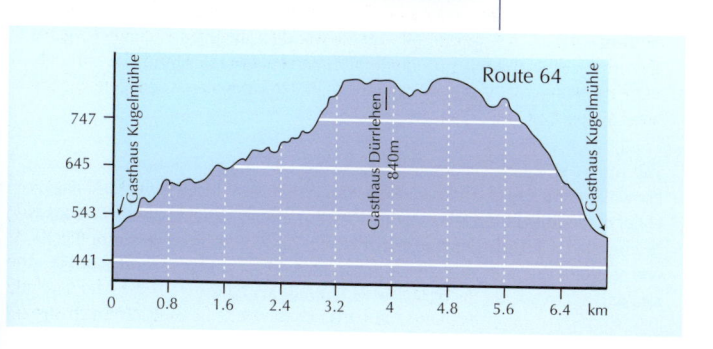

might spot a tiny dipper (Cinclus cinclus), the only member of the songbird family that can swim and dive under water. The fact that they can be found in the *Klamm* is proof that the water is of good quality as these birds are very sensitive to water pollution, and are now rare in many parts of Germany.

Instead of walking back the same way you can turn left just before the dam and walk uphill through the woods to **Gasthaus Dürrlehen**, which serves simple but hearty Bavarian fare and (very important for Bavaria) cheap beer! From here follow the signs back to the *Kugelmühle*. This last section of the route goes for the most part through forest, but there are still some nice views along the way.

ROUTE 65
Kehlstein: The Eagle's Nest

Start	Berchtesgaden
Parking	Car park opposite Obersalzberg-Seilbahn
Transport	Local buses
Distance	6.5km/4 miles
Height gain	820m (2690ft)
Time	3hrs
Grade	2
Refreshments	Café Sonneck, Kehlstein Haus
Map	Kompass-Wanderkarte No 14: Berchtesgadener Land – Chiemgauer Alpen

This route's goal is the infamous 'Eagle's Nest' (or 'Hitler's Teahouse' as it is also known). Referred to by Germans nowadays as Kehlstein Haus it was presented to Hitler on his 50th birthday by Martin Bormann. Hitler, however, seldom visited as he considered the trip there too risky. Having narrowly escaped destruction at the end of World War II the building is now preserved in its original form as a restaurant and a reminder of the dark days of National Socialism.

Route 65 – Kehlstein: The Eagle's Nest

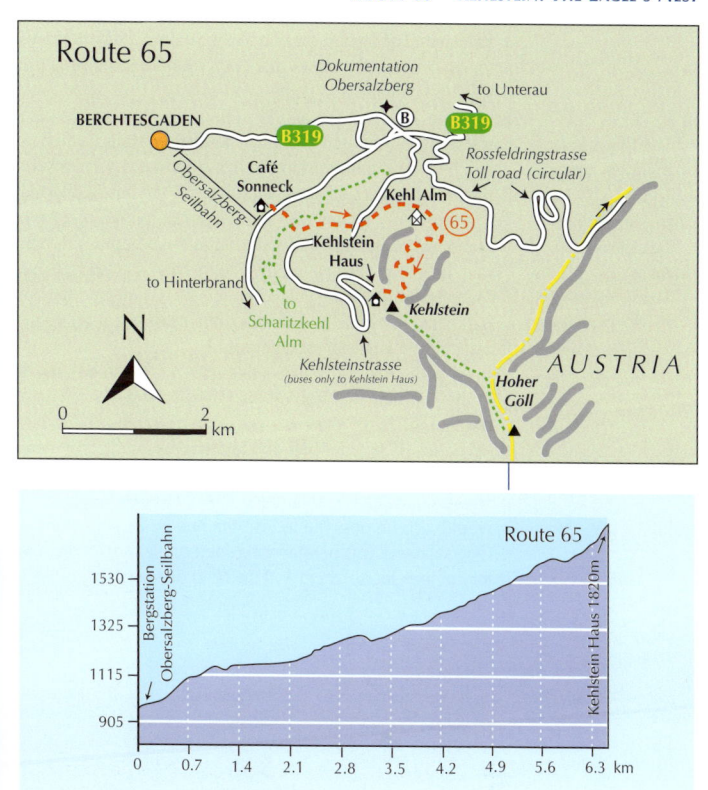

From the upper station of the Obersalzberg-Seilbahn walk a short distance uphill from **Café Sonneck**. Leave the asphalt road at the signposted trail to Kehlstein on the right. The track climbs into the woods and soon comes to a narrow, asphalted forestry road. Here the sign to Scharitzkehl Alm is followed right. After climbing awhile at a comfortable gradient another signposted fork is reached. Go left in the direction of Ofnerboden – Kehlstein, crossing at one point the Kehlsteinstrasse, which is only open for the buses up to Kehlstein Haus. After passing a track going downhill on the left the asphalt path begins its steep, winding ascent of the

This is as far as normal mountain walkers can go, as the Mannlsteig along the Mannlköpfe to the Hoher Göll (2522m) is only for properly equipped mountaineers.

Kehlstein. For the last section to the summit the path leaves the woods and the views that open up hold promise of the splendid panorama to come.

The ascent of the actual summit is only possible with the huge brass-lined lift up to **Kehlstein Haus**, which is reached via a tunnel from the bus stop below – tickets for the lift must be purchased beforehand at the bus stop kiosk. Crammed in together with the dozens of tourists that have come by bus the lift whisks you up to the cavernous restaurant. Instead of rushing to buy 'Eagle's Nest' souvenirs, leave the restaurant to be overwhelmed by a fantastic alpine panorama outside. The actual summit cross is a short uphill walk from the restaurant complex. ◄

For the return trip to Berchtesgaden take the bus down to the Kehlstein bus stop on the Obersalzberg – purchase a ticket at the kiosk. Here it is necessary to catch another bus (RVO bus 9538 from bus stop at the 'Dokumentation' centre; ticket from driver) for the rest of the ride back to town. However, instead of continuing directly to Berchtesgaden it would also be possible to visit the nearby Dokumentation Obersalzberg. This permanent exhibition deals with the history of the Obersalzberg and the Nazi dictatorship.

Kehlstein Haus

The Dokumentation Obersalzberg is open Mon–Sun from 09.00–17.00 (last entry 16.00), Apr–Oct; Tues–Sun from 10.00–15.00 (last entry 14.00), Nov–Mar. Website: www.obersalzberg.de; tel: (08652) 947960.

ROUTE 66
Jenner (1874m)

Start	Königssee
Parking	Large car park next to Jennerbahn
Transport	Bus 841 and 843 from Berchtesgaden to the lake
Distance	14.7km/9 miles
Height gain	1247m (4091ft)
Height loss	1247m (4091ft)
Time	5½ hrs
Grade	2
Refreshments	Mitterkaser Alm, Schneibstein Haus, Königsbach Alm
Accommodation	(Carl von Stahl Haus), Schneibstein Haus
Map	Kompass-Wanderkarte No 14: Berchtesgadener Land – Chiemgauer Alpen

Despite the fact that the Jenner is one of the most popular destinations in the Berchtesgaden region the first section of this route is guaranteed to be free of crowds. The reason is simple: everyone takes the cable car. We don't – it is the 'challenge' of the steep ascent that makes reaching the summit all the more satisfactory. You feel as though you have earned the fantastic view at the top – more so than would be the case after the short stroll from the cable-car station (and after the effort of the climb a snack at the hut is doubly enjoyable!). Anyway, the Jennerbahn can be saved for another day, perhaps for Route 67, where the climb to the Jenner would make the route difficult to achieve in a day.

WALKING IN THE BAVARIAN ALPS

In the vicinity of Mitterkaser Alm there are plenty of marmots and you might also spot chamois grazing on the nearby slopes. On the last section of the descent route back to Königssee note the old votive paintings nailed to some of the trees flanking the track. They usually commemorate a tragedy that took place in the vicinity; a fall over a precipice, a fatal accident while felling timber, or even the murder of some unlucky fellow who got in the way of a poacher.

Votive paintings can be seen nailed to some trees on the descent back to Königssee

Leave the valley station of the Jennerbahn along Jennerbahnstrasse, which is followed uphill into Richard-Voss-Strasse. Ignore a turn-off to the right into Hochbahnstrasse (signposted Jenner – Königsbachalm – Gotzenalm) and continue climbing towards a cluster of houses marked as **Holz** on the map. After a steepish climb leave Richard-Voss-Strasse along the Brandkopfweg, a narrow road going very steeply uphill on the right. On reaching the edge of the woods this asphalt road dwindles to a rocky mountain path, which is followed for the rest of the ascent up to the Vorderbrandstrasse.

At Vorderbrandstrasse follow the now-level trail right, still going through forest, in the direction of the Jennerbahn's Mittelstation. To the left you can follow the asphalted Vorderbrandstrasse downhill to the restaurant at Vorderbrand (5mins). After passing a waterfall come to a fork, where you bear left at first in the direction of the Mittelstation and Jenner Haus (Dr Hugo-Beck-Haus). A short distance later, a small trail on the left (signposted Krautkasersteig) is reached. Follow this track steeply uphill

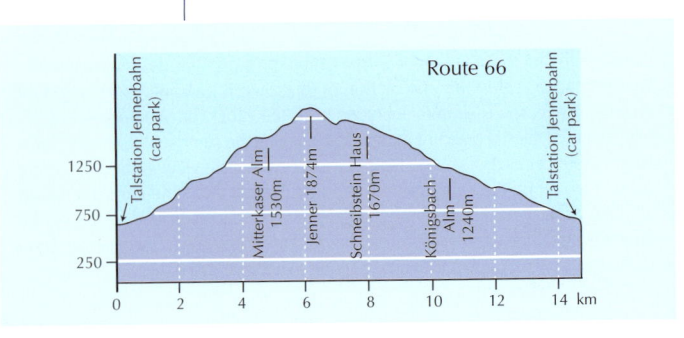

ROUTE 66 – JENNER

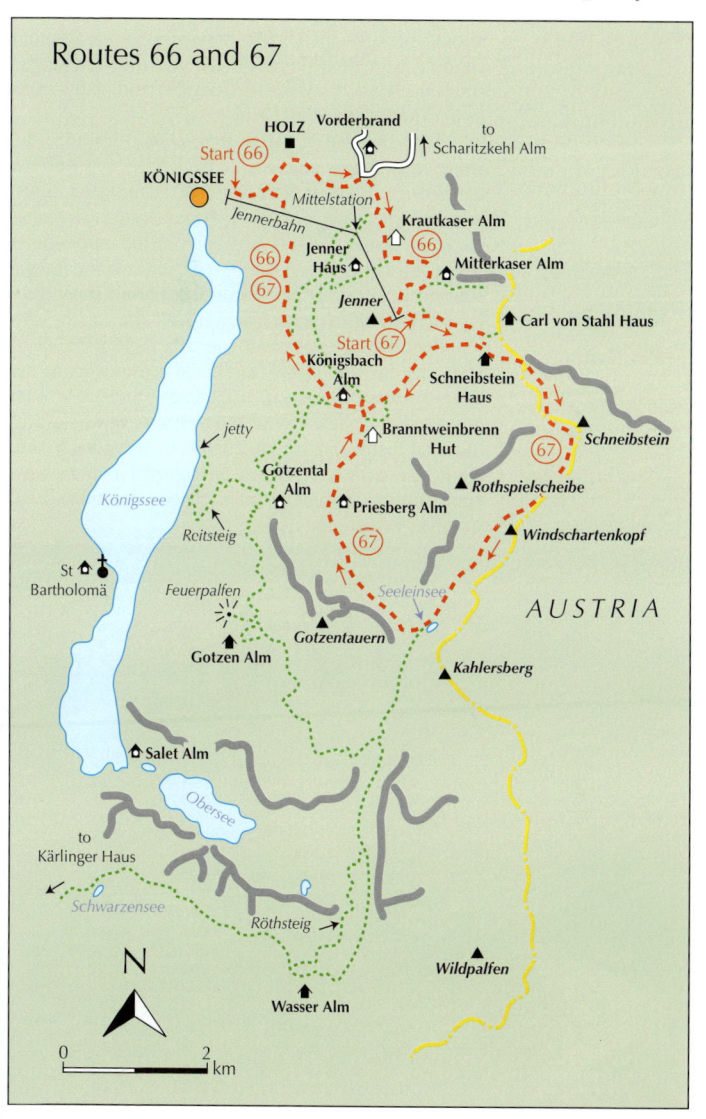

Routes 66 and 67

through pastures, then lightly wooded slopes, to where it connects with the wide gravel road from the Mittelstation and Jenner Haus. Continue up along this road (trail 498 on map) to **Mitterkaser Alm** (1530m).

From the hut a steep trail climbs towards the Jennerbahn's upper terminus. At the intersection with the trail down to Carl von Stahl Haus and Schneibstein Haus, turn right and continue past the cable-car station to the summit of the **Jenner** (1874m). After enjoying the superb views return the same way to the intersection. Now continue downhill in an easterly direction to **Schneibstein Haus**, passing a turn-off on the left to Carl von Stahl Haus on the way.

Those who are prepared to spend the night at the hut, or at nearby Carl von Stahl Haus, could continue along the route described in Route 67 the next day. Otherwise, path 498 leads downhill, through the meadows of Königsberg Alm and then along wooded slopes to **Königsbach Alm**. From here path 493 crosses the forested slopes above Königssee back towards the valley station of the Jennerbahn.

View of Königssee from the Jenner

ROUTE 67
The Hagengebirge above Königssee

Start	Königssee
Parking	Large car park next to Jennerbahn
Transport	Bus 841 and 843 from Berchtesgaden to the lake
Distance	17km/10.5 miles
Height gain	475m (1558ft)
Height loss	475m (1558ft)
Time	5½–6hrs (via Gotzen Alm 2 days)
Grade	2
Refreshments	Schneibstein Haus, (Gotzen Alm), Priesberg Alm, Königsbach Alm
Accommodation	Schneibstein Haus, (Gotzen Alm), (Wasseralm)
Map	Kompass-Wanderkarte No 14: Berchtesgadener Land – Chiemgauer Alpen

Great alpine scenery, tremendous views over the Königssee from the Jenner or the Feuerpalfen (longer alternative) and a lonely alpine tarn are among the scenic highlights of this route over the Hagengebirge. Apart from a long steep climb to the top of the Schneibstein the walking is not too strenuous. However, it pays to bring plenty to drink as there is quite a lot of ground to be covered between Schneibstein Haus and the next place where refreshments are available (Priesberg Alm).

Considering the length of this route it is best to make use of the Jennerbahn (check timetable) rather than undertake the long, uphill climb from the valley. From the Bergstation (upper station) of the cable railway it is only a 10min stroll to the viewpoint on the **Jenner**'s summit (1874m). The views over the Königssee are spectacular. ▶

Back at the Bergstation the onward route to **Schneibstein Haus** is clearly signposted. A well-beaten (and heavily eroded) path takes you downhill in an easterly direction, past

Near the southern end of the lake is the church of St Batholomä, a favourite with visitors to Berchtesgaden (accessible by boat from the tourist village at the northern end – see Route 68).

Schneibstein Haus

the fork to Carl von Stahl Haus (10mins) to the large hut which is run by the Naturfreunde (Naturefriends). Beautiful views across alm pastures and forest to the Watzmann massif. A track leads uphill (east then southeast) from the hut through dense groves of the ubiquitous dwarf pine. After a while the pines thin out and give way to grassy slopes. The final stretch to the top of the **Schneibstein** (2277m) is very steep. It is with a feeling of relief that you collapse on the spacious grass summit (1½hrs from Schneibstein Haus), no doubt hot and perspiring. Needless to say this is the place for a longer rest, after which you can enjoy the great panoramic views.

Continue southwest. As far as the Windscharte (2100m), a saddle, it is fairly easy walking with only a few relatively minor dips and rises in the trail. A track goes down from the saddle to Hinterschlum Alm in Austria, but this

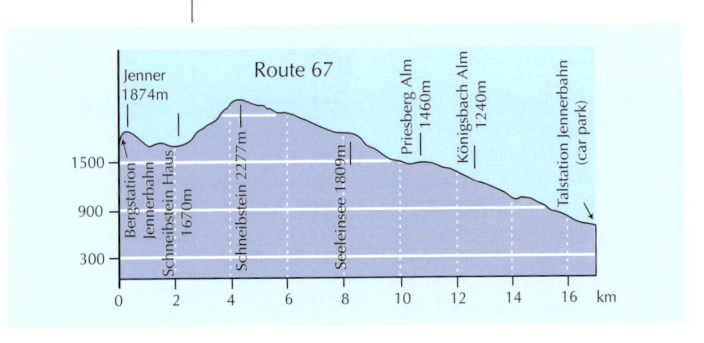

Route 67 – The Hagengebirge above Königssee

route continues south around the **Windschartenkopf**. There are more ups and downs now as the trail picks its way through rugged, rocky terrain towards a small tarn known as the Seeleinsee. Its blue-green waters contrast dramatically with the bleak grey of the surrounding rock cliffs. Herds of chamois can often be seen in the vicinity. It is altogether a beautiful, lonely spot.

A short distance further on from the tarn the trail forks and you have the choice of taking either the direct route back to the Königssee via Priesberg Alm and Branntweinbrenn Hut (waymark 497) or the longer route via Gotzen Alm (416, 493). If the weather is playing along then the longer variant (continue south) is well worth the extra effort.

Gotzen Alm is rated as the most beautifully situated alm in the entire Berchtesgaden region, in large part due to the famous view over the Königssee and the Watzmann's east face from the nearby **Feuerpalfen** (1741m). This alternative would require staying at the alm, however, as you would no longer have enough time to catch the last boat back to Dorf Königssee from the jetty at Kessel. You could walk all the way back to the car park, but at least in autumn you would have no chance of getting back before dark.

Fine views over Königssee from the last wooded section of the track before reaching the starting point

Those who have decided on the direct route turn right and start descending through an area of loose boulders and rocks. The track gradually improves, and after walking through open woodland you enter meadows prior to reaching **Priesberg Alm**. The path widens into a gravel road, then passes through an area of moorland (Priesberger Moos) on its way to the picturesque **Branntweinbrenn Hut** (1352m). At a fork just after the hut go left and downhill. Continue along the road past Königsbach Alm, but after another 1km turn left and follow path 493. Though this pleasant footpath goes through the woods it still allows a few glimpses of the Königssee far below. Magnificent colours in autumn. Before you know it you reach the first group of houses and are soon back at the car park.

'Great Round the Lake Walk' (4–5 days)

This is a continuation of the above tour and links it to Route 68 at Kärlinger Haus. It is best to spend the first night at either **Carl von Stahl Haus** or **Schneibstein Haus** so as to ensure the earliest possible start in the morning. Walk as described above as far as the Seeleinsee, but instead of descending to either Priesberg Alm or Gotzen Alm continue on along path 416 to **Wasser Alm** (hut is open all year but there is no catering). Spend the night here then next day follow path 416 northwest, then southwest past the Schwarzensee and Grünsee to Kärlinger Haus. From there continue as described in Route 68.

ROUTE 68
A Three-day Hike through Berchtesgaden National Park

Start	Königssee
Parking	Large car park near Jennerbahn (parking fee)
Transport	Bus 841 and 843 from Berchtesgaden to Königssee and Bus 846 from Wimbachbrücke (Wimbach Bridge) to Berchtesgaden; boat to St Bartholomä
Distance	36km/22.5 miles
Height gain	1585m (5200ft)
Height loss	1561m (5121ft)
Time	3 days
Grade	2–3
Refreshments	St Bartholomä, Kärlinger Haus, Riemann Haus, Ingolstädter Haus, Wimbachgrieß Hut, Wimbachschloss
Accommodation	Kärlinger Haus, Riemann Haus, Ingolstädter Haus, Wimbachgrieß Hut
Maps	Kompass-Wanderkarte No 14: Berchtesgadener Land – Chiemgauer Alpen and No 30: Saalfelden – Leoganger Steinberge

This tour from the Königssee to the Wimbachtal offers some of the most stunning scenery to be seen anywhere in the Bavarian Alps. The lake is certainly one of Germany's most beautiful (in the opinion of the authors *the* most beautiful) and is a fitting introduction to the National Park which has been formed around it. All the huts that are used as overnight quarters during the tour are superbly situated and would make pleasant bases for longer stays. The walking is fairly easy (Grade

2 or an 'easy' Grade 3), but some stretches are quite long or steep. If visibility is bad the Steinernes Meer should be avoided.

Large sections of this tour also follow the 'Purple Trail' of the Via Alpina, which links the alpine regions of Slovenia, Austria and Germany. Day 1 follows the Purple Trail to Kärlinger Haus, then on Day 2 to Riemann Haus. From here the Purple Trail leaves the described route to continue on to Saalfelden in Austria. An alternative stretch of the Purple Trail is followed on Day 3 through the Wimbachtal. **Note** Remember to take your passport with you.

Day 1 (4hrs)

The tour begins with a cruise on the beautiful Königssee. If, like the dutiful wanderer you are, you have made an early start (check first boat departure) you will be able to avoid the crowds that descend on the lake later in the day. The launches are powered by electric motors and glide noiselessly over the water. At one point the boat stops and the fellow who collected your ticket plays a few notes on a trumpet. The resulting echo is quite impressive; it often sounds more in tune than the original! After some 45mins the pretty church of **St Bartholomä** presents itself on a small peninsula at the foot of the Watzmann's imposing east face – a classic picture-postcard motif which has most passengers grabbing excitedly for their cameras.

Once ashore follow the path running south from the jetty. It runs along the edge of the lake at first, then starts climbing through the woods. The footbridge over the Schrainbach stream is reached in about 20mins. A little further on, at a

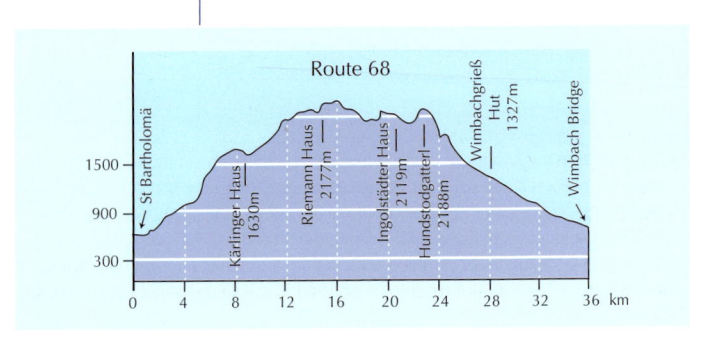

Route 68 – A Three-day Hike through Berchtesgaden National Park

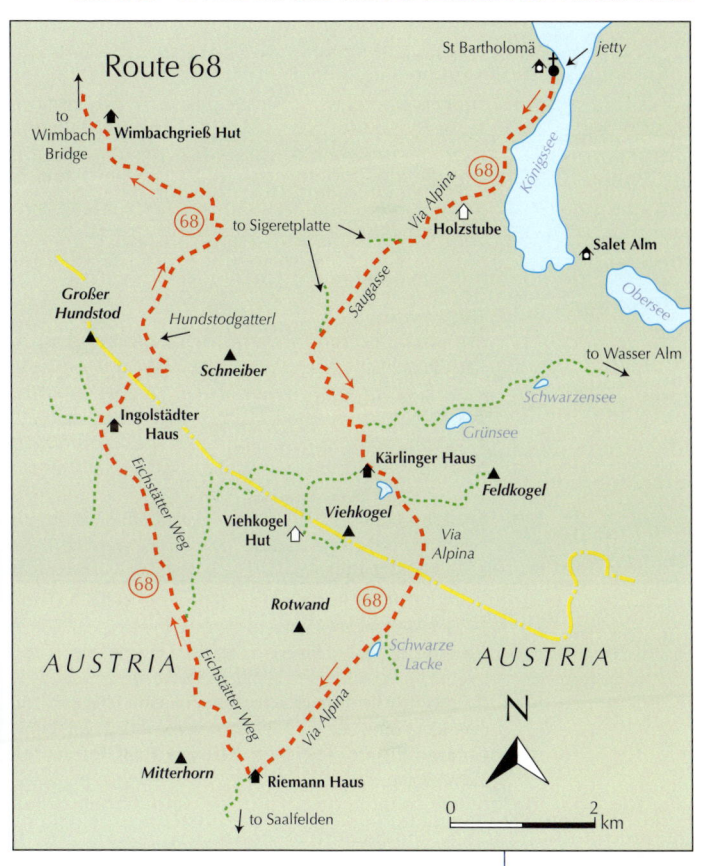

sharp bend in the trail, you have good views over Sallet Alm at the southern end of the lake. This is also where the track starts zigzagging very steeply up the so-called Hochstieg. Eventually it levels out and arrives at a hut marked on the map as '**Holzstube**'. As the hut has a nice location next to the Schrainbach stream it might be a pleasant spot for a break after the strenuous climb. Continue across the stream until you come to a fork. ▶ This route continues left to the Saugasse, some 30mins away.

The path to the right goes over the Sigeretplatte and then over the Trischübel Pass to Wimbachgrieß Hut (3hrs).

297

Karlinger Haus reflected in the waters of the Funtensee

It takes roughly 45mins to climb up this steep gully, and even the slightest of breezes is received in gratitude. At the top the trail continues to climb, but more gently now, as it threads its way through a rugged mountain landscape of ever-increasing beauty. After passing the fork down to the Grünsee it is no longer far to **Kärlinger Haus**, the goal of today's route.

Kärlinger Haus (or Funtensee Haus) is a large hut with a magnificent situation just above a pretty tarn known as the Funtensee. In summer it tends to be filled to capacity, but in autumn is usually much less crowded. Those who decide to sleep in one of the *Matrazenlager* will experience what it is like to be a sardine: the dozen or so mattresses are placed right next to one another. In the interests of a good night's sleep you will probably find it more comfortable if you ask for a *Bett*, a small bunkroom which sleeps four. In spring or late autumn you will probably have the room all to yourself. All in all it is quite a pleasant hut where you could base yourself for a few days if you wished to explore the environs at more leisure.

Route 68 – A Three-day Hike through Berchtesgaden National Park

Excursions from Kärlinger Hut

Those who still have the energy can make a very worthwhile late afternoon excursion from the hut along path 423 to the **Feldkogel** (1886m, 1hr). On the way you pass through meadows alive with marmots. These fat, furry little creatures are not at all shy, so it is not hard to get quite close to them. From the Feldkogel summit you have a wonderful view north over the Königssee. In autumn yellow larches add that extra touch of beauty to the scene.

If you do plan on staying longer at the hut an interesting 2½hr excursion can be made to the **Viehkogel** (2158m), just to the south. Path 412 is followed up a very steep slope (plenty of perspiring faces on this stretch) but at the point where it forks to Ingolstädter Haus (northwest) you curve instead to the left and walk past a rock face to **Viehkogel Hut** which lies on Austrian territory. The path continues its curve left to a point almost directly south of the summit, then climbs in a northwesterly direction to the top. Magnificent views over the Steinernes Meer. Return the same way.

Day 2 (5½hrs)

Continuing on from **Kärlinger Haus** next morning the trail (path 413) heads south into Austria and an area known as the Steinernes Meer (Stone Sea). This desolate karst landscape is reminiscent of the Gottesacker Plateau in the Allgäu Alps (see Route 11) and is equally fascinating. The bizarrely eroded limestone rocks are virtually devoid of vegetation except for little 'islands' of dwarf pines. For some reason these karst plateaux seem to be a favourite habitat of ptarmigan – they are numerous both here and on the Gottesacker. It will take about 2½hrs to pick your way through the rocky terrain to **Riemann Haus**. Magnificently situated at an altitude of 2177m, and with great views over the Saalachtal to the mountains beyond, the hut is the perfect place for a longer rest.

The onward trail continues northwest through the Steinernes Meer along the so-called Eichstätter Weg (Eichstätter Trail). This route poses no problems, but orientation can be very difficult when it is misty – if conditions are bad stay at the hut until they improve. After around 1½hrs of up and down walking a fork is reached: right goes back to

Kärlinger Haus (2½hrs), left to the Weißbachlscharte. **Ingolstädter Haus** lies straight ahead and is reached in another 1½hrs. A smaller hut than either Kärlinger Haus or Riemann Haus it is situated at the foot of the Kleiner (2263m) and **Großer Hundstod** (2593m).

Day 3 (4–6hrs)

Next day continue in a northeasterly direction back into Germany. In just under 1hr the track (path 411) brings you to a fork where you turn left. This is the start of the steep climb up to the **Hundstodgatterl** (2188m), a saddle between the Grosser Hundstod and Schneiber (2330m). Here the tour resembles a scramble rather than a walk and in a few places it is necessary to use your hands. Fantastic views at the top over the Steinernes Meer to the Simetsberg and Viehkogel (near Kärlinger Haus). The trail now descends quite steeply towards the abandoned Trischübel Alm (path 411). Fortunately, the magnificent scenery helps you ignore the extra strain on your knees. After one particularly steep section (could be rather tricky if the track is wet) the track climbs again briefly before descending to the point where it joins path 421 from the Sigeretplatte. The fork is signposted, and the trail is followed left (northwest) to **Wimbachgrieß Hut** (1hr). It is downhill all the way now, with breathtaking views of the mountains surrounding the hut.

Those who wish can spend the night at Wimbachgrieß Hut (probably the best solution). Otherwise continue down the Wimbachtal to the Wimbach Bridge (see Route 60). This takes about 2hrs. There is a bus stop right next to the bridge, on the right-hand side. Buses run directly to Berchtesgaden railway station (*Bahnhof*). From here catch a bus to Königssee and the Jennerbahn car park.

The Via Alpina is the longest of the multi-day tours through the Bavarian Alps

PART VII
MULTI-DAY TOURS: THE VIA ALPINA

PART VII
MULTI-DAY TOURS: THE VIA ALPINA

There are innumerable possibilities for lengthy hut-to-hut tours in the Bavarian Alps. At many places in this guidebook suggestions are given for tours of 2–3 days or longer. With the help of the recommended maps it should not be difficult to work out even more long-distance routes by linking the single-day tours described. An excellent network of huts ensures that the daily walking stages need not be too long – see the Introduction and Appendix B for more information on mountain huts.

Many of the routes in this guidebook follow sections of the Via Alpina long-distance walk: here on the way to Meiler Hut (Route 26)

VIA ALPINA

The international long-distance walk network of the Via Alpina consists of five routes linking the alpine regions of Italy, Slovenia, Austria, Germany, Liechtenstein, Switzerland, France and Monaco. The longest of these is the 'Red Trail', which links all the above-mentioned nations in 161 stages – a truly epic long-distance route! The other routes are the 'Purple Trail' (Slovenia, Austria, Germany), the 'Yellow Trail' (Italy, Austria, Germany), the 'Green Trail' (Liechtenstein, Switzerland) and the 'Blue Trail' (Switzerland, Italy, France). Obviously, the German sections of these routes are of most interest here.

Many of the routes mentioned in the guidebook touch on the German sections of the Via Alpina. Where a longer stretch of the Via Alpina coincides with a significant part of any route attention is drawn to the fact. The newest versions of the Kompass walking maps, which are recommended, all show the route of the Via Alpina through the Bavarian Alps.

Descriptions of all the various stages with sketch maps and altitude profiles are available at www.via-alpina.com. The website also provides map recommendations and occasional information on walking without luggage on sections of the trail. An interesting feature of the site is that you can use it to search for someone to accompany you on your chosen route.

ROUTE 69
Via Alpina: Bavarian section of the Purple Trail

Location	Travelling east to west from Saalfelden in Austria through the Bavarian Alps to Oberstdorf (Allgäu)
Distance	Approx 400km/248 miles
Time	26–28 days
Grade	2–3
Accommodation	Mountain huts, villages en route
Maps	Kompass maps

The Purple Trail branches off the Red Trail in the Triglav region of the Julian Alps (Slovenia), crosses the Karawanken (Slovenian–Austrian border) and passes through the Lower Tauern, Dachstein and Salzburg Alps in Austria to reach the Berchtesgaden Alps in Germany. The section outlined here (a slightly shorter variation of the official route) starts with Stage 39 of the Purple Trail (Stage 1 below) and ends with Stage 66 (Stage 26) in Oberstdorf.

Berchtesgaden Alps to the Tegernsee and Schliersee Mountains

1. Saalfelden – Riemannhaus (2177m)
2. Riemannhaus – Kärlingerhaus (1630m)
3. Kärlingerhaus – St Bartholomä (604m) – ferry to Königssee village – Grünstein Hut – Engedey
4. Engedey – Söldenköpfl – Neue Traunsteiner Hut (1560m)
5. Neue Traunsteiner Hut – Unken
6. Unken – Peitingsköpfl (1720m) – Heutal (968m) – Laubau – Ruhpolding
7. Ruhpolding – Hochfelln (1664m) – Hochgern (1743m) – Marquartstein
8. Marquartstein – Niedernfels (590m) – (Hochplatte chairlift) – Piesenhausener Hochalm – Steinlingalm (1550m) – Kampenwandhaus/Sonnenalm (1467m)

9   Sonnenalm – Hintere Dalsenalm (1000m) – Weitlahner (1615m) – Roßalm – Priener Hut (1411m)
10 Priener Hut – Sachrang (738m) – Spitzsteinhaus (1335m)
11 Spitzsteinhaus – Mühlgraben (470m) – Oberaudorf
12 Oberaudorf – Hocheck (823m) – Brünntal – Brünnsteinhaus (1342m)
13 Brünnsteinhaus – saddle between Großer and Kleiner Traithen (1640m) – Beim schweren Gatter (830m) – Silberghaus (1060m) – Soinsee (1459m) – Taubensteinhaus (1567m) – Schönfeld Hut – (1410m) or Albert-Link-Hut (1000m)
14 Albert-Link-Hut – Stümpflingbahn upper station – Suttenbahn valley station – Risserkogel (1826m) – Kreuth
15 Kreuth – Schwarzentenalm (1027m) – Rauhalm (1400m) – Seekarkreuz (1601m) – Lenggrieser Hut (1388m) – Lenggries

Tegernsee and Schliersee Mountains to the Allgäu Alps
16 Lenggries – Brauneckbahn upper station (1530m) – Latschenkopf (1712m) – Tutzinger Hut (1327m)
17 Tutzinger Hut – Glaswandscharte (1324m) – Staffelalm Jocheralm (1381m) – Kesselberghöhe (850m) – Herzogstandhäuser (1575m)
18 Herzogstand (1731m) – Heimgarten (1790m) – Asamklamm – Pustertal-Jagdhütte – Weilheim Hut (1946m)
19 Weilheim Hut – Esterbergalm (1264m) – Wank (1780m) – Garmisch-Partenkirchen
20 Garmisch-Partenkirchen – Kramer (1985m) – Stepbergalm (1583m) – Rotmoosalm (1206m) – Linderhof (948m)
21 Linderhof – Sägertal-Diensthütte- Bäckenalm (1309m) – Bäckenalm Saddle (1536m) – Kenzen Hut (1285m)
22 Kenzen Hut – Fensterl (1916m) – Fritz-Putz-Hut (1185m) – Hohenschwangau – Füssen
23 Füssen – Saloberalpe (1089m) – Falkenstein (1267m) – Pfronten-Steinach (850m)
24 Pronten-Steinach – Bad Kissinger Hut (1788m) – Enge (1210m) – Berg (1097m) – Tannheim
25 Tannheim – Älpele (1526m) – Willersalpe (1456m) – Jubiläumsweg – Prinz-Luitpold-Haus (1847m)
26 Prinz-Luitpold-Haus – Laufbachereck – Edmund-Probst-Haus (1930m) – Oberstdorf

ROUTE 70
Via Alpina: Bavarian section of the Red Trail

Location	German–Austrian border between Scharnitz (Austria) and Oberstdorf
Distance	Approx 120km/74 miles
Time	7 days
Grade	2
Accommodation	Mountain huts, villages en route
Maps	Kompass Wanderkarten Nos 5, 4 and 3

The Red Trail begins in Trieste and ends in Monaco (or vice versa). The section outlined below passes through the Wetterstein Mountains near Mittenwald and Garmisch-Partenkirchen, then continues weaving its way through Austria and Germany to end in the Allgäu at Oberstdorf. It offers magnificent alpine scenery along trails that are not unduly difficult.

The section through the Bergleintal to Meiler Hut, and from there to Knorr Hut, is described in detail under Routes 25, 26 and 27. The last stretch of Day 7 is covered by Route 5. Of the various stages of the tour Day 1 is probably the toughest. It involves a steep 4½hr climb up to Meiler Hut from Ahrn.

1. Scharnitz – Leutasch-Ahrn (1094m) – Bergleintal – Meiler Hut (2375m)
2. Meiler Hut – Schachenhaus (1866m) – Bock Hut (1052m) – Reintalanger Hut (1370m)
3. Reintalanger Hut – Knorr Hut (2051m) – Gatterl – Seebensee – Coburger Hut (1917m)
4. Coburger Hut – Biberwier – Wolfratshauser Hut (1751m)
5. Wolfratshauser Hut – Berwang – Weißenbach am Lech
6. Weißenbach – Eibles Hut (1113m) – Prinz-Luitpold-Haus
7. Prinz-Luitpold-Haus – Wildenfeld Hut (1692m) – Oberstdorf

APPENDIX A:
Further Reading

Walking guidebooks

Apart from this book, there is virtually no walking literature in English on the Bavarian Alps. *Mountain Walking in Austria* by Cecil Davies (Cicerone) does include a few routes on the German side of the border. This book would be very useful for those who plan to do a bit of border-hopping, as some of the Austrian routes described are also easily reached from the base towns in this book.

Another Cicerone book of interest is *Klettersteig – Scrambles in the Northern Limestone Alps* by Paul Werner. It covers the more ambitious Via Ferrata routes in the region.

A useful book covering Berchtesgaden, available locally, is *Your Complete Guide to Berchtesgaden* (Plenk Verlag). Apart from tips for hiking in the region, it also provides plenty of background information on the area and its sights.

For the Zugspitze region there is *Around the Zugspitze* by Dieter Siebert (Bergverlag Rudolf Rother, Munich). This is a translation of the German original and is available from amazon.co.uk

There are plenty of relevant German publications. The series *Rother Wanderführer* (Bergverlag Rudolf Rother, Munich) and *Kompass Wanderbuch* (Deutscher Wanderverlag, Stuttgart) cover the Bavarian Alps in exhaustive detail. The routes are clearly graded according to the degree of difficulty. It should not be difficult to obtain any of these at local German bookshops.

General guidebooks to Bavaria and the Bavarian Alps

Bavaria by Rodney Bolt (Cadogan Guides)

Covers all of Bavaria with a chapter devoted to the Alps.

Drive Around Bavaria & The Austrian Tyrol: Your Guide to Great Drives by Brent Gregston (Thomas Cook Publishing)

With the motorist in mind, this covers the border region of Germany and Austria.

Frommer's Munich and the Bavarian Alps by Danforth Prince (Wiley Publishing)

A practical guide that is regularly updated. The emphasis is on Munich, with a short chapter on the Bavarian Alps.

Munich & Bavaria by Andrea Schutle-Peevers, Jeremy Gray and Catherine Le Nevez (Lonely Planet)

Once again Munich dominates. Useful practical information.

Munich and the Bavarian Alps Eyewitness Travel Guide by Izabella Galicka (Dorling Kindersley Publishers)

Lavishly illustrated with photos and 3D models, this is a guide for those who find that a picture tells more than a thousand words…

Flora and wildlife

The Wild Flowers of Britain and Northern Europe by R. Fitter, A. Fitter and M. Blamey (Collins)

Collins Tree Guide by Owen Johnson and David More (Collins)

Mammals of Britain and Europe by David W. MacDonald (Collins)

The New Birdwatcher's Pocket Guide to Britain and Europe by P. Hayman and Rob Hume (Mitchell Beazley)

Collins Bird Guide: The Most Complete Guide to the Birds of Britain and Europe by Lars Svensson (Collins)

APPENDIX B:
Alpine Hut Accommodation

Listed here are only those huts mentioned in the route descriptions. For a comprehensive listing of AV huts (only in German) visit the German Alpine Club's website at www.alpenverein.de. Near the start or towards the end of the walking season it is advisable to ring the huts to see if they are open; the local tourist offices can assist you with this. When ringing Austrian huts from outside Austria dial 0043, then drop the first zero of the area code; for example, for Fiderepaß Hut tel: 0043 (0)664 3203676.

AV = Alpenverein or Alpine Club
DAV = German Alpine Club
OeAV = Austrian Alpine Club

NaturFreunde Huts (Naturefriends) There is a full listing of huts at the German-language site www.naturfreunde.de. For more information about Naturefriends, visit the British website at www.naturefriends.org.uk.

ALLGAU ALPS

AV Huts
Bad Kissinger Hut 1792m (Pfrontner Hut), DAV, Cat I
DAV-S Bad Kissingen
Pater-Reinisch-Weg 2
D-97688 Bad Kissingen
Hut: Tel: (0676) 373 11 66 (Austria)
Valley: tel./fax: (05677) 20 088 (Austria)
Website: www.dav-kg.de
Open: May–end Oct

Edmund-Probst-Haus 1930m, DAV, Cat II
DAV-S Allgäu-Immenstadt
Grüntenstr. 5
D-87527 Sonthofen
Hut: tel: (08322) 4795, fax: (08322) 8594
Website: www.dav-allgaeu-immenstadt.de/prohaus.html
E-mail: probsthaus@yahoo.de
Open: Whitsun–Oct, 20 Dec–first Sun after Easter

Fiderepaß Hut 2070m, DAV, Cat I
DAV-S Oberstdorf/Allgäu
Karweidach 1
D-87561 Oberstdorf
Tel: 0664 3203676 (Austria)
or (08322) 700 151 (Hut Hotline)
Fax: 05517 3157 (Austria)
Website: www.fiderepasshuette.de
Open: Whitsun–mid-Oct

Landsberger Hut 1810m, DAV, Cat I
DAV-S Landsberg
Malteserstr. 425f
D-86899 Landsberg
Hut: tel: (05675) 6282 (Austria)
(reservations)
Valley: tel: (05632) 386 (Austria)
Website:
www.tannheimertal.at/landsberg
Open: Whitsun–15 Oct

Prinz-Luitpold-Haus 1846m, DAV, Cat I
DAV-S Immenstadt
Grüntenstr. 5
D-87527 Sonthofen
Tel: (08322) 700 154,
fax: (0721) 151 305 728
Website: www.prinz-luitpoldhaus.de
E-mail: post@prinz-luitpoldhaus.de
Open: Whitsun–Oct

Other Huts
Schwaben Haus 1500m
(Berghaus Schwaben)
Tel: (08326) 438,
fax: (08326) 384 860
Website: www.berghaus-schwaben.de
Open: All year, restaurant closed Tues
(reservations necessary)

Widderstein Hut 2009m
(Widdersteinalpe)
Tel: (0664) 391 2524 (Austria)
E-mail: widdersteinhuette@aon.at
Open: June–mid-Oct
(reservations necessary)

AMMERGAU ALPS

AV Huts
Brunnenkopfhäuser 1602m, DAV, Cat I
DAV-S Bergland
Kyreinstr. 6
D-81371 Munich
Hut: tel: (0175) 654 0155
Valley: tel: (08821) 71 319
Website: www.dav-bergland.de
E-mail: brunnenkopf@t-online.de
Open: May–Oct
(according to snow conditions)

Hörnle Hut (Hörndl Hut) 1390m,
DAV, Cat II
DAV-S Starnberg
Hans-Walter Zeeb
Wangener Str. 59
D-82319 Starnberg/Leutstetten
Hut: tel: (08845) 229
Open: All year, except Apr and Nov
(reservations recommended)

August-Schuster-Haus (Pürschling Haus)
1564m, DAV, Cat II
DAV-S Bergland
Kyreinstr. 6
D-81371 Munich
Hut: tel: (08822) 3567
Valley: tel: (08822) 4195
Website: www.dav-bergland.de
Open: All year, except Nov

Other Huts
Gasthaus Bleckenau 1167m
Tel: (08362) 81181
Open: Mid-May–mid-Oct
Kenzen Hut 1285m
Tel: (08368) 390, fax: (08861) 256 1420
Website:
www.kenzenhuette-ammergebirge.de
Open: Ascension–end Oct
(reservations only by phone)

Kolben Alm 1040m
Lorenz Gröbmüller

APPENDIX B – ALPINE HUT ACCOMMODATION

Kolbenalm 1
D-82487 Oberammergau
Tel: (08822) 6364, fax: (08822) 923 770
Website: www.kolbenalm.de
E-mail: lenz@kolbenalm.de
Open: All year

Tegelberg Haus 1707m
Tegelberg 1
D-87645 Schwangau
Tel: (08362) 8980,
fax: (08362) 88 265
Website: www.tegelberghaus.de
E-mail: tegelberghaus.skara@t-online.de
Open: All year (accommodation in winter only by prior arrangement)

WETTERSTEIN, ESTER AND WALCHENSEE MOUNTAINS

AV Huts

Brunnstein Hut 1560m, DAV, Cat I
DAV-S Mittenwald
Max Schmidt
Matthias-Klotz-Str. 26
D-82481 Mittenwald
Hut: tel: (0172) 890 9613,
fax: (0172) 890 9614
Valley: tel: (08823) 94 385
Website: www.brunnsteinhuette.de
E-mail: brunnstein@t-online.de
Open: May–Oct

Hochland Hut 1623m, DAV, Cat I
DAV-S Hochland
Koboldstr. 78
D-81739 Munich
Hut: tel: (0174) 989 7863
Valley: tel: (08823) 5686
Open: June–mid-Oct

Höllentalanger Hut 1381m, DAV, Cat I
DAV-S Munich
Bayerstr. 21
D-80335 Munich
Hut: tel: (08821) 8811
Website:
www.alpenverein-muenchen-oberland.de
Open: June–mid-Oct

Knorr Hut 2052m, DAV, Cat I
DAV-S Munich
Bayerstr. 21
D-80335 Munich
Hut: tel: (08821) 2905
Website:
www.alpenverein-muenchen-oberland.de
Open: End May–end Sept

Kreuzeck Haus 1652m, DAV, Cat II
DAV-S Garmisch-Partenkirchen
Hindenburgstr. 38
D-82467 Garmisch-Partenkirchen
Hut: tel: (08821) 2202, fax: (08821) 96587
Website: www.alpenverein-ga-pa.de/
kreuzeckhaus.html
Open: Mid-May–early Nov;
mid-Dec–mid-Apr

Krinner-Kofler Hut 1407m, DAV, Cat I
DAV-S Mittenwald
Max Schmidt
Matthias-Klotz-Str. 26
D-82481 Mittenwald
Valley: tel: (08823) 5584
Website: www.dav-mittenwald.de
E-mail: davsmittenwald@aol.com
Open: June–mid-Oct

Krottenkopf Haus 1955m
(Weilheimer Hut), DAV, Cat I
DAV-S Weilheim
Hofstr. 17
D-82362 Weilheim
Hut: tel/fax: (0170) 270 8052
Valley: tel: (08825) 2023
Website: www.dav-weilheim.de
Open: Whitsun–mid-Oct

Meiler Hut 2366m, DAV, Cat I
DAV-S Garmisch-Partenkirchen
Hindenburgstr. 38
D-82467 Garmisch-Partenkirchen
Hut: tel: +49 (0)171 522 7897

WALKING IN THE BAVARIAN ALPS

Valley: tel: (08821) 2701
Website: www.meilerhuette.de/
meilerhuette_1.html
Open: Mid-June–early Oct

Münchner Haus 2964m, DAV, Cat II
DAV-S Munich
Bayerstr. 21
D-80335 Munich
Hut: tel: (08821) 2901
Website:
www.muenchner.wachterhaus.com
E-mail: muenchnerhaus@t-online.de
Open: Mid-May–end Sept
(no reservations on weekends possible)

Oberreintal Hut 1525m, DAV,
Cat I (self-catering)
DAV-S Garmisch-Partenkirchen
Hindenburgstr. 38
D-82467 Garmisch-Partenkirchen
Hut: tel: (08821) 2701, fax: (08821) 71 994
Website: www.oberreintalhuette.de/
oberreintalhuette.html, or www.hbgap.de
E-mail: info@oberreintalhuette.de
Open: June–early Oct

Reintalanger Hut 1366m, DAV, Cat I
DAV-S Munich
Bayerstr. 21
D-80335 Munich
Hut: tel: (08821) 2903
Website:
www.alpenverein-muenchen-oberland.de
or www.charly-wehrle.de
E-mail: info@reintalangerhuette.de
Open: End May–mid-Oct

Soiern Haus 1616m, DAV, Cat I
DAV-S Hochland
Koboldstr. 78
D-81739 Munich
Hut: tel: (0171) 546 5858
Open: Whitsun–mid-Oct

Tutzinger Hut 1327m, DAV, Cat I
DAV-S Tutzing
Postfach 1146
D-82323 Tutzing
Hut: tel: 0175 164 1690
(mobile/cell phone)
Valley: tel: (08851) 7418
Website: www.dav-tutzinger-huette.de
Open: May–c5 Nov

Wank Haus 1780m, DAV, Cat II
DAV-S Garmisch-Partenkirchen
Hindenburgstr. 38
D-82467 Garmisch-Partenkirchen
Hut: tel/fax: (08821) 56 201
Website: www.wank-haus.de
Open: All year

Other Huts
Dammkar Hut 1650m
Tel: (0173) 351 4659
Website: www.dammkarhuette.de
Open: Easter–end Sept
(reservations necessary)

Forsthaus (Alpenhotel) Graseck 900m
Graseck 4
D-82467 Garmisch-Partenkirchen
Tel: (08821) 943 240, fax: (08821) 55 700
Website: www.forsthaus-graseck.de
Open: All year

Gasthaus Ferchensee
Am Ferchensee 1
D-82481 Mittenwald
Tel: (08823) 1409
Website: www.mittenwald-ferchensee.de
Open: All year

(Holiday apartment for 1 or 2 persons)
Herzogstandhäuser 1575m
Tel: (08851) 234, fax: (08851) 244
Website:
www.berggasthaus-herzogstand.de
E-mail:
s.zauner@berggasthaus-herzogstand.de
Open: All year, except mid-Nov–Christmas
(reservations necessary)

APPENDIX B – ALPINE HUT ACCOMMODATION

Hotel Lautersee 1016m
Am Lautersee 1
D-82481 Mittenwald
Tel: (08823) 1017, fax: (08823) 5246
Website: www.hotel-lautersee.de
E-mail: info@hotel-lautersee.de
Open: All year

Hubertushof (Hotel)
Familie Pfeffel
Reindlau 230a
A-6105 Leutasch (Austria)
Tel: (05214) 6561, fax: (05214) 6961
Website: www.erlebnishotels.org
E-mail: office@hubertushof-leutasch.at
Open: All year

Kranzberg Haus 1391m
Kranzberghaus
D-82481 Mittenwald
Tel: (08823) 1591, fax: (08823) 928 551
Website: www.kranzberghaus.de
E-mail: kranzbergwirt@aol.com
Open: All year

Schachen Haus 1866m
Tel: (08821) 2996 or 0172 876 8868
Website: www.schachenhaus.de
E-mail: info@schachenhaus.de
Open: June–mid-Oct

Tiroler Hut 2154m
Tel: 0179 453 0056
Open: June–early Oct

TEGERNSEE AND SCHLIERSEE MOUNTAINS

AV Huts

Aiblinger Hut 1311m, DAV,
Cat I (self-catering)
DAV-S Bad Aibling
Heimatsberger Str. 9
D-83043 Bad Aibling
Tel: (08061) 1850
Website: www.alpenverein-aibling.de
E-mail: info@alpenverein-aibling.de
Open: Apr–Dec
(accommodation weekends only)

Brauneck Hut 1540m, DAV, Cat II
DAV-S Alpiner Ski-Club
Eulenspiegelstr. 55a
D-81739 Munich
Hut: tel: (08042) 8786
Website: www.brauneckgipfelhaus.de
Open: All year except mid-Nov–mid-Dec,
mid-Apr–mid-May

Brünnstein Haus 1360m, DAV, Cat I
DAV-S Rosenheim
Von-der-Tann-Str. 1a
Münchner Str. 9
D-83022 Rosenheim
Hut: tel: (08033) 1431
Website: www.breunnsteinhaus.de
Open: All year except mid-Mar–end Apr,
Nov–26 Dec, weekends only

Freisinger Hut 1050m, DAV,
Cat I (self-catering)
DAV-S Freising
Seilerbrücklstr. 3
D-85354 Freising
Tel: (08161) 12236
Website: www.dav-freising.de
Open: All year, key necessary
(obtainable from above address)

Lenggrieser Hut 1338m, DAV, Cat I
DAV-S Lenggries
Alfred Kellner
Karwendelstr. 18
D-83661 Lenggries
Hut: tel: (0175) 596 2809,
fax: (0175) 596 2004
Website: www.dav-lenggries.de
Open: All year, closed Tues
(plus Mon in winter)

Guffert Hut 1475m (Ludwig-
Aschenbrenner Hut), DAV, Cat I
DAV-S Kaufering
Franz-Senn-Weg 1

WALKING IN THE BAVARIAN ALPS

D-86916 Kaufering
Hut: tel: (0676) 629 2404
Website: www.dav-kaufering.de
E-mail: huette@dav-kaufering.de
Open: Mid-May–end Oct

Rotwand Haus 1737m, DAV, Cat I
DAV-S Turner-Alpenkränzchen
Preysingstr. 71
D-81667 Munich
Hut: tel/fax: (08026) 7683
Website: www.rotwandhaus.de
Open: All year except Nov–mid-Dec

Taubenstein Haus 1567m, DAV, Cat II
DAV-S Bergbund
Karl Lichtinger
Margaretenstr. 10
D-82152 Krailling
Hut: tel: (08026) 7070
Website: www.bergbund-muenchen.de
Open: All year except Nov–mid-Dec

Tegernseer Hut 1650m, DAV, Cat I
DAV-S Tegernsee
Freihausstr. 29
D-83707 Bad Wiessee
Hut: tel: (0175) 411 5813
Valley: tel: (08042) 917 378
Website:
www.heimat.de/tegernseer_huette
or www.dav-tegernsee.de
Open: Mid-May–first weekend Nov

Other Huts

Berggasthaus Riederstein 1080m
(Berggasthaus Galaun)
Frau Elisabeth Wagner
Postfach 352
D-83702 Bad Wiessee
Tel: (08022) 273 022
Website:
www.tiscover.de/berggasthof-galaun
Open: All year, except 3 weeks from end
Jan; restaurant closed Tues

Breitenberg Hut 1050m
NaturFreunde
St Margarethen 9½
D-83098 Brannenburg
Tel: (08034) 8663
Open: 20 Feb–17 Jan, closed Tues

Blauberg Alm 1540m
Tel: 0043 664 230 6719 (cell phone)
Open: June–end Oct

Buchstein Hut 1240m
Tel: (08029) 244
Open: Dec–mid-Nov

Kessel Alm 1285m
Kesselalm 2
D-83730 Fischbachau-Birkenstein
Tel: (08028) 2602
Website: www.kesselalm.de
E-mail: info@kesselalm.de
Open: Apr–Oct, closed Mon;
Mar and Nov weekends only

Wallberg Haus 1512m
Tel: (08022) 6288
Open: All year except Nov–Christmas

CHIEMGAU ALPS

AV Huts
Priener Hut 1410m, DAV, Cat I
DAV-S Prien
Margit Ossman
Seestr. 56
D-83209 Prien am Chiemsee
Hut: tel: (08057) 428, fax: (08057) 904 869
Website: www.priener-huette.de
Open: All year

Straubinger Haus 1600m, DAV, Cat I
DAV-S Straubing
Fraunhoferstr. 10
D-94315 Straubing
Hut: tel: (05375) 6429
Website: www.straubingerhaus.de
Open: May–early Nov

APPENDIX B – ALPINE HUT ACCOMMODATION

Traunsteiner Ski Hut 1160m, DAV, Cat II
DAV-S Traunstein
Dürrnbachhornweg 14
D-83242 Reit im Winkl
Hut: tel: (08640) 8140
Website: www.alpenverein-traunstein.de
Open: All year, except 24 Apr–7 May and 13 Nov–2 Dec

Other Huts
Alpengasthof Winklmoosalm 1160m
Dürrnbachhornweg 6
D-83242 Reit im Winkl-Winklmoosalm
Tel: (08640) 97440, fax: (08640) 974 444
Website: www.winklmoosalm.com
E-mail: info@winklmoosalm.com

Hochgern Haus 1510m
Tel: (0864) 61919
Website: www.hochgernhaus.de
Open: All year

Sonnen Alm
Kampenwandseilbahn
An der Bergbahn 8
D-83229 Aschau im Chiemgau
Tel: (08052) 4411, fax: (08052) 2508
Website: www.kampenwand.de
E-mail: info@kampenwand.de
Open: All year

Zwiesel Alm 1386m
Tel: (08651) 3107
Open: Mid-May–mid-Oct

BERCHTESGADEN ALPS

AV Huts
Blaueis Hut 1680m, DAV, Cat I
DAV-S Berchtesgaden, Kurgarten
Maximilianstr. 1, D-83471 Berchtesgaden
Hut: tel/fax: (08657) 271
Valley: tel: (08657) 546
Website: www.blaueishuette.de
E-mail: info@blaueishuette.de
Open: Mid-May–end Oct
(reservations advisable)

Carl von Stahl Haus 1736m, OeAV, Cat I
ÖAV-S Salzburg
Nonntaler Hauptstr. 86
A-5020 Salzburg
Hut: tel: (08652) 2752,
fax: (08652) 63940 (Germany)
Website: www.carl-von-stahl-haus.com
Open: All year, except 24 Dec

Ingolstädter Haus 2119m, DAV, Cat I
DAV-S Ingolstadt
Franz Mayr
Ludwigstr. 4
D-85049 Ingolstadt
Hut: tel/fax: (06582) 8353 (Austria)
Valley: tel: (06582) 73921 (Austria)
Website: www.ingolstaedter-haus.de
E-mail: info@ingolstaedter-haus.de
Open: Mid-June–mid-Oct

Kärlinger Haus 1631m, DAV, Cat I
DAV-S Berchtesgaden
Am Kurgarten
Maximilianstr. 1
D-83471 Berchtesgaden
Hut: tel: (08652) 2995
Valley: tel: (08652) 2796
Website: www.kaerlingerhaus.de
E-mail: info@kaerlingerhaus.de
Open: Whitsun–mid-Oct

Neue Traunsteiner Hut 1560m (Karl-Merkenschlager-Haus), DAV, Cat I
DAV-S Traunstein
Bahnhofstr. 18b
D-83278 Traunstein
Hut: tel/fax: (0171) 437 8919
Website: www.traunsteinerhuette.com
E-mail: office@traunsteinerhuette.com
Open: Mid-May–end Oct

Riemann Haus 2177m, DAV, Cat I
DAV-S Ingolstadt
Franz Mayr
Ludwigstr. 4
D-85049 Ingolstadt
Hut: tel: (0664) 211 0337 (Austria)

Valley: tel/fax: (06582) 73300 (Austria)
Website: www.riemannhaus.de
E-mail: info@riemannhaus.de
Open: Mid-June–start Oct

Stöhrhaus 1894m, DAV, Cat I
DAV-S Berchtesgaden
Am Kurgarten
Maximilienstr. 1
D-83471 Berchtesgaden
Hut: tel/fax: (08652) 7233
Website: www.dav-berchtesgaden.de
Open: Mid-May–mid-Oct

Wasseralm 1423m, DAV,
Cat I (self-catering)
DAV-S Berchtesgaden
Am Kurgarten
Maximilienstr. 1
D-83471 Berchtesgaden
Tel: (08652) 2207
Website: www.dav-berchtesgaden.de
Open: All year, hut warden in summer

Watzmann Haus 1930m, DAV, Cat I
DAV-S Munich
Bayerstr. 21
D-80335 Munich
Hut: tel: (08652) 964 222
Valley: tel: (08652) 65 7523
Website:
www.alpenverein-muenchen-oberland.de
Open: Mid/end May–mid-Oct

Other Huts
Gotzen Alm 1685m
Tel: (08652) 690 900,
fax: (08652) 979 115
Website: www.gotzenalm.de
Open: Mid-May–mid-Oct

Kühroint Hut 1420m
Tel: (08652) 7339
Open: June–Sept/mid-Oct
Berghotel Predigtstuhl 1583m
Tel: (08651) 96 850, fax: (08651) 968 518
Website: www.predigtstul-bahn.de
E-mail: empfang@predigtstuhl-hotel.de
Open: All year

Schneibstein Haus 1666m
NaturFreunde
Tel: (08652) 2596, fax: (08652) 66 918
Website: www.schneibsteinhaus.de
E-mail: info@schneibsteinhaus.de
Open: May–end Oct and 26 Dec–6 Jan

Toni-Lenz Hut 1550m
Tel: (0664) 134 1690 (Austria)
Website: www.eishoehle.net
Open: 30 May–end Oct

Wimbachgrieß Hut 1327m
NaturFreunde
Tel: (08657) 344
Open: May–end Oct

APPENDIX C:
Useful Addresses

German National Tourist Offices

Great Britain
PO Box 2695
London W1A 3TN
Tel: 020 7317 0908, Fax: 020 7317 0917
Website: www.germany-tourism.co.uk
E-mail: gntolon@d-z-t.com

USA
122 East 42nd Street
New York, NY 10168-0072
Tel: (212) 661 7200
Toll free: (800) 651 7010
Website: www.cometogermany.com
E-mail: mailto:GermanyInfo@d-z-t.com

PO Box 59594
Chicago, IL 60659-9594
Tel: 773 539 6303
E-mail: heike.pfeiffer@gntoch.com

133 Parkview Ave, Suite 300
Manhattan Beach
Los Angeles, CA 90266
Tel: 310 545 1350
E-mail: info@gntolax.com

480 University Ave, Suite 1410
Toronto, ON M5G 1V2
Tel: (416) 968 1685
E-mail: info@gnto.ca

Canada
480 University Ave, Suite 1410
Toronto, ON M5G 1V2
Tel: (416) 968 1685
E-mail: info@gnto.ca

Regional Tourist Offices

Bayern Tourismus Marketing GmbH
Website: www.bayern.by
Information on Bavaria

Tourismusverband München-Oberbayern e.V.
Radolfzeller Str. 15
D-81243 Munich, Germany
Tel: 0049 (0)89 829 2180
Website: www.oberbayern-tourismus.de
E-mail: touristinfo@oberbayern.de
Information on Upper Bavaria

Allgäu Marketing GmbH
Allgäuer Str. 1
D-87435 Kempten, Germany
Tel: 0049 (0)8321 8004 569
Website: www.allgäu.info
E-mail: info@allgaeu.de
Information on the Allgäu Alps

Tourismusgemeinschaft Zugspitz-Region C/O
Garmisch-Partenkirchen Tourismus
Richard-Strauss-Platz 1a
D-82467 Garmisch-Partenkirchen,
Germany
Tel: 0049 (0)8821 1804 84
Website: www.zugspitz-region.de
E-mail: info@zugspitz-region.de
*Information on the Ammergau Alps and
the region around Garmisch*

Tourismusverband Bayerisches Oberland e.V.
Tegernseer Str. 20a
D-83734 Hausham, Germany
Tel: 0049 (0)8026 920 700
Website:
www.tegernsee-schliersee-wendelstein.de
E-mail:
info@tegernsee-schliersee-wendelstein.de
*Information on the Tegernsee and
Schliersee Mountains*

Chiemgau Tourismus e.V.
D-83278 Traunstein, Germany
Tel: 0049 (0)861 58 223
Website: www.chiemgau-tourismus.de
E-mail: info@chiemgau-tourismus.de
Information on the Chiemgau Alps

Berchtesgadener Land Tourismus GmbH
Bahnhofplatz 4
D-83471 Berchtesgaden, Germany
Tel: 0049 (0)1805 865200
Website: www.berchtesgadener-land.com
E-mail: info@berchtesgadener-land.com
Information on the Berchtesgaden Alps

APPENDIX D:
Glossary

English is widely spoken in Germany, and younger people especially are quite fluent. Nevertheless, it does not hurt to master a few simple phrases; many people will be more than pleased that you have made an effort! The following lists of terms and phrases do not attempt to replace a good phrase book, but provide a very basic vocabulary specific to the needs of hikers in the border region of the German and Austrian Alps.

Note 'ß' sometimes replaces 'ss' in German.

Useful words and phrases

Arzt/Zahnarzt	doctor/dentist
Bahnhof	railway station
Bergstation	upper station (cable car, etc)
Bergwacht	mountain rescue
Bitte	please
Campingplatz	camping ground
Danke (schön)	thank you (very much)
Haltestelle	bus stop
Ferienwohnung	holiday flat
Gondelbahn	gondola-lift
Grüß Gott!	hello (a common greeting in Bavaria, which literally means 'God bless you')
Jugendherberge	youth hostel
Mittelstation	middle station/terminus (cable car, etc)
Nein, nein danke	no, no thank you
Nur für Geübte	only for the experienced (signposted at the start of trails requiring experience in alpine terrain)
Öffnungszeiten	opening times
Privatzimmer	room in a private house, often with breakfast
Ruhetag	day on which a restaurant is closed
Servus!	informal hello, or as a friendly farewell: so long! (common greeting/farewell along German–Austrian border)
Sesselbahn	chairlift
Spezi	a mixture of coke and lemonade, a favourite non-alcoholic drink of German hikers
Talstation	valley station (cable car, etc)
Verkehrsverein	tourist office
Wanderkarte	walking map

APPENDIX D – GLOSSARY

Wanderweg	walking trail
Weg	path, trail
Zahnradbahn	rack railway, cogwheel railway
Zimmer frei	room vacancies

Topographical and other terms

Commonly used on German maps or in this guidebook.

Alm/Alp/Alpe	alp, alpine pasture
Alpen	Alps
Bach	stream
Bergwachthütte	mountain rescue hut
Blatt	map sheet
Diensthütte	hut used eg by forestry workers, ie no accommodation
Gebirge	mountain range
Gipfel	summit, peak
Gletscher	glacier
Grat	ridge
Haus	often used instead of Hütte (hut)
Höhenweg	high-level route or trail
Höhle	cave
Hütte	hut
Jagdhütte	hunting lodge
Jausenstation	especially in the Austrian Alps; a small restaurant serving snacks, or simple meals
Kamm	mountain crest or ridge
Kar	cirque
Klamm	narrow gorge
Klettersteig	via ferrata (ambitious mountain track)
Maßstab	scale
Paß	pass
Quelle	spring
Sattel	saddle
Scharte	narrow saddle or col
Schlucht	gorge
See	lake or tarn
Steig	steep mountain trail
Tal	valley
Tobel	ravine
Topographische Karte	topographical map
Verfallen	abandoned (in respect of hut or alm)
Wanderkarte	walking map
Wasserfall	waterfall

LISTING OF CICERONE GUIDES

BACKPACKING
The End to End Trail
Three Peaks, Ten Tors
Backpacker's Britain Vol 1 – Northern England
Backpacker's Britain Vol 2 – Wales
Backpacker's Britain Vol 3 – Northern Scotland
The Book of the Bivvy

NORTHERN ENGLAND LONG-DISTANCE TRAILS
The Dales Way
The Reiver's Way
The Alternative Coast to Coast
A Northern Coast to Coast Walk
The Pennine Way
Hadrian's Wall Path
The Teesdale Way

FOR COLLECTORS OF SUMMITS
The Relative Hills of Britain
Mts England & Wales Vol 2 – England
Mts England & Wales Vol 1 – Wales

UK GENERAL
The National Trails

BRITISH CYCLE GUIDES
The Cumbria Cycle Way
Lands End to John O'Groats – Cycle Guide
Rural Rides No.1 – West Surrey
Rural Rides No.2 – East Surrey
South Lakeland Cycle Rides
Border Country Cycle Routes
Lancashire Cycle Way

CANOE GUIDES
Canoeist's Guide to the North-East

LAKE DISTRICT AND MORECAMBE BAY
Coniston Copper Mines
Scrambles in the Lake District (North)
Scrambles in the Lake District (South)
Walks in Silverdale and Arnside AONB
Short Walks in Lakeland 1 – South
Short Walks in Lakeland 2 – North
Short Walks in Lakeland 3 – West
The Tarns of Lakeland Vol 1 – West
The Tarns of Lakeland Vol 2 – East
The Cumbria Way & Allerdale Ramble
Lake District Winter Climbs
Roads and Tracks of the Lake District
The Lake District Angler's Guide
Rocky Rambler's Wild Walks
An Atlas of the English Lakes
Tour of the Lake District
The Cumbria Coastal Way

NORTH-WEST ENGLAND
Walker's Guide to the Lancaster Canal
Family Walks in the Forest Of Bowland
Walks in Ribble Country
Historic Walks in Cheshire
Walking in Lancashire
Walks in Lancashire Witch Country
The Ribble Way

THE ISLE OF MAN
Walking on the Isle of Man
The Isle of Man Coastal Path

PENNINES AND NORTH-EAST ENGLAND
Walks in the Yorkshire Dales
Walks on the North York Moors, books 1 and 2
Walking in the South Pennines
Walking in the North Pennines
Walking in the Wolds
Waterfall Walks – Teesdale and High Pennines
Walking in County Durham
Yorkshire Dales Angler's Guide
Walks in Dales Country
Historic Walks in North Yorkshire
South Pennine Walks
Walking in Northumberland
Cleveland Way and Yorkshire Wolds Way
The North York Moors

DERBYSHIRE, PEAK DISTRICT, EAST MIDLANDS
High Peak Walks
White Peak Walks Northern Dales
White Peak Walks Southern Dales
Star Family Walks Peak District & South Yorkshire
Walking In Peakland
Historic Walks in Derbyshire

WALES AND WELSH BORDERS
Ascent of Snowdon
Welsh Winter Climbs
Hillwalking in Wales – Vol 1
Hillwalking in Wales – Vol 2
Scrambles in Snowdonia
Hillwalking in Snowdonia
The Ridges of Snowdonia
Hereford & the Wye Valley
Walking Offa's Dyke Path
Lleyn Peninsula Coastal Path
Anglesey Coast Walks
The Shropshire Way
Spirit Paths of Wales
Glyndwr's Way
The Pembrokeshire Coastal Path
Walking in Pembrokeshire
The Shropshire Hills – A Walker's Guide

MIDLANDS
The Cotswold Way
The Grand Union Canal Walk
Walking in Warwickshire
Walking in Worcestershire
Walking in Staffordshire
Heart of England Walks

SOUTHERN ENGLAND
Exmoor & the Quantocks
Walking in the Chilterns
Walking in Kent
Two Moors Way
Walking in Dorset
A Walker's Guide to the Isle of Wight
Walking in Somerset
The Thames Path
Channel Island Walks
Walking in Buckinghamshire
The Isles of Scilly
Walking in Hampshire
Walking in Bedfordshire
The Lea Valley Walk
Walking in Berkshire
The Definitive Guide to Walking in London
The Greater Ridgeway
Walking on Dartmoor
The South West Coast Path
Walking in Sussex
The North Downs Way
The South Downs Way

SCOTLAND
Scottish Glens 1 – Cairngorm Glens
Scottish Glens 2 – Atholl Glens
Scottish Glens 3 – Glens of Rannoch
Scottish Glens 4 – Glens of Trossach
Scottish Glens 5 – Glens of Argyll
Scottish Glens 6 – The Great Glen
Scottish Glens 7 – The Angus Glens
Scottish Glens 8 – Knoydart to Morvern
Scottish Glens 9 – The Glens of Ross-shire
The Island of Rhum
Torridon – A Walker's Guide
Walking the Galloway Hills
Border Pubs & Inns – A Walkers' Guide
Scrambles in Lochaber
Walking in the Hebrides
Central Highlands: 6 Long Distance Walks
Walking in the Isle of Arran
Walking in the Lowther Hills
North to the Cape
The Border Country – A Walker's Guide
Winter Climbs – Cairngorms
The Speyside Way
Winter Climbs – Ben Nevis & Glencoe
The Isle of Skye, A Walker's Guide
The West Highland Way
Scotland's Far North
Walking the Munros Vol 1 – Southern, Central
Walking the Munros Vol 2 – Northern & Cairngorms
Scotland's Far West
Walking in the Cairngorms

Walking in the Ochils, Campsie Fells and Lomond Hills
Scotland's Mountain Ridges
The Great Glen Way
The Pentland Hills: A Walker's Guide
The Southern Upland Way
Ben Nevis and Glen Coe

IRELAND
The Mountains of Ireland
Irish Coastal Walks
The Irish Coast to Coast

INTERNATIONAL CYCLE GUIDES
The Way of St James – Le Puy to Santiago cyclist's guide
The Danube Cycle Way
Cycle Tours in Spain
Cycling the River Loire – The Way of St Martin
Cycle Touring in France
Cycling in the French Alps

WALKING AND TREKKING IN THE ALPS
Tour of Monte Rosa
Walking in the Alps (all Alpine areas)
100 Hut Walks in the Alps
Chamonix to Zermatt
Tour of Mont Blanc
Alpine Ski Mountaineering Vol 1 Western Alps
Alpine Ski Mountaineering Vol 2 Eastern Alps
Snowshoeing: Techniques and Routes in the Western Alps
Alpine Points of View
Tour of the Matterhorn
Across the Eastern Alps: E5

FRANCE, BELGIUM AND LUXEMBOURG
RLS (Robert Louis Stevenson) Trail
Walks in Volcano Country
French Rock
Walking the French Gorges
Rock Climbs Belgium & Luxembourg
Tour of the Oisans: GR54
Walking in the Tarentaise and Beaufortain Alps
Walking in the Haute Savoie, vol. 1
Walking in the Haute Savoie, vol. 2
Tour of the Vanoise
GR20 Corsica – The High Level Route
The Ecrins National Park
Walking the French Alps: GR5
Walking in the Cevennes
Vanoise Ski Touring
Walking in Provence
Walking on Corsica
Mont Blanc Walks
Walking in the Cathar region of south west France
Walking in the Dordogne
Trekking in the Vosges and Jura
The Cathar Way

PYRENEES AND FRANCE / SPAIN
Rock Climbs in the Pyrenees
Walks & Climbs in the Pyrenees

The GR10 Trail: Through the French Pyrenees
The Way of St James – Le Puy to the Pyrenees
The Way of St James – Pyrenees-Santiago-Finisterre
Through the Spanish Pyrenees GR11
The Pyrenees – World's Mountain Range Guide
The Pyrenean Haute Route
The Mountains of Andorra

SPAIN AND PORTUGAL
Picos de Europa – Walks & Climbs
The Mountains of Central Spain
Walking in Mallorca
Costa Blanca Walks Vol 1
Costa Blanca Walks Vol 2
Walking in Madeira
Vía de la Plata (Seville To Santiago)
Walking in the Cordillera Cantabrica
Walking in the Canary Islands 1 West
Walking in the Canary Islands 2 East
Walking in the Sierra Nevada
Walking in the Algarve
Trekking in Andalucia

SWITZERLAND
Walking in Ticino, Switzerland
Central Switzerland – A Walker's Guide
The Bernese Alps
Walking in the Valais
Alpine Pass Route
Walks in the Engadine, Switzerland
Tour of the Jungfrau Region

GERMANY AND AUSTRIA
Klettersteig Scrambles in Northern Limestone Alps
King Ludwig Way
Walking in the Salzkammergut
Walking in the Harz Mountains
Germany's Romantic Road
Mountain Walking in Austria
Walking the River Rhine Trail
Trekking in the Stubai Alps
Trekking in the Zillertal Alps
Walking in the Bavarian Alps

SCANDINAVIA
Walking In Norway
The Pilgrim Road to Nidaros (St Olav's Way)

EASTERN EUROPE
The High Tatras
The Mountains of Romania
Walking in Hungary
The Mountains of Montenegro

CROATIA AND SLOVENIA
Walks in the Julian Alps
Walking in Croatia

ITALY
Italian Rock
Walking in the Central Italian Alps
Central Apennines of Italy
Walking in Italy's Gran Paradiso
Long Distance Walks in Italy's Gran Paradiso

Walking in Sicily
Shorter Walks in the Dolomites
Treks in the Dolomites
Via Ferratas of the Italian Dolomites Vol 1
Via Ferratas of the Italian Dolomites Vol 2
Walking in the Dolomites
Walking in Tuscany
Trekking in the Apennines
Through the Italian Alps: the GTA

OTHER MEDITERRANEAN COUNTRIES
The Mountains of Greece
Climbs & Treks in the Ala Dag (Turkey)
The Mountains of Turkey
Treks & Climbs Wadi Rum, Jordan
Jordan – Walks, Treks, Caves etc.
Crete – The White Mountains
Walking in Western Crete
Walking in Malta

AFRICA
Climbing in the Moroccan Anti-Atlas
Trekking in the Atlas Mountains
Kilimanjaro

NORTH AMERICA
The Grand Canyon & American South West
Walking in British Columbia
The John Muir Trail

SOUTH AMERICA
Aconcagua

HIMALAYAS – NEPAL, INDIA
Langtang, Gosainkund & Helambu: A Trekkers' Guide
Garhwal & Kumaon – A Trekkers' Guide
Kangchenjunga – A Trekkers' Guide
Manaslu – A Trekkers' Guide
Everest – A Trekkers' Guide
Annapurna – A Trekkers' Guide
Bhutan – A Trekker's Guide
The Mount Kailash Trek

TECHNIQUES AND EDUCATION
The Adventure Alternative
Rope Techniques
Snow & Ice Techniques
Mountain Weather
Beyond Adventure
The Hillwalker's Manual
Outdoor Photography
The Hillwalker's Guide to Mountaineering
Map and Compass
Sports Climbing Handbook
An Introduction to Rock Climbing

MINI GUIDES
Avalanche!
Snow
Pocket First Aid and Wilderness Medicine
Navigation

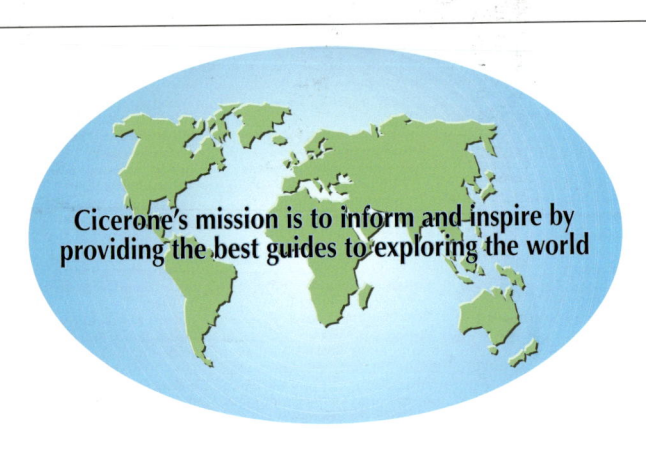

Cicerone's mission is to inform and inspire by providing the best guides to exploring the world

Since its foundation over 30 years ago, Cicerone has specialised in publishing guidebooks and has built a reputation for quality and reliability. It now publishes nearly 300 guides to the major destinations for outdoor enthusiasts, including Europe, UK and the rest of the world.

Written by leading and committed specialists, Cicerone guides are recognised as the most authoritative. They are full of information, maps and illustrations so that the user can plan and complete a successful and safe trip or expedition – be it a long face climb, a walk over Lakeland fells, an alpine traverse, a Himalayan trek or a ramble in the countryside.

With a thorough introduction to assist planning, clear diagrams, maps and colour photographs to illustrate the terrain and route, and accurate and detailed text, Cicerone guides are designed for ease of use and access to the information.

If the facts on the ground change, or there is any aspect of a guide that you think we can improve, we are always delighted to hear from you.

Cicerone Press
2 Police Square Milnthorpe Cumbria LA7 7PY
Tel:01539 562 069   Fax:01539 563 417
e-mail:info@cicerone.co.uk   web:www.cicerone.co.uk

CICERONE